THE SOUL NEVER DIES

Past Lives, Near-Death Experiences, Life Between Lives, and Mysteries: Our True Spiritual Origin

HERMELINDA

"

"What happens after death is so unspeakably glorious that our imagination and our feelings do not suffice to form even an approximate conception of it [...] But in this reality we know little or nothing about that state of being. And what will we discover about this world after death? The dissolution into eternity of our time-limited form brings no loss of meaning."
(C.G. Jung)

"And remember: no man who existed died. They turned into light and as such still exist."
(Nikola Tesla)

CONTENTS

INTRODUCTION

We live in a mysterious world; we suddenly found ourselves here without knowing our origins and why we are here. It is a material world in which we are surrounded daily by a recurrent, constant and certain phenomenon: death. We begin to become aware of it when we closely live it, for example, since our early youth, when our grandparents are the first to leave. Over the years, other loved ones leave us. We are therefore faced with this unknown event that initially causes dismay and disorientation, and we are disbelieving and desperate when a loved one leaves. But the most important thing is that we find ourselves before the greatest mystery of human life, which gave rise to all speculations, religions, philosophies, literature and art.

Many people are so busy in their daily struggle for survival that they do not even have time to think about it.

The universe is vast, no one knows its origin or end, when creation really took place or if it will ever end. What we know is that on this planet there are billions of living beings that are born and die. The human mind seems to contain more incredible mysteries than one could have ever imagined, and often surprises us with its knowledge and sudden insights.

The origin of life itself is a mystery that goes far beyond the short and ephemeral parenthesis between the birth and death of a single individual. That Origin, the source of everything, is seen as a necessary force for man to reconnect with himself and rediscover the meaning of his existence.

We spend much of our lives hiding behind masks, investing in training and education, earning money for survival, caring for beauty and body health, identifying ourselves in certain social roles and in our work. But when death is closing in, these masks and identifications begin to fall one by one, revealing our true faces. All identifications, goals and desires are revealed in their ephemeral being.

Sometimes in our existence, we feel something pushing and driving us in ways that often escape rationality. What underlies such sensations is obscure, as it seems to come from the very depths of one's awareness.

Death makes us wonder not only about "where we are going" and "where we will go", but also about "where we come from" and therefore about our mysterious origins. There is no human being who has not asked himself these questions at least once in his life. There is something in every human being that gives us the feeling that, beyond the appearances of the ordinary external world, there is much more. We can perceive in ourselves an intuition that goes beyond the limits of science and official religions with their dogmatic creeds. Many scholars from different fields of knowledge have dealt with this enigma. Esotericism and spirituality provided us with broad perspectives on the interpretation of the life-death phenomenon and opened a door to a dimension different from that of the ordinary material world. But the real turning point came when professionals in the scientific and medical fields started to get interested in what lies beyond the commonly understood physical life, no longer being able to ignore that there is something that goes far beyond the boundaries of academic science. In recent decades, therefore, several researches have been carried out, aimed in particular at the phenomena of Near-Death Experiences (NDEs), based on the accounts of patients who came back to life following situations of temporary clinical death.

John Mack, professor of psychiatry, is aware that science, psychology and spirituality are coming into contact after centuries of separation. Contemporary physics and depth psychology are showing a universe in which everything is connected and reveal to us that there are states of consciousness attainable by the human being, which confirm the reality of the mystical experiences of the saints, and which testify that the human self is able to go beyond the narrow limits of what is considered "reality".

The human being can rediscover in himself the traces of his unity with the Whole and his immortality beyond space-time.

I began to write this book following a series of events, signs and coincidences, which led me to give a new meaning to my personal journey, which I talk about in the book "A Mystical Journey: Meetings with Extraordinary Masters, Magicians and Shamans", and to become aware that what is considered *Afterlife* is much more than a mere concept. I therefore engaged in studies and research, and with an extensive bibliography, I wanted to offer a synthesis of what can currently be found in the literature on topics related to the perspective of the survival of the soul after death. This does not claim to be complete but at least exhaustive and coherent. I will cover several topics since this is a quite developed field of study and it is connected to different areas of knowledge, and eventually I will culminate in spirituality.

The present work aims foremost to give an overview of what religious and spiritual traditions teach us about life and death. Subsequently, it will focus on the phenomenon of near-death experiences, according to the experience and research of doctors, psychologists and numerous subjects who lived them. The investigation will continue towards the latest discoveries in the field of past-life regression hypnosis, following the research of leading experts. Then the phenomenon of reincarnation will be analysed. Following this thread, other studies are discovered, in particular by Dr. Michael Newton, concerning an even deeper area of investigation: the "life between lives", that is, what the soul experiences when it is in the spiritual worlds between one incarnation and another, and what the methods of choosing its next physical life are. Along this path, we will find the subsequent research of Dra. Dolores Cannon who, during her long professional practice, came across interesting and sensational discoveries regarding not only past lives and the spiritual life between physical incarnations, but also the link between human beings' life and the evolution of the Earth in relation to the universe. We will inevitably come into contact with a "lost knowledge" that is closely connected to the greatest mysteries. Precisely for this reason, during the discussion a digression will be made to briefly analyse the UFO and alien phenomenon. We will continue with a brief overview of the phenomenon of mediumship and the body of knowledge that the doctrine of spiritism has offered us. We will enter the field of psychotherapy to analyse the grief elaboration process, but also to discover unexpected perspectives of communication with the deceased through the IADC method, founded by Dr. Allan Botkin. The mysteries of dreams and out-of-body experiences will be investigated later, approaching the true spiritual nature of our being. In the following chapters, we will face science, dissecting its limits, as well as its possibilities, and we will study the new frontiers of quantum physics. These seem to confirm the existence of spiritual dimensions that cannot be perceived by the physical senses and offer us an excellent perspective on the possibility of the survival of the soul after death. Finally, the right tribute will be given to what Western and Eastern esoteric sciences, in particular Alchemical Hermeticism and Tibetan Buddhism, have to offer us not only to understand the mystery of life and death, but to invite us to undertake a journey of research and spiritual work to face death with a new awareness.

CHAPTER 1

HISTORY OF LIFE AND DEATH IN DIFFERENT TRADITIONS

*"There is no Death—that what we call Death is but
'the other side' of Life, and one with it."*
(Yogi Ramacharaka)

The idea that the soul has an existence beyond life appears in different times, places and cultures.

According to the ancient civilization of Mesopotamia, the dead are like shadows and descend into an underground world where they will receive judgment. The afterlife is considered as a place without light, from which one cannot return.

The hero Gilgamesh, king of Uruk, an ancient Sumerian city, had founded cities and brought back numerous triumphs in battle and personal victories, but he was tormented by the idea of death and by the search for the meaning of temporary human existence.

The death of his only friend Enkidu, after a long agony, made him feel anguished and frightened him, animating him with the desire to discover the secret of immortality and conquer death. He began searching for answers and met Utnamishtim, who was granted eternal life by the gods. Utnamishtim told him about the plant of youth, but once Gilgamesh had found it, a snake ate it. So Gilgamesh went back to Uruk and accepted his destiny as a mortal man. The Sumerians considered death sad and depressing, an event that left neither the possibility of a ransom or an ascent to another dimension nor a rebirth.

However, this was not the case in Ancient Egypt: they did not consider death as the end, but as something closely connected to life. The Pharaohs lived waiting for the moment of death, which is why they invested time and resources in the construction of the pyramids.

Death was like a rebirth, a renewal, a journey to another dimension, in which the deceased was accompanied by the God of the Sun. According to Egyptian beliefs, after death the deceased made a long journey in which he passed through twelve doors and fought bravely against frightening demons.

From the Egyptian book of the Dead (1250 BC) we learn that, after the death of the physical body, the soul made a journey into the "underworld", but before being able to enter the afterlife, it was supposed to face the final judgment of Osiris. For this reason, they weighed the heart of the deceased and the heavier it was, the more sins he had committed in life. If it was too heavy for its negative actions, the soul ended up in hellish worlds. On the other hand, if the heart was lighter, the soul could be welcomed in the presence of the Sun God, to enjoy a blessed immortality.

However, the civilization of India gives us a completely different idea of life and death.

"There was neither existence nor non-existence then.
There was neither sky nor heaven beyond it.
What covered it and where? What sheltered?
Was there an abyss of water?
There was neither death nor immortality.
There was nothing telling night from day.
The One breathed breathless autonomously.
There was nothing else."
(Hymn of Creation — Rig Veda)

According to the Vedas, after death, the deceased is subjected to a final judgment. Those who behaved well will go to the "World of the Fathers", a kind of paradise. Otherwise, they will go to the "House of Clay", as the Brihadaranyaka Upanishad said: *"Now, these are, verily, the three worlds: the world of men (Manushyaloka), the world of the Manes (Pitriloka) and the world of the Gods (Devaloka)."*

A paradise is therefore identified as the place for the major deities and pure souls; the Antariksa represents an intermediate region between heaven and earth and here there are the semi-gods. The house of Clay is located underground in darkness and is home to demons and damned souls. While reincarnation was not mentioned in the Vedas, the Upanishads introduced the idea of the cycle of birth and rebirth. One's destiny after death is determined by karma, which is the cause and effect law relating to all actions performed both in the present life and in past lives.

"As the embodied soul continually passes, in this body, from boyhood to youth to old age, the soul similarly passes into another body at death. The self-realized soul is not bewildered by such a change. Those who are seers of the truth have concluded that of the non-existent (the material body) there is no endurance, and of the eternal (the soul) there is no change. This they have concluded by studying the nature of both. Know that which pervades the entire body is indestructible. No one is able to destroy the imperishable soul.

The soul is neither born, nor does it ever die; nor having once existed, does it ever cease to be. The soul is without birth, eternal, immortal, and ageless. It is not destroyed when the body is destroyed. As a person puts on new garments, giving up old ones, the soul similarly accepts new material bodies, giving up the old and useless ones."

"What exists cannot cease to exist." (Bhagavad Gita).

According to Krishna's words, the body is the abode of the soul, which is eternal and invisible to the physical eyes. If the soul manages to have dominance over the body and its passions, it can rise to regions of pure spiritual beings, in direct contact with the Highest Divine. If, on the other hand, the soul is overwhelmed by matter, physical instances and ignorance, it is held back in lower regions. Indian spirituality believes that the divine Being, apparently superior to the human being, is within each of us, but must be found by carrying out a process of purification towards a state of perfection that will take it beyond the cycle of deaths and rebirths.

"Before this world was manifest, there was only existence; one without a second. He, the One, thought, 'Let me be many and let me grow forth'. Thus, out of himself he projected the universe; he entered every being. He is the truth; He is the subtle essence of all. And you are That."
(Chandogya Upanishad)

"The whole multitude of beings in creation manifested from the eternal source like thousands of sparks from a fire."
(Mandokya Upanishad)

In the Rig Veda, the deities Indra (air), Agni (fire), Surya (sun), Varuna (cosmic order) are propitiated through sacrifices. According to the ancient Indians, deceased ancestors have influence over those who live and can be propitiated through rituals. The deceased are in a different state of being in which they maintain their identity and have the ability to bless those who are still alive, granting births and prosperity. Rituals and offerings are important to ensure the deceased, immediately after his death, the transition to his new dimension of existence.

"Going and coming is a pure illusion; the soul never goes nor comes. Where should it go when all the space is in the soul? What should be the time of arrival and departure, when all time is in the soul?"

According to the Upanishadic texts, the human soul is immortal. With *soul* we refer to the true Self, Atman, which by its nature is immortal and has a substantial identity with the supreme Brahman.

"The all-knowing Self was never born, Nor will it die. Beyond cause and effect, This Self is eternal and immutable."
(Katha Upanishad)

According to Patanjali, when a yogi, after a life of balance and detachment, evolves spiritually, he obtains knowledge of the reason for his birth and of his past. Paramahansa Yogananda states that evolved souls maintain continuity of consciousness from one life to another.

"Each individual decides on his or her number of births and the duration of each birth. Every action of ours has its own reaction that we must face. If we don't face them in this life, we'll face them in another."
(Satchidananda)

"We are the King of the Children of the universe and we have run away from home. We have forgotten our divine heritage because we have been locked up in

a body for so long."
(Paramahansa Yogananda)

According to Gregory Shushan, there are similarities between Egyptian/Indian beliefs and near-death experiences studied in the contemporary age, which suggests that they were aware of such phenomena and that their religions and spirituality were based on such knowledge.

In ancient Persia, the cradle of Zoroastrianism, the main monotheistic religion in the world before the advent of the Roman Empire, people believed in the continuation of life after death. According to Zoroastrianism, there is a relationship between every thought, word and action of human life and destiny after death. The eternal law of Asha determines this destiny: the soul of a righteous person goes to a heaven of infinite light, the "Vangheush Demana Manangho", while others go to hell, the "Aschishtaya Demana Manangho". This religion does not see heaven and hell as places, but as states of consciousness. According to such beliefs, three days after death the soul meets three judges and is then directed over a bridge by a guiding figure who actually represents its consciousness.

The civilization of Ancient Greece, whose treasures still live in Europe, was able to express in new forms the solemnity of Eastern wisdom through poetry, music, literature and philosophy and provided us with important details about the meaning of life and death.

According to Plato, the soul has full and perfect knowledge as long as it descends into the physical world. The paths of life will be different depending on how much the eternal truths of justice, temperance, knowledge, and beauty are treated.

Plato believes that in life, the immortal soul is imprisoned in the body, while death is an awakening to true life. The world in which we live is illusory, a shadow of the true reality of the spiritual world, defined by him as the "world of ideas", which transcends space and time.

Plato compares human beings to prisoners locked and chained inside a cave. There is a light behind their bodies, but they look ahead at the shadows reflected on the wall, thinking that these are the true reality. They do not realize that the light behind them is the true reality.

The reflected shadows are the sensory perceptions received during earthly life. They imprison the human being, making him believe that this is the only existing world and making him live in a real banishment from the Light, his true home.

According to Plato, each soul lives multiple existences and chooses, in line with its nature, the circumstances to which it will return in each subsequent life.

After being purified through human lives, the soul will gain the status of "pure immortal intelligence".

"The living come from the dead, and consequently, souls exist after death."
(Plato, Phaedrus)

Death is seen as the separation of the soul, the spiritual part, from the body, that is, the material part. The soul has very few limits compared to the body. The spiritual world is described as timeless; what we on Earth call "time", according to Plato, is nothing more than "an unreal reflection of time". The soul separated from the body can meet and dialogue with spirits, and is guided by guardian spirits through the transition from physical life to the spiritual world. On spiritual planes, the soul is more lucid than before, and the thought is clearer.

The body is therefore a prison for the soul, reducing it to a state of sleep, oblivion, unconsciousness. So death will be a liberation that will mark the return to the spiritual worlds, an awakening and a re-membering.

"Once free from the body, the soul is able to see the truth clearly, because it is purer and remembers the pure ideas it knew before," Plato writes in Phaedo.

It is said that each soul passed into the human form at the price of forgetting the other world, especially because it has stuck to the body and therefore being "dragged into the dimension of the imper-manent" it is confused. The soul therefore tends to identify with the body through physical sensations and pleasure, and believes every-thing that the body makes it believe.

Socrates says in Phaedo: *"And what is this thing called death, if not the separation and liberation of the soul from the body?"*

"Divine Souls! Return to your mortal bodies; you are about to embark on a new path. Here are all the destinies of life, choose freely; the choice is irrevocable."
(Plato, Republic)

In his work "Republic", Plato introduces the legend of Er, a sol-dier who died in war.

Ten days after his death, they recovered his body, which was not yet decomposing. After two days, Er came back to life and told his experience of death, which included an out-of-body experience, a review of the life just spent, a passage to bright light, wonderful landscapes, disembodied souls, and the subsequent return to the body. Er describes his journey, saying that at first he found different souls who had just finished their lives and were reconsidering them.

From there, different directions coordinated by judges unfolded, towards the sky-Heaven or towards Tartarus-underground worlds, depending on how they had lived according to universal laws. It was revealed to Er that he was not there for his judgment but as a messenger to reveal to humans the inaccessible wisdom regarding the fate of souls after death. Er came into contact both with a group of bright and colourful celebratory souls, who told of their joys of Heaven, and with damned souls, who externalized the suffering and despair of living in underground worlds. His journey continued: he went through a paradisiacal gate, until he met a Being of Impersonal Light. He glimpsed the passage between Heaven and Earth, where souls prepared for rebirth, programming different life patterns for each soul. Er witnessed how each soul chose a sort of script, noting that evolved souls chose wisely, unlike younger souls, who instead were tempted by the possibility of enjoying life's riches and pleasures. Each soul was assigned a guardian-angel who would provide help and guidance through the existential events. Er witnessed how souls drank from the River of Forgetfulness, which would cause amnesia of what had been lived on those spiritual planes. He chose not to drink from the river, so as to bring back to Earth the memories of what he had seen. He finally saw how souls, like shooting stars, were directed towards what would be their earthly mothers.

According to the Neoplatonic philosopher Plotinus: *"Every man is his absolute caretaker, the dispenser of joy or pain to himself, the decree of his life, his reward, his punishment."*

"Before here, they will exist there. Each soul descends to its special, determined moment, and enters the Earth in a voluntary 'immersion', going into a suitable body."

The physical world is very far from the One, the original spiritual dimension, but it is the best place to evolve and to be able to return to the One with a new awareness. Plotinus found himself regretting life in the spiritual worlds and often took refuge in the contemplation of the divine through temporary mystical experiences. He wrote nostalgically: *"When our soul comes down from home, we are like children taken by our parents and taken away."*

Apuleius and Philostratus refer to apparitions, dreams and evocations of the spirits of the deceased.

In the Odyssey, Ulysses meets his mother's ghost. He tries to hug her but fails and suffers. His mother explains that, after death, the soul leaves the body. According to the beliefs of the ancient Greeks, the deceased begins the journey into Hades through the River Styx. There are three judges: Aeacus, Minos and Rhadamanthus, who will decide the destiny of the deceased based on the life he led. Those who lived according to noble ideals are sent to the Elysian fields, a kind of heavenly paradise full of joy where it is always spring. Those who stained themselves with sins in life are destined to go to Tartarus, a dark infernal region of eternal punishment. Those who are neither virtuous nor evil are sent to the Asphodel Fields, a limbo-purgatory.

Even in Roman culture, we find references to death and contact with the dead, for example, in the works of Lucan and Tacitus. Pliny the Elder tells the story of Corfidius, a nobleman who died and left his inheritance to his younger brother, who was supposed to take care of his funeral. However, after a few hours after his death, Corfidius came back to life, surprising everyone, and called his servants. He told them that he had met his brother in the afterlife, who had said that the funeral arrangements should be used for him instead. The brother confided to Corfidius the place where he had hidden the gold. The information received turned out to be true: his brother had indeed died unexpectedly under accidental circumstances, and the gold was located right in the place he had indicated.

In the Aeneid, we find a reference to the afterlife in the sixth book, when Aeneas meets his father Anchise in the Elysian Fields and learns the law of rebirth.

From Roman history, with Julius Caesar's "De bello gallico", it was possible to learn the Druids' traditions, one of the main classes of the Gallic society, a college of priests since the ancient Celtic peoples. They were wise priests who exercised a highly symbolic worship in which all the elements of nature, including forests, trees and stones, had sacredness and meaning. According to the Druids, the soul goes through four cycles: the "animal state", the "earthly state", made up of trials and cycles of reincarnations, and the "cycle of joy", reaching the spiritual worlds. Finally, it arrives at the "cycle of infinity", which is the fusion with the Absolute-God.

According to the Druids, the human being is master of his destiny and has the possibility to evolve through discipline and wisdom, transcending ephemeral and transitory pleasures through the daily battles of existence. The Druids maintained close contact with the unseen, in particular with the spirits of the dead. According to historical records, Vercingetorix, before the battle against Caesar, communicated with an invisible spirit who predicted his defeat. The commemoration of the dead is of Gallic origin: the Gauls had a sincere and deep respect for the souls of the dead, venerating them not in cemeteries, but in the same houses where they lived.

Outside Europe, other traditions give particular sacredness to death. In China, in line with the assumptions of Confucianism, for 4,000 years they believed in God, called Shang Di. There are several references to life after death and they practice a cult dedicated to ancestors, which also includes rituals of invocation of their "mana" in order to support the clans. The world of the dead is considered closely connected with that of the living. The world of the ancestors is seen as a dark realm, a yin space, which in some respects is similar to the world of the living. According to Taoism, the devotee who has had a conduct of compassion, confession and virtue, can go to heaven after a brief stay in an "underworld".

In Thailand, it is believed that the soul decides the length of life and when and how death will occur. Among the peoples of Sumatra, we can find the legend of leaves: each soul chooses a leaf, where there is a lesson to be learned, the duration of life and the circumstances of death.

Moving further, we discover that in Africa, the belief in survival after death is strongly rooted and rituals are organized to consolidate the bond between the living and the dead, considered members of the same community. Ancestors are considered living and spiritually present members, in a more decisive and influential way than when they were in their bodies: they are considered intermediaries between God and the living and capable of influencing the events and destiny of the members of the community. They are actively involved in the lives of individuals, their families and their social lives. Much attention is paid to funerary rituals, which aim to facilitate the passage of the deceased to the world of the ancestors.

According to the Zulus, the soul moves forward on different levels, from a disciple to a teacher, and then becomes the abakula-bantu, a perfect human being. At this point, the soul becomes one with the origin and no longer needs to reincarnate, although it could under certain circumstances.

References to reincarnation and the pre-life state are found among the Indian populations of America, particularly among the Lakota, who believe that, prior to reincarnation, souls roam the hills, scanning the tents, until they find parents suitable for them.

The Great Religions

In the Jewish Torah, it is written: *"All souls are One. Each is a spark of the original Soul, and this soul is entirely contained in all souls."* According to the tradition of the Midrash and Zohar, the basis of Kabbalah seen as a set of esoteric and mystical teachings of rabbinic Judaism, the soul is part of the Creator, feels lost in the body and longs to return to the place where it originates, where our souls were created.

"Before descending to Earth, an elder says to the soul that is about to incarnate, 'You are going on a long journey. Do your best. You will return and be asked how your trip went'."

According to Jewish tradition, death is the passage from one state of material consciousness to another spiritual state. The human soul has a "nefesh" essence that survives physical death. The "ruach" is awareness and the "neshama" is similar to the Jungian collective unconscious. Finally, there is a vital part that transcends the individual and projects him towards the supreme divine consciousness, made of unity and love.

The Jewish religion basically believes in an afterlife, but it emphasizes the resurrection of the body for the pure, which will take place at the end of time, so it does not go beyond the indissoluble unity of body and spirit. The dead are believed to descend into a world of shadows called Sheol. Any form of spiritual communication with the deceased is prohibited. The intervention of divine grace is essential, the active intervention of God.

The Christian religion, on the other hand, is based on different assumptions. The first verses of the Gospel according to John read as follows: *"In the beginning was the Word, and the Word was with God, and the Word was God. The same was in the beginning with God. All things were made by him; and without him was not any thing made that was made."*

The Bible includes many references to the immortal soul. Belief in an afterlife is rooted in the dogma of Jesus' resurrection. Jesus is seen as both human and divine. According to his teachings, eternal life is a new state of being that can be acquired in life. *"I am the life"*: to live in Jesus means to live with the divine life. *"As the son of God became man, so we can become God,"* says Athanasius, meaning that the human being can become like God.

"We are heirs of God"
(Acts of the Apostles).

As in the Jewish religion, Christianity also affirms the belief in the resurrection of the body, as well as in a spiritual existence between physical death and resurrection. The concept of Paradise can be interpreted as the idea of union with the creator, in immense bliss and infinite joy, full of ecstatic and unconditional love; a concept that cannot be described in ordinary human terms and that indicates a state of being and not a place. Instead, Hell would be a total separation from God — extreme suffering. However, according to the Christian perspective, God does not want anyone to go to Hell — He wants salvation for everyone. God gave human beings free will. It is as if Hell were a human creation, as a logical consequence of the use of freedom outside the kingdom of God. But God does not condemn or judge anyone. As if it were a deep part of ourselves that judges as a divine mirror. There will always be second chances. Then Purgatory: an intermediate state for those who need to be purified, souls assisted by the prayers of those who are still alive, a time of growth and transformation, so that they can see the face of God.

Early Christians believed in reincarnation. In the New Testament, there is a reference to a born-blind man, whom the apostles believed to be "punished with blindness for sins committed before he was even born". The Christians of the origins believed in the assistance of a cycle of souls, the "Gilgul". In the Acts of the Apostles there are some clues about communication with the spirits of the dead. In the letter to the Corinthians, St. Paul refers to "spiritual gifts" and believes that the gospel truth was communicated to him by the spirit of Jesus. John, however, said that he did not believe "every spirit, but test the spirits if they are of God."

The references to the resurrection in St. Paul's letter to the Corinthians are particularly interesting:

"But someone will say, 'How are the dead raised? And with what body do they come?'. You foolish one! That which you yourself sow is not made alive unless it dies. That which you sow, you don't sow the body that will be, but a bare grain, maybe of wheat, or of some other kind. But God gives it a body even as it pleased him, and to each seed a body of its own. All flesh is not the same flesh, but there is one flesh of men, another flesh of animals, another of fish, and another of birds. There are also celestial bodies, and terrestrial bodies; but the glory of the celestial differs from that of the terrestrial. There is one glory of the sun, another glory of the moon, and another glory of the stars; for one star differs from another star in glory. So also is the resurrection of the dead. The body is sown perishable; it is raised imperishable. It is sown in dishonour; it is raised in glory. It is sown in weakness; it is raised in power. It is sown a natural body; it is raised a spiritual body.

There is a natural body and there is also a spiritual body. So also it is written, 'The first man Adam became a living soul. The last Adam became a life-giving spirit'."

This passage was quoted by Raymond Moody in his "Life After Life"; according to his interpretation, the apostle Paul seems to describe the spiritual body of those who have found themselves in a state of "Out-of-body experience", as we will see later: immateriality, lack of physical substance, strength opposed to weakness of the physical body, completeness, lack of limits of space and time.

In the Alexandrian school, which intended to combine the teachings of Pythagoras and Plato with those of the Vedas and Christianity, almost all philosophers considered themselves inspired by superior spirits: Plotinus, Porphyry, Philo, Ammonius Sacca and Iamblichus.

"Why not attribute these works to the spirits of the dead and not believe that divine Providence uses everything to instruct men, console and correct them?" St. Augustine says this, referring to the "teletes", practices of theurgy that led to communicating with angelic spiritual entities.

Other references can be found in St. Clement of Alexandria and St. Gregory of Nyssa who say: *"The immortal soul must be healed and purified, if not in this earthly life, in future and subsequent lives."*

According to Gnosticism, the soul is a divine spark; each soul is a spark of individualized spiritual essence, contained in the depths of human consciousness. The roots of a human being come from another world. It is just like a divine spark falling into this world. According to Gnosticism, when the soul falls into matter, its true centre, its true knowledge, is forgotten.

"I have said unto you indeed from the beginning that ye are not of the world."
(Pistis Sophia)

Origen synthesizes Christianity and Greek philosophy, theorizing that previously every soul lived with God since the dawn of time, and then went to live in various worlds, from life to life, until it was purified and returned to a spiritual state, the apocatastasis. However, his doctrine was censured at the Council of Constantinople in 553 AD.

In the Muslim religion, Muhammad gives voice to God Allah in the Koran: *"I was a hidden treasure, I wanted to be known, so I created this world of form and life."* The Sufis express the relationship between body and soul with metaphors, comparing the soul to a fish out of water, or a caged parrot. In the Koran it is stated that:

"No one dies, because the soul carries in itself the signs of its eternity."

Comparing the ancient religions of different eras, places and cultures, common elements emerge that lead to the belief in life after death and in the fact that the type of life led affects the modalities of our passage to the afterlife. The concept of God as creator, revealer and guide is also recurrent.

Apparently, believing in an afterlife is deeply rooted in human beings since the beginning of time.

CHAPTER 2

DOCTORS FROM THE AFTERLIFE

"Near-Death Experiences" are defined as the memory of experiences lived during a special state of consciousness that can occur in the event of clinical death or, as witnessed in rare cases, even in sudden situations due to altered states of consciousness or to particular medical situations such as fainting, coma, near drowning, high fever or asphyxiation. Recent studies suggest that millions of people around the world experienced an NDE: people who do not know each other, who live in different countries and belong to different cultures. The increase in the incidence of NDEs in recent decades is due to the development and refinement of resuscitation techniques, which has therefore let to an increased chance of survival following a critical and potentially fatal medical event.

Carl Gustav Jung

Very significant is the near-death experience of the Swiss psychiatrist Carl Gustav Jung following his myocardial infarction in 1944 at the age of 43. He described it in his autobiographical book "Memories, Dreams, Reflections", with his typical intensity of being attentive to inner and spiritual experiences:

"It seemed to me that I was high up in space. Far below I saw the globe of the Earth, bathed in a gloriously blue light. I saw the deep blue sea and the continents. Far below my feet lay Ceylon, and in the distance ahead of me the subcontinent of India. My field of vision did not include the whole Earth, but its global shape was plainly distinguishable and its outlines shone with a silvery gleam through that wonderful blue light.

In many places the globe seemed coloured, or spotted dark green like oxidized silver. Far away to the left lay a broad expanse — the reddish-yellow desert of Arabia; it was as though the silver of the Earth had there assumed a reddish-gold hue. Then came the Red Sea, and far, far back — as if in the upper left of a map — I could just make out a bit of the Mediterranean. My gaze was directed chiefly toward that. Everything else appeared indistinct. I could also see the snow-covered Himalayas, but in that direction it was foggy or cloudy. I did not look to the right at all. I knew that I was on the point of departing from the Earth.

Later I discovered how high in space one would have to be to have so extensive a view — approximately a thousand miles! The sight of the Earth from this height was the most glorious thing I had ever seen."

Jung then recalls the vision of a large stone-meteorite, in which a temple was excavated, which was accessed through a door framed by lighted lamps. To its right there was a Hindu in the position of the lotus. At that point Jung approached the steps leading to the entrance and had the feeling that *"everything was being sloughed away; everything I aimed at or wished for or thought, the whole phantasmagoria of earthly existence, fell away or was stripped from me—an extremely painful process.*

Nevertheless, something remained; it was as if I now carried along with me everything I have ever experienced or done, everything that had happened around me. I might also say: it was with me, and I was it. I consisted of all that, so to speak. I consisted of my own history, and I felt with great certainty: this is what I am. I am this bundle of things that have been and that have been accomplished. This experience gave me a feeling of extreme poverty, but at the same time of great fullness. There was no longer anything I wanted or desired. I existed in an objective form; I was what I had been and lived."

Jung continued to approach that temple, having the distinct feeling that he was about to enter an illuminated room, where he would meet *"all those people to whom I belong in reality"* and where he would have the real understanding of the meaning of his life. But he found himself looking again towards the globe of the Earth, in the direction of Europe, where his doctor was calling him back, as if there were *"a protest against my going away [...] I had no right to leave the earth and must return."*

This experience was crucial for Jung, who would later live to the age of 86 — for another 43 years — and would never forget the beauty and intensity of what he had experienced in that dimension. So safe in an *"immeasurable emptiness but full of an intense feeling of happiness."* From that moment Jung realized that physical life is nothing more than a small fragment of existence, related to a merely three-dimensional universe, but that in reality it is much broader. He had the impression that reality on Earth was like a prison that reduced people to a state of hypnosis, leading them to believe that it was the only reality. As a result of his near-death experience, Jung produced his major works, in the wake of new insights.

It is important to note that, at the time Jung lived his near-death experience, there were still no photos of the Earth seen from space, since the first space flights came after. It is therefore surprising that Jung was able to see so realistically what would later be confirmed by pictures taken by space astronauts, portraying our blue globe enveloped by white clouds. How else could he see the Earth except through an out-of-body experience?

George G. Ritchie

In Texas, when he was still a medical student and enlisted in the military, the psychiatrist George Ritchie fell ill with a severe form of pneumonia and experienced an NDE. In his book "Return from Tomorrow", published 42 years after the event, he tells the details of this experience. He was in an isolation room in the hospital of the military base and, when a nurse went to check on him in the evening, he was found without any sign of life. He was visited by a medical officer who found the total absence of breathing and heart-beat and was therefore declared clinically dead. He was immediately taken to the morgue, where he was left covered by a sheet up to his face. Meanwhile, Ritchie was very alert and rational, but not in his body; after hearing a continuous buzzing sound inside his head that became more and more intense, he was practically out of his body. He was not yet aware that he was in something like a "spiritual body", so he sat down and even looked for a clock. He noticed that all his belongings, including his watch, had been taken away and, when he turned to the bed, he saw with extreme dismay that some-one was lying there motionless, which seemed impossible since he had just gotten out of that bed. At the moment he did not worry about it and headed towards the corridor, where he met a sergeant who was carrying a tray of tools covered with a cloth. When Ritchie asked him if he had seen the nurse on duty, he was blatantly ig-nored, he recalls: *"In fact, he didn't even look at me. He continued straight towards me with his step, without slowing down."* Ritchie was alarmed because the sergeant walked towards him, risking hitting him, but he noticed that a moment later the sergeant was behind him, and he could not understand how he managed to avoid touching him. In out-of-body experiences, as we will see later, not only people are not seen by normally incarnated people, but the "astral body" can pass through solid surfaces and even through people. Ritchie con-tinued walking until he reached the metal door at the end of the corridor with the intention of getting out of there and even taking a train to reach Richmond. He found himself outside but noticed that his movements were very agile and quick: he found himself floating quickly over the desert and the will to go to Richmond gave the direction of this journey that took place at a speed "*a hundred times faster than that of any train on this Earth.*" Suddenly his movements slowed down and he found himself in front of a building with a sign depicting a beer and the luminous words "café". Ritchie was suspended in the air several meters high, until he saw a man who was walking and then manifested the will to descend on the sidewalk to ask where he was. He was able to see that his thoughts were closely linked to his actions. When he approached the passer-by, he noticed that he had not even noticed his presence, despite walking beside him and despite the questions he asked him insistently. The man arrived at the cafe and was about to open the door, when Ritchie tried to urge him: "*I raised my left hand to tap him on his shoulder, but there was nothing there.*"

"*I stood there in front of the door, gawking at him as he opened the door and disappeared into the room. It was like touching the air, as if there was no one there.*" Ritchie was stunned, aware that he had clearly seen that man, even noticing particular details about his beard. When he tried to lean on a telephone pole, he noticed that his body was passing through that surface, as if there was nothing there. Ritchie's clearness of mind was of considerable intensity and particularly animated by the strangeness of the situation. He could not understand what was happening to him and feared that he had lost his "physical form" or his ability to get in touch with the world. Suddenly he remembered the young man he had seen on the bed and doubted that this was precisely his physical body from which he had separated. When Ritchie focused his attention on his body, manifesting a willingness to reach it and go back to that hospital room in Texas, it began to move again, floating quickly in the direction it had come from, soaring over nighttime landscapes of rivers, lakes, and hills. Finally, he found himself in front of the hospital of the military base, "*and so began one of the strangest searches that have ever taken place: the search for myself*": he entered every room until he found a dead man in a bed covered with a sheet wearing his ring on his finger. That man was exactly him. *"But I wasn't dead! How could I be dead, and still be so awake? I thought, I had experiences... Death was something different: it was... I didn't know... the complete darkness, the absolute nothingness. I was me, fully awake, though lacking the physical body to function with."* Ritchie had a momentary anxious reaction, tried to pull down the sheet, but again could not interact with any physical object. He realized that everything around him was bright, with a light that progressively increased. It was a non-physical and "impossible" light, as if it were produced by a million light bulbs. At that moment, he noticed a man made of light who had entered the room. He had the feeling that that being of light, who emanated power, unconditional love, *"a breath-taking love, a love beyond what I could have ever imagined"*, was "the son of God" and that he knew everything about him. He felt that he was deeply loved and accepted by him, while the episodes of his life were reviewed simultaneously, as if they took place at the same time, or rather in a timeless line of synchronicity. *"Every detail of twenty years of living was there to be looked at. The good, the bad, the high points, the run-of-the-mill. And with this all-inclusive view came a question. It was implicit in every scene and, like the scenes themselves, seemed to proceed from the living light beside me. 'What did you do with your life?'."* At that point, Ritchie realized that it was difficult to find something that had value facing the pure radiance of that being. He revealed his life was animated by constant concern for himself and that he had done nothing for others. To understand the intensity of that moment, we need to read Ritchie's own words:

'The answering thought, however, held no trace of judgment. Death, – the word was infinitely loving, – can come at any age.'

'What about the insurance money coming when I'm seventy?' The words were out, in this strange realm where communication took place by thought instead of speech, before I could call them back. If I'd suspected before that there was

mirth in the presence beside me, now I was sure of it: the brightness seemed to vibrate and shimmer with a kind of holy laughter – not at me and my silliness, not a mocking laughter, but a mirth that seemed to say that in spite of all error and tragedy, joy was more lasting still.

And in the ecstasy of that laughter, I realized that it was I who was judging the events around us so harshly. It was I who saw them as trivial, self-centred, unimportant. No such condemnation came from the glory shining around me. He was not blaming or reproaching. He was simply... loving me. Filling the world with himself and yet somehow attending to me personally. Waiting for my answer to the question that still hung in the dazzling air. 'What have you done with your life to show me?'

The question, like everything else proceeding from him, had to do with love. How much have you loved with your life? Have you loved others as I am loving you? Totally? Unconditionally? Hearing the question like that, I saw how foolish it was even to try to find an answer in the scenes around us. Why, I hadn't known love like this was possible."

Then Ritchie noticed that he was moving, flying very high, towards a bright spot that was a big city, with illuminated buildings, crowded streets, smoke coming out of the chimneys. Beyond the lights there seemed to be a stretch of water that could be an ocean or a large lake. He found himself in front of several scenes in which the incarnated people did not notice the spirits of the deceased who tried to interact with them. Ritchie asked his luminous guide why such souls were so desolate and why they kept trying to talk to people who couldn't hear them. The light conveyed to him the thought that these were souls who had left the body following suicide. Looking at the living people, Ritchie noticed that they were surrounded by a faint luminous glow that enveloped their bodies, unlike inanimate objects. On the other hand, the souls of the deceased did not have this luminous glow, which therefore seemed the prerogative of the physical body.

Ritchie found himself witnessing the assault of non-embodied souls on living people who were addicted to alcohol. These souls desperately tried to satisfy their desire, but in vain, as they no longer had a physical body. Ritchie observed a sailor who fainted and noticed that the luminous glow split and one of the non-embodied beings tried to rush towards that opening. He guessed that this aureole of light was like a protective shield against "non-solid" beings, who had probably had a physical body in the past and, after death, had brought their addiction to alcohol to the afterlife, which, however, they could no longer realise, except if they could briefly take possession of a physical body of some poor guy. He noticed that the sailor's luminous cocoon was opening and beginning to split, slipping away like a film from the top of his head. Ritchie realised that that invisible dimension, so close to the Earth almost able to interact spiritually with living beings, was like a level of "hell": *"But what if one level of hell existed right here on the surface – unseen and unsuspected by the living people occupying the same space. [...] What if it meant remaining on earth but never again able to make contact with it."*

Ritchie began to identify the characteristics of the spiritual dimension in which he found himself, realising that disembodied beings tend to be attracted to similar ones. His journey continued in dimensions where there seemed to be thousands of distressed disembodied beings fighting each other as if they were on a battlefield, but no one was hurt. These creatures seemed locked into habits of mind and emotion, into hatred, lust, destructive thought-patterns. In those dimensions they were completely exposed: every thought was no longer private but perceptible by others and in resonance with everything that was happening around him. Ritchie felt that, somehow, those dimensions mirrored his deepest internality and all that persisted in him as unresolved. He was always guided by the luminous being, who radiated compassion and total lack of any form of judgment or condemnation. Now they moved to a higher dimension in a sunny park, in a building that reminded him of a well-planned

university full of souls focused on intellectual activities and sophisticated experiments. In other buildings he could hear complex music
different from the terrestrial one, complicated rhythms, tones not on
a scale he knew. Ritchie and his guide visited a huge library where
"the important books of the universe" were assembled. *"The calm, the brightness, they were surely heaven-like! So was the absence of self, of clamouring ego.
When these people were on earth did they grow beyond selfish desires?'*

*'They grew, and they have kept on growing.' The answer shone like sunlight
in that intent and eager atmosphere. But if growth could continue, then this
was not all. Then... there must be something even these serene beings lacked."*

In that dimension that he would call "kingdom of mind and intellect" or "kingdom of scientific and religious knowledge", Ritchie
was realising that it is not true that a human being after death does
not learn or evolve, instead everything goes on. Souls who have developed the greatest interest in a particular field of life's endeavour,
want to keep on researching and learning more in their particular
fields.

"Now, however, we seemed to have left the earth behind.

*And then I saw, infinitely far off, far too distant to be visible with any kind
of sight I knew of, a city. A glowing, seemingly endless city, bright enough to be
seen over all the unimaginable distance between. The brightness seemed to shine
from the very walls and streets of this place, and from beings which I could now
discern moving about within it. In fact, the city and everything in it seemed to be
made of light, even as the figure at my side was made of light."*

At that point Ritchie felt the peace, joy and love of the beings that
populated that city and thought he was really in heaven.

In that context, his guide showed him some images of what the
future of the Earth could be, with different scenarios based on the
free will of human beings and on what they would learn to love un-

conditionally. And that's how the guide finally announced to Ritchie that he had to return to earth.

When Ritchie "returned to his body", the nurse noticed a slight movement of the chest, although still without breathing and heartbeat and suggested to the medical officer to perform an intrathoracic injection of adrenaline, an unusual procedure at that time. The patient had remained in a condition of clinical death, therefore without a heartbeat and without respiratory activity, for about ten minutes.

It was in this way that Ritchie was "resurrected" and could only regain consciousness four days later. The spiritual value of such an experience was unbelievable and would change his life forever. This event prompted him to devote his life to studying the phenomenon of near-death experiences.

Eben Alexander

The neurosurgeon Eben Alexander has focused his studies and research on the nervous and endocrine system, in particular the complications of aneurysm, specializing in Cerebrovascular Neurosurgery and operating on hundreds of patients in desperate brain conditions. He has contributed to the development of technical procedures for neurosurgery guided by the most modern scan-imaging technologies to operate on complex tumours or vascular diseases. With hundreds of publications, he considered himself devoted to science, with the desire to learn as much as possible about the functioning of the human brain and body. He thought that if the brain had shut down and ended its functioning, there would be no chance that consciousness would continue to function. Eben Alexander thought that the brain was a machine producing the phenomenon of consciousness. Although scientists had not discovered exactly how neurons do this, he believed it was only a matter of time. "*I loved the absolute honesty and purity of science. I respected the fact that it leaves no room for fantasies or rough thinking. If a fact could be established as tangible and trustworthy, it was accept-*

ed. Otherwise, it was rejected." This approach did not leave room for the spirit, for something that subsisted beyond physical death.

In his book "Proof of Heaven", Eben Alexander tells that at the age of 44 he suddenly woke up at dawn with a violent headache and back pain. In a few hours he lost consciousness and his wife could no longer wake him up. He was immediately taken to the emergency room and the first tests showed damage both to the cerebral cortex — precisely the area responsible for the cognitive processes of perception, thought, language and memory — and to the brainstem that regulates breathing, blood pressure, heartbeat, sleep/wake rhythm. The doctors believed his chances of survival were minimal. Alexander was in a deep coma for several days, on life support. During his coma, his brain was not working at all and the neocortex was not active. As a neurosurgeon, he would only later realise the disconcerting implication of what had happened to him.

Further investigations revealed that there was pus in the brain cavity, and this situation detected the presence of a serious infection of the brain: severe meningitis. Unlike the prognosis and expectations of the doctors, he woke up after six days, unable to speak, with motor problems and memory loss. However, he had vivid memories of an experience lived in another context and was able to talk about it a few days later. He revealed that he had found himself in a place full of lights and colours, flowers, waterfalls, celestial music and that he had experienced an intense level of awareness, feeling out of the physical body. He had met several luminous beings, including a female figure who seemed to be a guide and communicated with him telepathically. He then remembered having met a great divine being, comparable to God. He also reported seeing specific people outside his family around his intensive care bed, a situation that was later confirmed. Four months after his near-death experience, Alexander, who had been adopted at birth, met his family of origin who showed him the picture of a sister he had never met, who had died ten years earlier. He recognised the female figure who had led him into the afterlife.

Bruce Greyson, a doctor who studies NDEs, as we will see later, wanted to analyse his colleague's medical record, noting that he had really been on the threshold of death and that his brain activity was actually suspended. It was not a medically induced coma, but it had been caused by the delicate conditions of his compromised clinical picture. Eben Alexander himself was astonished to see from his medical record how serious his situation was: deep damage to the neocortex caused by the attack of the bacterium.

He realized: *"My experience showed me that the death of the body and the brain is not the end of consciousness. [...] The place I went to is real. Real in a way that, in comparison, makes the life we are living here and now completely like a dream."*

From that experience, he thinks he has gained knowledge about the nature and structure of the universe, which is beyond his understanding:

"It will take me years to understand, using my mortal and material brain, what I understood so instantly and easily in the world of the afterlife, free of the brain."

Alexander believes that science is not against what he has learned from his experience, although most of his colleagues in the scientific community support the incompatibility of science and spirituality.

He states that the brain tends to block and veil the perception of the spiritual worlds that are our true nature. It is therefore necessary to recover this knowledge when you are still alive, when the brain is still in its full functioning.

Alexander had never read anything on the NDE topic before his illness and chose not to do so until he had written down his personal experience in detail, in order to avoid being influenced by it. This process took him two years to be completed. According to his medical training, for a subject in a deep coma, it would be impossible to live any kind of experience or have memory of it.

When he finally examined the publications on the topic, he found considerable analogies with his own experience, as well as the same difficulty that others had had in expressing in words what they had experienced beyond the threshold.

To those who objected to the authenticity of his experience, attributing everything to a dream, to a psychedelic experience induced by DMT or to the effect of drugs administered in intensive care, he replied in the same way as Dr. Pimmel — as we will see later —, emphasizing that nothing he experienced could ever manifest itself in the absence of the functioning of the neocortex.

Everything that Eben Alexander had learned in decades of study about the human brain, the universe, and reality, had turned out to be totally in contrast to what he had experienced during the seven days in a deep coma.

> *"I became more convinced that my discovery wasn't just interesting or dramatic. It was scientific."*

Even with Eben Alexander's experience, human consciousness was therefore the greatest mystery that scientific research could face, showing itself to be much more than a mere product of psychic processes.

Mary C. Neal

Mary Neal, an orthopaedic surgeon and director of spinal surgery at the University of South Carolina, had already survived a car accident when she was just a teenager and a scuba diving accident. She attended the Methodist church, trying to constantly nurture her relationship with God and pass Christian values to her children. In her work "To Heaven and Back: A Doctor's Extraordinary Account of Her Death", she tells the details of her near-death experience during a holiday in southern Chile, when she suffered a kayak accident along a river, ending up trapped inside a waterfall. She was found drowned, without life and breath, and was later subjected to the cardiopulmonary resuscitation procedure. She reports that when she was drowning she had the feeling that her soul was being "sucked out" from her body, as if it was getting rid of a heavy outer layer. She met a group of souls who greeted her with incredible joy. She had the feeling she knew some of them, including some deceased relatives and friends; although she could not identify them all, she had the clear feeling that she had known them forever. She perceived them as distinct forms, but not as real bodies of earthly appearance. Communication took place telepathically, through the transmission of thoughts and emotions. She had the feeling that those beings were there to guide her and help her with immense love.

> *"The intensity, depth, and fullness of these feelings and sensations were greater than I could describe in words and far greater than anything I have experienced on Earth."*

She found herself walking along a path with those spiritual companions, aware that she was "returning to God", towards a bright room. However, suddenly she brought attention to the image of her husband and children expressing despair. Mary Neal noted that whenever she heard her husband and children begging her to go back and breathe, she felt compelled to return to her body and stop her journey into the afterlife. When she arrived with her spiritual companions at the entrance to the luminous hall, she sensed a sadness on their part and was told that her time to cross the threshold had not yet come, as her journey on Earth had not yet ended. She therefore had to return to her body, and so it happened — to her great regret. Dr. Neal has returned from this experience with new strength and a new awareness of the meaning of her life. She changed the way she interacted with patients, pursuing a much broader concept of healing than that commonly understood by conventional medicine to "fix mechanical problems". He had the opportunity to hear stories from some of her patients who were in critical condition. For example, a patient who, after a spinal surgery, in the process of death had "seen the angels" and described "paradise" to his wife.

CHAPTER 3:

STUDYING NEAR-DEATH EXPERIENCES

Raymond Moody, an American physician, psychologist and para-psychologist, is one of the leading experts in research on near-death states. He was the first to coin the term "Near-Death Experience". His teacher was George Ritchie, whose exciting personal experience we have just seen.

After Raymond Moody published his book, in the following years he was contacted by numerous fellow doctors, nurses, health professionals and social workers who, during their clinical experience, had the opportunity to collect testimonials from patients who had experienced NDEs. A meeting took place between Raymond Moody, Bruce Greyson, the psychologist Ken Ring, the cardiologist Michael Sabom and the sociologist John Audette. On that occasion, the Association Iands was founded in order to study and provide information on the phenomena of the NDE.

To follow this research, it is necessary to understand the relationship between immaterial consciousness and material brain support, and to ask ourselves what happens to consciousness in a state of sleep, total anaesthesia, coma, and precisely in clinical death.

The moment a heart attack occurs, the respiratory centre ceases to function, and therefore the breathing process stops. The loss of consciousness following a heart attack occurs in about eight seconds. Blood flow to the brain is interrupted and electrical activity in the cerebral cortex completely ceases, a situation detected by a flat line EEG. Twenty seconds later, brain functions cease, making it impossible for consciousness to persist and memory to function.

During resuscitation procedures, cardiac massage tries to induce blood circulation so that it reaches the brain and nourishes it with oxygen and nutrition in order to avoid brain damage in the event of a return to life. Hypothermia is also used, as the lowering of brain temperature prevents brain damage and deterioration in a situation of no heartbeat.

The possibility that there still is some cerebral electrical activity was evaluated; however, it was confirmed that the electroencephalogram as early as ten seconds after the heart attack does not record any electrical activity in the cerebral cortex, which is responsible for thoughts, perceptions, language and memory.

According to cardiologist Michael Sabom, whose research we will see later: *"There is no definable moment of death, but only a process of dying that starts with life and eventually ends in death [...] and whether the journey ends in life or in death is determined not only by physical factors, but by events not seen by everyone, except the dying patient, in a state of unconsciousness."*

Sam Parnia, a doctor specialised in anaesthesia and resuscitation, also believes that death is a process that begins when the heartbeat and breathing cease and brain functions are interrupted.

In order to explain how it could happen that thought processes can coexist with serious brain dysfunctions, Parnia says that many studies have shown that brain processes are mediated by multiple areas of the brain. Even assuming the presence of a minimal blood flow in a restricted area of the brain, it is still known that the activity of thoughts is generated by a global function of the brain, so if there is no breathing and complete blood circulation, no type of conscious activity should occur.

However, the near-death experience is an experience of the soul and not the brain. For this reason, it cannot be monitored through equipment that can only detect brain activity.

We can derive information on NDEs from multiple sources, which include numerous written testimonies gathered in a structured format. We can find it on thematic websites, among which the most important is the NDER-F.org-Near Death Experience Research Foundation, founded and managed by Jeffrey and Joy Long, which gathers over 5,000 testimonies collected over more than twenty years. Hundreds of conferences, interviews and discussion forums run by different associations and even universities can be found online. Then there are books that deal with the subject in a theoretical-scientific, philosophical or psychological way, based on the most up-to-date studies and research on the subject. There are also scientific studies and research published by reputable and prestigious organizations.

An NDE must have occurred during a state of clinical death, in a hospital setting. The testimonies are first-person accounts of subjects aged 14 and over, considering that at that age there is a better chance of verbalizing the experience to the best of our ability.

Pim Van Lommel, a Dutch cardiologist and researcher, first became aware of the NDE experiences in 1969, when he was still a resident, since he witnessed the resuscitation of a patient in cardiac arrest. Surprised by the possibility that a conscious experience could occur in a state of cardiac arrest, which was considered impossible by ordinary medical science, he began to carry out investigations and research among the patients who survived that clinical condition.

In his "Consciousness Beyond Life", as in Raymond Moody's work "Life After Life", Pim Van Lommel accurately describes the different elements that characterize an NDE.

An important element is the out-of-body experience (OBE). In a study of 53 verified OBE reports, 43% were confirmed by independent witnesses; 92% were accurate, 6% had some errors, and 1% were incorrect. The OBE experience is not a hallucination or a psychotic episode. For example, there is the case of a patient blind from birth, who had suffered a car accident and reported a serious head injury that had reduced her to a coma. She had a near-death experience, in which she "saw" different details that she obviously could never have perceived because of her blindness. The accurate physical descriptions of the accident scene and rescuers were true to life. Another example is about a patient who had suffered a heart attack and who, after coming back to life with the resuscitation procedures, knew perfectly well where the CCU nurse had kept his dentures, even though his body was clinically dead at the time.

In the out-of-body experience, a feeling of strangeness from the physical body is often reported. Some subjects feel not like they are in another body, but instead like they are pure consciousness, as if they were able to see everything around them, but without occupying any space. In this state, the subject can see other people and fully perceive their thoughts, although they cannot see them in turn.

Another element of the NDE concerns the meeting with deceased relatives, people never known before, or people whose deaths could not have been known.

In most cases, they also talk about luminous beings, which seems to be what has the greatest meaning.

The luminous being is not just any being, but a defined identity with which one has a special bond that radiates unbelievable light,

warmth and love. Wonderful is the feeling of being loved and accepted.

It is possible that such beings are attributed religious identities,
based on their background. "Being of Light" is the basic definition,
whatever the identity attributed to the entity. The luminous being
seems to telepathically communicate a recurring idea that sounds like
a question: "Are you ready to die? What did you do with your life that
you can show me?". There is no accusation or judgment, but full acceptance and love, with the sole purpose of making the person think
about the life just spent. This meeting is described as a moment of
extraordinary intensity and emotion.

Such encounters with spiritual beings take place to give relief to
the dying in the state of transition or to warn him that the time to die
has not yet come and that he must therefore return to Earth.

In most cases, people refer to see a "light" with an intensity never
seen before. It does not destabilize or blind, precisely because it is
not seen with the physical eyes but with the soul. This light does not
prevent you from seeing other things around you.

The encounters in other dimensions are mainly described as spiritual beings gathered in groups. There are different levels of experience and categories of beings. There are "spirits" who guide those
who have just found themselves in those dimensions. They are like
spiritual beings, angels radiating love, wisdom, and power. They do
not have a definite human form, although they seem to be wrapped
in white clothes, and give the impression of being surrounded by a
luminous aura. Often those who lived the experience report feeling
connected to such guides as if they had known them for thousands
of years, even if there is no feeling of a physical personal recognition. They communicate with these entities through thought. Positive emotions of joy, love, gratitude and freedom are experienced
near them.

Many subjects describe having found themselves in contact with a "being of light", which they experienced as a point of origin of the whole, therefore a being identified as God. Those who lived this experience said that they felt part of this light, of this origin, as if their soul were a piece of an atom separated from the universe and that therefore in that circumstance they had the opportunity to re-join it. It has been attributed to this being the closest identity to their religious background, so it is not unusual for a Christian to consider this entity as Christ, as for example happened to George Ritchie. Regarding the concept of God experienced in that dimension, the testimony of this subject, collected by Moody, expresses the ineffa-bility of the deep spirituality lived in that circumstance: *"I think that human beings want to create a box and put God inside, because in that way they can define God and control the result. But I realized that God is much greater than that."*

It is as if one has access to universal knowledge that leads to un-derstand anything, not so much as a pre-packaged God, but a cos-mic consciousness. One has the feeling of instantly assimilating a vast knowledge, as with a "download" of something that one has the feeling of having always possessed but then having forgotten, and of having finally found it in that mysterious circumstance. Many are aware that, unfortunately, very little of that knowledge is then brought back to earth at the time of their return to life. The reason is unclear.

There are many descriptions of the landscapes seen in those di-mensions. They often describe a type of crystalline water that ra-diates energy, in a moving flow, like a fountain. Sometimes water is represented as a boundary not to be crossed. Cities of light are de-scribed, often surrounded by large stone walls, with structures simi-lar to the Greco-Roman style. The buildings that are most described are large libraries that seem to be a source of knowledge that tells us about the wisdom and meaning of life. Everything has wonderful and bright colours that seem something more than those in the ordinary physical-material dimension.

We can say that all the different descriptions and representations of this spiritual dimension have multiple elements in common, as if they were several ways of seeing the same world. We could also think that that level is simultaneously created by all the beings that populate it, as if it were a shared lucid dream, a co-created environment that nevertheless has objective existence. Of course, each mind represents that dimension in more familiar and understandable ways based on their cultural and spiritual background. The variety of representations does not mean there is no reality of these worlds: they are composed of extremely subtle matter and therefore extremely modifiable by thoughts, emotions and imaginations.

Many reported the presence of wonderful and heavenly music, which has no similarity to those heard on Earth, even with the best masterpieces of classical music. The music seems to resonate along with the colours, in a fusion of auditory and visual experiences. The absence of body implies the total lack of physical sensations such as cold, hunger, thirst, fatigue and any kind of discomfort. In addition, a particular absence of thoughts or worries is experienced: a sense of total calm, extreme peace, the feeling of being one with everything.

Another recurring element in the NDEs is the "tunnel". Many report being pulled very quickly through a dark space, which can also be defined with images other than the tunnel, but which define a single background idea, for example as a cave, a well, a void, a cylinder. These images suggest the interpretation of the transition from a physical dimension to a "non-local" one, where everything and every person are connected in a unity, beyond time and space. It is a dimension of unconditional love where you feel at home.

The recurring and very important element of the NDEs is that of the revision of one's own life: events are relived, as spectators but at the same time actors, as if in a film in which one lives not only one's own thoughts, but also those of others, in particular the effects of one's actions on others. One understands how every single thought, word and action has had an important impact not only on oneself, but also on other people. Everything seems to be connected in an eternal present. The review of one's life is lucid, precise and accurate and causes deep reflection. It can happen both in the absence and in the presence of the being of light; in the latter case the experience will be more intense, emotional and significant. You feel the intense power and love of the luminous being who has always been beside you as a loving guide.

The review of life happens from an external, impersonal point of view, as if you were another person. It seems there is the opportunity to assume the different identities of the people with whom you interacted. There are no judgments or punishments: as if in those moments you were the only judge. You can know both the happiness and the pain caused by your actions. You may initially perceive regret or shame, but you soon understand that the aim of such retrospection is not provoking feelings of guilt or punishment, but transmitting teachings in order to understand what was really important in your existence. Particular importance is given to love and the will to create good on Earth, starting with small acts of kindness. You can see how your decisions influenced others and their lives. You are now aware that you could have handled some situations differently.

Many saw their memories clearly, backwards or in progression, with different scenes that can be selected as you like. It is like a film or a book, from which you can understand what was really essential in your life and what was not. This is how new meanings are discovered, in a change of consciousness.

"Your life in retrospect is more coherent than it is when you're living it," says psychiatrist John Mack.

Dr. Goran Grip, an anaesthesiologist professor at Uppsala, experienced an NDE as a young man and described it as being at a two-dimensional table representing life and different points representing each action performed. He had the opportunity to see each point from different angles, with a different inclination in order to contemplate all the events that become consequences of a single action. On a horizontal level, one can see the consequences that the actions had not only for oneself, but also for the other people with whom one interacted.

"I saw all the moments of my life at the same time"

"All the pieces of the puzzle were put together again"

"Oddly enough, I felt no fear or judgment, and absolutely no guilt or shame. I relived every thought, word, and action of each life experience when I focused on it. I was suspended in a world of unlimited dimensions [...]," is reported by some NDE witnesses.

From the testimonies, people also realized in what way every action, every thought, every gesture, not only influenced the person to whom it was addressed directly, but also other people with whom the latter will interact, and so on. All this represents a huge field of energy that influences yourself and others. Everything that has been thought, tried and accomplished has had importance and remains imprinted in those dimensions. The past and future are both present when you focus on it, but the experience of revision is carried out in a context in which there is neither time nor space. It turns out that you are connected to people, animals and plants, and that everything you do somehow comes back. One gets the impression that the Earth is like a school and that suffering is often the greatest teacher.

Raymond Moody developed an abstract model to derive consistent patterns in the dynamics of NDEs. According to Moody, there are many elements in the NDEs of a universal character, while others of a more subjective type, related to the personal contingent situation of the subject. The order of experiences can vary from subject to subject, although in most cases there seems to be a typical order. Moody found significant differences between those who had an NDE when they were close to death, compared to those who had actually been declared dead. In this second case, people lived deeper and more complete experiences.

Moody's research is mainly based on people stories and testimonies and, although not all the recurring elements in the patterns studied are present in a story, this does not mean that they did not occur, but that probably not everything has been reported by those who experienced it, often because no memory has been retained. The main difficulty consists in the very nature of the experience, defined by many as "inexpressible", "ineffable".

It seems to be "in the eternity". It is not possible to place those experiences in a defined time duration: it seems to be lasted for years, even if it actually happened in a very limited time of a few minutes.

Other classifications of NDEs were made by Kenneth Ring, an American psychologist and professor emeritus of Psychological Sciences at the University of Connecticut, in a study in which he distinguished five phases. The first phase is the affective one, which marks the end of suffering and is characterized by deep peace, calm and bliss. The second phase consists of the abandonment of the body, which in many cases is seen from the outside. In the third phase, there is the arrival in a dark environment full of peace; many see it as a tunnel that leads to a bright light, which seems to radiate something like unconditional love. The fifth phase is about another wonderful dimension, where one can meet deceased relatives or friends. In this context, you can review your life or receive anticipations regarding your future.

The NDE is like a gateway to the afterlife and not yet the afterlife itself.

Returning Transformed

The recurring element in most NDEs is a threshold not to be crossed, which can be displayed as a bridge, a gate, or an aquatic surface. You have the awareness of having to go back, or you find yourself directly in the body. If you know you have to return, it is because "your time has not yet come". This indication is somewhat mandatory, and it seems that there is no way to negotiate otherwise. You go back to your body despite you want to remain in that dimension. The return to life is often described as traumatic, with an indefinite alternation of negative emotions, physical discomfort and dismay. It is clear that the out-of-body state is preferred to the physical one.

Several psychologists have focused on studying the changes that occur in patients who have experienced NDEs. Many of them claim to have changed for the better after an NDE experience. As if in that dimension they lived in a standard of good, in contact with beings of light who have transmitted their wisdom, behaving in a non-judgmental way. From all this, therefore, comes the determination to change for the better.

Those who lived this kind of experience discovered a transpersonal point of view, that is, the possibility of transcending their personality and ego. As a result, a change in one's self-image results, which leads to giving less importance to the opinion or approval of others. You have the feeling of being a new person, as if you had actually died and later had a new spiritual rebirth. You begin to give less value to social conventions and instead give greater importance to what is really essential. You learn how to better manage stress, develop a new outlook on life, often manifesting new interests in philosophical and spiritual topics. Most of those who have returned from those dimensions say that love is the most important thing, that we are all part of a single great living universe, therefore it is unacceptable to hurt another person, without actually hurting themselves.

An authentic feeling of compassion for others arises in their hearts: an emotional development that goes in the direction of an unconditional love, which includes a greater ability to forgive, greater sensitivity and tolerance. You feel a need to help others, often by engaging in social activities. A real re-evaluation of the purposes of life is carried out, with a new list of priorities aimed at expressing affection for your loved ones.

There is more pleasure in spending time in nature.

They also noted the overcoming of the fear of death. The reason is that beyond that mysterious threshold, they had the opportunity to experience that the death of the body is not the end of everything, but the beginning of a new life in a different dimension, probably better than the physical-material one. This is how a new sensitivity and attention to the spiritual dimensions develops, feeling part of an infinite universe. They reported the tendency to not tolerate lights or loud noises, in general towards any type of perception that is too intense. Moreover, cases have been reported in which the person has developed intuitive-paranormal faculties: telepathy, clairvoyance, precognition, premonitory dreams, out-of-body experiences, visions, development of healing skills.

Speaking of healing, the example of Anita Moorjani, who had stage "4B" lymphoma, is very interesting. She was in intensive care, when the cancer had spread widely and she was suffering from a bilateral pleural effusion, with the very serious situation of multi-organ failure. She had undergone urgent chemotherapy treatment, but in her situation it could be seriously toxic. The doctors had told her husband that there was nothing left to do, as Anita's organs had stopped working, tumours had spread everywhere through the lymphatic system and her lungs had filled with fluid. From her spiritual body, Anita could hear her family and the doctors speaking and could sense her husband's emotions. In addition, she was aware that her brother was on a plane trip. She describes the feeling of expansion towards the eternal, beyond the physical world, living the experience of occupying "a wider space of consciousness". She experienced a great sense of freedom. She was aware to be in another dimension beyond space-time, and that emotional ties to her loved ones seemed to fade. She reports having met her father who had died ten years earlier, with whom she communicated telepathically, finding out that he had always remained spiritually close to the whole family in all these years. Anita also met her best friend who had died three years earlier and felt the presence of other beings around her, from whom she felt loved and protected. She describes her vision as *"all-round"*, with *"a total awareness of what was around me"*. *"I was simultaneously aware of everything that concerned me: the past, the present, the future. I was aware of past lives that had closed."* This is a form of temporal perception of simultaneity.

Anita was there not only without her body, but also without her identity, her beliefs, her culture: her consciousness subsisted regardless of all this. She felt free from cultural and social pressures. The revelation she received in those dimensions was important: *"I didn't have to do anything special. I deserved to be loved just for being in the world."* She perceived that all things in the world are interconnected and that pure unconditional love reigns in those dimensions. While she was there, doctors performed numerous tests on the functioning of her organs. Anita felt that the results of those exams depended on her decision to live or die: she felt a threshold, a border. If she had crossed it, she would never have been able to go back. She was realizing that her consciousness could affect the physical body, even healing from cancer, becoming aware of her connection to the Whole.

And so it was: she returned to her body, with a miraculous healing that left all the doctors amazed, especially when she reported the details of everything she had witnessed outside her body, such as the conversations that took place even in rooms other than that in which her body was. The reports of the analyses showed a total remission of the cancer. *"Ma'am, as I see it, you should be dead by now,"* commented the oncologist who studied cases of spontaneous remission of terminal cancer patients, adding: *"I guess that something (non-physical? Any information?) turned off the mutated genes or signalled a programmed cell death."*

Anita Moorjani believes that illness has a meaning connected to one's individual life path and purpose in existence. She reports that in those dimensions she understood why she was dying: she did not express herself, as she was hindered by a series of fears and concerns. She believes that her healing came from the extra-mental state: a spiritual state of pure awareness, which transcended any belief, dogma, or conviction. It was therefore a total reset. She realized that she was something "infinitely greater" than the physical body.

Another important element that is discovered with an NDE is the value of knowledge, seen more widely, as if in the spiritual dimensions there were a great university. You become aware that each human being is responsible for everything they do, that physical life is precious and must be lived to the fullest.

Whether one had previously been an atheist or had already had some notion of spirituality, one is aware that the experience of spiritual fullness lived in those other worlds cannot be limited by any religious doctrine. Religion is seen as a relative and limited human construction with respect to the deep spirituality lived beyond the threshold.

Kenneth Ring pointed out, among the fundamental aspects of change in those who have lived an NDE, that the transition is a peaceful experience; life does not begin with birth and does not end with death, it must be lived fully because it is precious. The body must be appreciated because it is a gift. Success and material things do not matter in life, but how much love we have been able to give. The difficulties of life must be considered as trials to be faced: everything that happens has a meaning and each person has a purpose in life, as well as a vocation to be recognized and valued.

In some cases, however, after an NDE, one may have encountered difficulties in readjusting to ordinary life, experiencing psychological discomfort, inevitably caused by the inability to share with others a mysterious experience, of such great scope and impact. One is afraid, in fact, of not being believed or, worse, of being ridiculed, so one tends to close in on oneself. Therefore, it is difficult to integrate those wonderful experiences with the problems and limits of the ordinary world and this could therefore lead to intrapsychic problems or serious problems in interpersonal relationships.

Studies and Research on NDEs

The first systematic study on NDEs has more distant origins: it was carried out in 1892 by the Swiss geologist Heim, who reported the description of thirty cases of mountaineers who survived fatal falls. Between 1979 and 2005, 42 studies involving more than 2,500 patients were published. These were retrospective studies based on voluntary testimonies following appeals and announcements. NDEs have been experienced by people of all ages, places, sexes, social classes, levels of education, professions, and religious beliefs.

Pim Van Lommel analysed the different scientific-medical interpretations. First of all, an attempt was made to provide a scientific explanation by elaborating "physiological theories", considering that the patient in a state of near-death or clinical death suffers from an oxygen deficiency, which could lead to hallucinations, chaos, agitation, mental confusion, fear and cognitive deficits. Yet, from the testimonies it is clear that, during an NDE, consciousness is lucid, with precise and defined memories, and that what is called "hallucinations" have very often turned out to be accurate images of situations and events that actually occurred near the patient who at that time was unconscious. The patient also suffers from an excess of carbon dioxide and his brain undergoes certain chemical reactions, including the production of ketamine and the blocking of brain receptors. There is a production of endorphins, which create a sense of peace and well-being, with the simultaneous production of psychoactive substances linked to serotonin: DMT produced by the epiphysis-pineal gland stimulated by hormones produced by the adrenal glands, cortisol, adrenaline, which are produced by the brain in large quantities in situations of psychological and physical stress, intolerable pain, accidents or cardiac arrest. Sceptics believe that consciousness cannot exist without the physical body. Susan Blackmore, a British psychologist researcher, seeks biochemical explanations for NDEs, which she says are induced by a blockage of NMDA receptors in nerve cell membranes, the level of endorphins and serotonin, stimulation of the limbic system, or a temporal lobe crisis.

"Psychological theories" were also formulated, according to which the experiences of NDE would be induced by the attempt to escape from the fear of death, or by religious and cultural expectations and beliefs, "thoughts and fantasies of shock". But very often the experience does not correspond at all to one's religion or atheist status. The NDE, in fact, does not seem at all to be linked to religious beliefs: it is not the subject who creates the experience, although the cultural background acts as a filter, through symbols and metaphors that have the function of giving meaning to reality.

The possibility of "depersonalization" would take over, that is, a process of detachment from the world and identity, with consequent alienation. However, in an NDE the sense of identity is preserved, accompanied by clarity and lucidity.

Other psychological theories speak of the possibility of dissociation, or escape from the reality of trauma through the annihilation of integrated functions of identity, memory and consciousness. Individual factors of personality, fantasy and imagination, and false memories would also be involved. These factors, however, are not relevant in an NDE, since the experiences of different individuals have detected patterns and dynamics in common. Other scholars have suggested the possibility of lies told in order to appear interesting and to impress. Finally, such NDEs could be interpreted as dreams. However, dreams physiologically assume greater brain activity, which certainly does not occur in an NDE, where brain functions have practically ceased.

Bruce Greyson, already mentioned before, an American psychiatrist and university professor, with many publications and awards, co-founder of Iands, "International Association for Near Death Studies", has dedicated 45 years of his life to research on NDEs. He got to know this kind of experience because of his patient Holly, who had been admitted to the intensive care unit after attempting suicide with an overdose. On that occasion, Greyson had been contacted by the emergency room, during his lunch break at the hospital, while he was eating tomato spaghetti and had just accidentally stained his tie with sauce. He was called because Susan, Holly's roommate, needed to talk to him about the events that had led her friend to collapse unconscious. After talking to Susan, Greyson went to visit Holly who, since the overdose, had never woken up, remaining in a state similar to a coma. The next day the patient woke up from her coma, and when Greyson went to visit her and introduced himself, she said she knew who he was and had seen him the night before while he was talking to her friend Susan in another room. She reported specific details of their conversation and Greyson immediately objected, considering it impossible for a comatose patient to get out of bed and go to another room. Holly, constantly supervised by the medical staff, had never woken up from the state of sedation before that morning. Holly then told Greyson an unequivocal and shocking detail: *"You were wearing a striped tie with a red stain."* The day before, Greyson had actually stained his tie while eating; later in the ward, he had his gown, but at the time of his meeting with Susan he had temporarily unbuttoned it, revealing the stain. Greyson was very surprised and looked for all possible rational and scientific explanations for this phenomenon, but in vain. He was completely shocked when he came to the conclusion that somehow a part of Holly, endowed with consciousness and visual and auditory perception, had detached itself from the body and was present in the room where he had spoken to Susan. He writes in his book After: *"The question whether our minds survive death has challenged my personal view of how the world works. Nothing in my background or scientific education had prepared me to interact with such a frontal attack on my world view."*

Thus began his journey to study these phenomena from a scientific point of view. He became director of the psychiatric emergency room at the University of Virginia just as Raymond Moody began his internship there, and that gave him the opportunity to confront his experiences. All this challenges ordinary scientific certainties and the very concept of who we are as human beings—our very concept of consciousness.

During his research he interviewed a thousand cardiology patients. 116 of these had a heart attack.

Greyson noted that some of them did not want to tell about their experience of NDE for several reasons: either because they were not ready to talk about it or because they were having difficulties adapting to ordinary life and were therefore afraid of being considered mentally ill, or worse, of being ridiculed.

In a "Near-Death Scale" study, Greyson divided NDE experiences into four groups: cognitive, affective, paranormal and transcendental. The two affective components, namely the feeling of peace, happiness and unity with the cosmos, and the transcendental one, indicating an otherworldly journey and the encounter with spiritual beings and deceased persons, are those most frequently reported in NDE reports.

The American psychologist and hypnosis expert Phyllis Atwater became interested in the NDEs because she had experienced it first-hand. She began her scientific research, accompanied by accurate statistical data, which lasted fifteen years and included over 3,000 interviews with people who had experienced an NDE. In particular, Atwater studied changes in consciousness and the loss of fear of death, which is therefore conceived as a passage to another world.

Sam Parnia, a British doctor, was in daily contact with patients in emergency conditions. His interest in NDEs stemmed from having listened directly to the numerous accounts of near-death experiences. He collaborated with neuropsychiatrist Peter Fenwick. He ran research on 63 patients at Southampton General Hospital who were brought back to life after being declared clinically dead following cardiac arrest. Among these, six patients reported having experienced an NDE according to the dynamics already studied. The research convinced Parnia that NDEs are real experiences and that the human soul really travels: consciousness survives brain death, considering that, as a doctor, Parnia was well aware of what a heart attack entails and the consequent interruption of brain activity. Through resuscitation manoeuvres, an attempt is made to restore the heartbeat, but before this can happen, it would not be possible for the brain to resume functioning. Yet the experiences had during the state of clinical death reveal complex thought activities, characterized by lucid reasoning and awareness of memories, consciousness functions that therefore seem to have no origin in the brain, in addition to perceptual activities of what is happening around the temporarily dead body.

Cardiologist Michael Sabom is the author of the book "Recollections of Death", an important work in this field that collects numerous cases of NDEs occurring in his cardiology patients. Sabom examined the detailed accounts of patients regarding their resuscitation during a state of temporary clinical death. Patients reported observing from above and from the outside the resuscitation manoeuvres carried out on their bodies and precise details, later confirmed by the health personnel involved. These details concerned moments during which the patients were declared clinically "dead" and therefore could not have been aware.

At the beginning, like other colleagues, Sabom with his solid academic and scientific background, was sceptical of the authenticity of such experiences. In 1994, he founded the "Institute Atlanta Study", born with the purpose of carrying out longitudinal studies, including research on fifty subjects brought back to life after resuscitation procedures, who remembered and reported in detail events, thoughts and emotions that occurred in the operating room or even occurred in other rooms, while their brains were practically dead. The results of these investigations were published in the work "Light and Death", which mentions in particular the case of Pam Reynolds, a patient who had undergone an operation to remove a brain aneurysm. It was a risky operation, as the large aneurysm was in a very delicate position. Pam underwent an innovative surgical procedure, the "hypothermic cardiac arrest", which consists of bringing the patient to a temperature of 15.5 °C, thus interrupting the heartbeat and the respiratory process. This causes the suspension of brain function also through the aspiration of blood from the brain. Basically, a state of death was artificially induced. At that temperature, it is possible to interrupt blood circulation for about an hour, without damaging the tissues. Her aneurysm was successfully excised and the temperature was gradually brought back to the normal 37 °C. The patient was then brought back to life. As she later reported, during her state of death, Pam lived an experience of NDE, finding

herself outside her body. She witnessed in detail the operating procedures and speeches in the operating room, despite her complete
brain inactivity. Later, according to what she reported, her consciousness moved away from the operating room and she found herself into a tunnel, at the end of which she met deceased friends and
relatives, including an uncle who induced her to return to her body.
The patient reported that they told her that she could not proceed
beyond that light, otherwise she would not be able to go back into
her body. She said, *"I felt more capable of conscious attention than I have
ever been in my entire life."*

Whenever a door to understanding NDEs is opened, other aspects
to explore will be found, as Moody reveals.

Laurin Bellg, in her work "Near Death in the ICU", tells her experiences as an intensive care and resuscitation unit doctor and also
her personal experiences and the conclusions she reached after all
this. She criticizes the closed approach of the medical community
to such phenomena and the scientific world's view that sticks to the
dogmatic belief that every phenomenon originates exclusively from
the material world and that only in this it can exist; they ignore and,
worse, ridicule the possibility of the existence of something beyond
the physical-material dimension. She supports the need for health
personnel to be prepared to interact in a respectful and welcoming
way with patients who experience such phenomena. They should not
dismiss their experiences in other dimensions as hallucinations or
dreams that have never happened, as this would hurt their sensitivity.
On the other hand, they have no doubt about the reality and authenticity of what they have lived beyond the threshold of physical death.

Thanks to the research of several brave scholars, following the
publication of "Life after Life" by Raymond Moody, a large amount
of research was produced with accurate scientific methodology.

You might notice almost divergent results between certain categories in both prospective and retrospective studies, as the method used in collecting data for each study varies.

In a study conducted at the University of California by Timothy Green and Penelope Friedman, they interviewed 41 people who had suffered an accident and had lived a period of clinical death. They highlighted the variety of experiences that can be lived in a similar situation, with different traits. According to Moody, the experiences should not necessarily be the same, as indeed happens in life when we visit a place: everyone will have their own personal experience, often unique and unrepeatable.

Van Lommel performed a prospective longitudinal study on 344 patients resuscitated after cardiac arrest. This study was published in the journal Lancet in 2001, conducted on a large scale, using statistical analyses of factors that contribute to the onset of an NDE. This study disproved the physiological, psychological and pharmacological theories that tried to explain the NDE phenomenon.

Other prospective studies on NDEs were carried out in the USA by Bruce Greyson himself, involving 1,595 patients, and in the UK by Sam Parnia and Peter Fenwick, with fewer patients. The data collected in the latter study suggest that there is evidence that consciousness is not localized exclusively in the brain. We should always remember that NDEs occur in a state of unconsciousness, when any type of experience could not be possible, much less that a lived experience is memorized. The hypothesis of mainstream medicine is that consciousness is the product of the brain. But how then could there be consciousness when, in coma or brain death, the brain shows no trace of activity? Cerebral electrical activity ceases completely, and the relative EEG becomes flat, about 6.5 seconds after cardiac arrest. However, NDEs show the existence of lucid awareness, with articulate and complex logical thought processes. We need to ask ourselves about the relationship between consciousness and the brain, as we will see later.

In the early '80s, Greyson invented an NDE scale, in order to standardize such experiences, using as references 16 characteristics to be evaluated with 0.1 or 2 points. The validity of this scale was confirmed by the analysis of independent researchers, and it was confirmed that it measures a type of experience that is the same for men and women of all ages and cultures. In addition, the score is the same even if many years have passed since the experience. Greyson, however, recognizes that a simple closed-ended questionnaire cannot reveal to us the complexity and richness of NDEs.

He administered the "SCL-90-R scale" test to several patients who had experienced NDEs and was able to exclude the connection between experiences of NDE and mental illness.

Regarding NDE memories, Greyson and the psychiatrist Lauren Moore used the MCQ (Memory Characteristics Questionnaire), a scale widely used to distinguish memories of real events from those of fantasies or dreams. Their research showed that memories related to NDEs have the same characteristics as those related to memories of real events.

A team of Italian scholars measured the brain waves of subjects remembering their NDEs. They found out that the types of brain waves are the same waves that usually develop when remembering events that really happened. Another research analysed whether there were traces of REM activity usually associated with dreams in the brain activity of the person evoking an NDE. The outcome revealed that in such cases there are no typical EEG patterns of the REM phase, but those typical of memory.

The "Evergreen study", carried out by James Lindley, Sethyn Bryan, Bob Cenley of the University in Olympia, Washington, involved

49 Americans in the northwest of the United States. They were subjected to an interview with a standard method, following the initial, uninterrupted report of their experiences on the edge of death. The questions, taken from Kenneth Ring's questionnaire, investigated the difficulties of telling that kind of experience in words, the awareness of being close to death, the emotions during the experience, the feeling of being travelling, if it had been an out-of-body experience, and the encounter with other individuals or with beings of light. In addition, they investigated the presence of scenes from one's past life, if there was a kind of threshold of no return, if one was tempted to stay in those dimensions or go back to the physical world. Finally, other questions investigated whether the subjects felt different in their way of being, and to what extent, and whether they are still afraid of death and what is currently the meaning attributed to it.

Children and the NDEs

The best evidence of a life after death comes from children, as they are free from the social and cultural conditioning typical of adults and have not yet been shaped by religious beliefs and life experiences. Therefore, the NDEs experienced in childhood prove that these are not influenced by religious or cultural factors, or by any type of external elements. Children have a different perception of the world than adults. At the age of 7, children usually consider death as temporary, as if it were a holiday period from which they will then return. From 7 to 10 years old, death is seen as a magical concept or as if it were a monster that will eat them. The look that a child can have towards the afterlife will have a considerable influence on his future life.

Several scientific studies have been carried out on childhood NDEs, which have turned out to be very similar to those experienced by adults.

The paediatrician and neuroscientist Melvin Morse studied NDEs in childhood; after his initial scepticism, he changed his mind. Being in daily contact with children in the hospital, he was able to witness the numerous accounts of those who had experienced an NDE and learned important knowledge regarding the meaning of life. He believes that NDEs are as real as any other human experience and therefore should not be devalued and considered as "hallucinations of a dying brain". He affirms that it is possible to have such experiences even in life, developing spiritual faculties not ordinarily used, since our brain is in close connection with the entire universe through our consciousness. In particular, the right hemisphere of the brain acts as a receiver and transmitter of information from the universal mind. He says, *"I've been sceptical for a long time. One day I read a long article in a medical journal that tried to explain NDEs as tricks of the mind. I've studied NDEs extensively since then, and none of those explanations made sense."*

Religion and Cross Culture

Everything that one experiences beyond the threshold of the afterlife seems to be the sum of various religions, which however does not adhere to any specific doctrine, as if each religion were a piece of the mosaic. The message received from thousands of people who have lived this experience is similar to what prophets and teachers have told us, namely that "love is all there is" and "life is like a dream". This immensity of truth is beyond our human comprehension. There are different paths that lead to God, but they are all the same in their essence. A more inclusive type of spirituality is proposed, without doctrines or dogmas, from which no one is left out and everyone is welcomed in the same way. It is no coincidence that an NDE experience often leads to a religious-spiritual re-evaluation or reorientation.

NDEs have a cross-cultural essence and, despite differences in language, stories, cultural idiosyncrasies and interpretations, such experiences have the same basic meaning: it is what happens when we die. Of course, such experiences are lived differently based on one's background of beliefs, interests, and inclinations.

The British anthropologist Edward Burnett Tyler reported in his work "Primitive Culture", a Polynesian story of a woman who came back to life after being declared dead, having left her body, crossed a river and met deceased relatives. When she came back to life, she claimed that she came back because she needed to take care of her son. Despite cultural differences, the NDE experience appears to be the same between different populations. The anthropologist Oscar Luiss in his work "The Children of Sanchez" reports his studies on a Mexican family. He had the opportunity to witness the story of one of the family members, about an NDE experience.

Not everyone lives the NDE experience. Lauren Bellg reports the example of her patient coming out of prolonged resuscitation after cardiac arrest. This woman had great interest in NDEs and had read a lot about it. When the doctor asked her if anything particular and unusual had happened to her during her heart attack, she said no with great frustration, expressing her disappointment. So the experience, at least the one imprinted in the memory, does not happen to everyone and the beliefs, inclinations and interests do not affect the manifestation or not of the phenomenon. On the other hand, several individuals who have experienced an NDE had no knowledge in this regard and no belief system that predisposed them to such an event. Many of them were atheists or had no particular religious or spiritual beliefs, so their way of facing life underwent a strong change.

Other Witnesses

In the work "Crossover Experience: Life after Death", written by Pim Van Lommel, Gregory Shushan and DJ Kadagian, valuable testimonies are mentioned.

"I began to feel an extraordinary release of my soul from my body. It was as if I had been freed from a life-long sentence, as if my body had been my prison."

"One of my first feelings is that I was still 'me'. The importance is hard to explain, but it was a surprise to me and a deep joy. I was not a mistake and I was who I was supposed to be."

"At first, I found myself in absolute darkness, but I was totally aware of everything and knew I was dead. There was no fear or anxiety along with that awareness. I knew that I was 'in death' [...] I had no reference point, nothing. Just myself in a void."

"I felt happy and loved, but this feeling was not separate from the light [...] Everything was an experience! Nothing was separate from nothing."

"Now I know there's an afterlife. Now I know there is no other hell but the one we create ourselves. I know that the most important thing is the love between people and all beings. I know that I am here to learn and reflect in others. Now I know that those who have died, sometimes visit me and follow what happens in my life. Now I know that all my children have chosen me as a mother, with love. Now I know that I have loved; I know that I am here in this life, among other things, to learn to love myself. Now I know there's a meaning to it all, why we're here."

"The higher I floated, the smaller the people and places became, until I could see the Earth itself becoming smaller. I begin to feel and see a complete connection in everything, every creature, every plant, every rock — everything. I could see how we're all connected, part of each other, and part of God."

"At the moment of death, my body and soul separated. I was in a dual existence. When my soul left my body, I felt like a new being, leaving behind all my old senses, thoughts, emotions. I could still see, hear, and sense the world around me, and I was aware of my inner mind. However, the cognitive processes were remarkably different. I no longer had any boundaries of bodies and physical limits."

Such people perceive they have freed themselves from the body as if this were an old coat. They are amazed to maintain their identity, consciousness, sight, thoughts, emotions.

"Nothing in my life compares to the moment I came into the light to become one with it! It was a true experience of inexpressible love. It was a love that could never be properly described in words. A love that could only be experienced. I was in the light, I was the light, and the light was God."

"I felt completely united, one with the universe. I felt as if a great light had absorbed me. It was a light free from all suffering. The light was of peace, understanding, acceptance and total calm."

They often report seeing an "intense light that does not blind", a light brighter than the sun, which occupies a defined space and is often seen at the end of the tunnel. Although it is not a diffused light, it could contribute to the complex brightness of the environment of that size. It is described in different ways — it is pulsating, all-pervading, radiating in all directions. It is something more than a light and is often described as a being of light. It is ineffable, beyond words, and its description could often be conditioned by one's cultural and religious background. For this reason, in some cases it could be perceived as Christ, Buddha or Shiva.

"It revealed to me that death is a lie that men tell themselves. We never really die. You leave this Earth when you have learned all you can, and then return to the spirit world. [...] Here in the physical world we have total free will."

"The golden light saturated my every cell, my entire being. It had a presence other than darkness. I was filled with so much joy that the feeling was more real and intense than any emotion I had ever felt in my best moments on Earth."

"It was like I was seeing the world for the first time with my own eyes. It was like taking off a pair of fogged sunglasses."

Moody listened to the testimony from his colleague physician in South Dakota who had a minor accident while on his way to work at the hospital. He had accidentally bumped into a car and was worried about receiving a large damage claim. That morning, at the hospital, the doctor was resuscitating a patient who had suffered a cardiac arrest. The next day that patient, who had survived thanks to his resuscitation manoeuvres, reported to the doctor that he had had an out-of-body experience — just as he was doing the resuscitation manoeuvres. The doctor asked him a few questions: the patient answered correctly by providing accurate details, including the instruments used during resuscitation and in what order they had been used. This surprised the doctor, who was further impressed when the patient told him another detail, "Doctor, I know you were worried about that accident you had. But there's no reason to be worried about things like that. You give your time to other people. No one will hurt you."

This experience reveals the ability of people living an NDE to read the minds of those around them, intimately perceiving their thoughts and emotions. Such experiences really challenge even the most sceptical scientist.

Moody, in his book "Reflections on Life After Life", researched examples of NDEs taken from history in different times and cultures and brought some of them to light, including Saint Bede's story. He was an English monk, and in his work "Ecclesiastical History of the English People," he told the story of a return from death in Brittany, with a man who became seriously ill until he died in the early hours of the night. While all his loved ones were crying around his body, in the early morning he came back to life and sat down. Everyone ran away in terror, except for his beloved wife, to whom he revealed: *"I am really reborn from the grip of death and I am allowed to live among men again. However, I shouldn't live as I did before; I must adopt a very different way of life than before. [...] A man in bright clothes was my guide [...] he led me out of the darkness into a clear light environment, and led me further into that bright light [...] The guide told me: 'You must return to your body and live among men once again, but if you act in great care and keep your words virtuous and simple, then when you die, you will have a home among these happy spirits you see' [...] When he told me this, I was very reluctant to return to my body, because I was ecstatic about the pleasantness and beauty of the place I could see and the company I saw there [...] I don't know how, I suddenly found myself living among human beings once again."*

Among the elements in common with contemporary NDEs, there are resistance to going back and the feeling that the soul has become something different from the body.

The following is an example of an NDE in which a meeting with deceased people took place, narrated in Roy Abraham's work, "There is Life After Death". Jack, a 36-year-old patient hospitalized with severe pneumonia, had met the nurse Anita, who had told him that that weekend was her birthday and, for the occasion, her parents would visit her. That evening, Jack's clinical condition plummeted and he experienced an NDE in which he found himself meeting the nurse Anita. Anita told him that he absolutely had to go back and asked him to tell her parents that she was so sorry for destroying the car they had given her for her birthday and that she loved them very much. Soon after, Anita crossed a fence and headed for a green valley, after telling Jack he could not go any further. When Jack came back to life after his experience, he told another nurse what Anita had told him. This nurse, a great friend of Anita's, burst into tears and left. Shortly afterwards, Jack found out that her parents had indeed visited Anita that weekend and had given her a sports car for her birthday. Unfortunately, while she was driving it for the first time, Anita had had a fatal accident. How could Jack know the details of events that took place in another place and even when he was in a deep coma? There are countless other such examples, drawn from the testimonies of different patients.

However, it should be noted that not everyone who has survived a clinical death remembers having experienced something. And if a person does not mention a certain element when telling the NDE experienced, this does not mean that this element was missing. In fact, it is possible to forget or remove several details.

From the different testimonies, ultimately, there are two recurrent and essential elements: love and knowledge. One is confronted with the meaning of love, an unconditional love, aimed at others despite their faults, imperfections and mistakes. Love is what really matters, that love that leads us to take care of the other persons and to be attentive to their needs.

And what kind of knowledge is it? The basic things, the causes of things, the basic universal principles, what holds the universe together: it is a knowledge linked to the soul. It is wisdom, a learning that does not cease with death but continues in other dimensions and lives. The same meaning of the Greek "Sophia", wisdom, both ethical and practical dimension, a morally practical ethics. Wisdom is gained when intellectual knowledge is transformed into something that is deeply imprinted, on an emotional level.

There are definitely elements in common between NDEs and mystical experiences. William James in his work "The Varieties of Religious Experience", identifies certain characteristics of mystical visions: ineffability, which does not allow translaing experience into words; the noetic quality, that is, experiences that are like knowledge, intuition of deep truths; transience, namely the impossibility of prolonging experience; passivity, as if something higher induced experience. In addition, there is an altered sense of time and space and a causal effect between experience and the future.

Years ago I found myself having a personal experience of something very similar to an NDE, after feeling a strong physical discomfort and have fainted. In that circumstance I experienced an OBE, out-of-body experience, which was not new to me, but in that circumstance seemed very different from the usual. I talked about this experience in "A Mystical Journey: Meetings with Extraordinary Masters, Magicians and Shamans" and I quote it here:

"One evening, I felt bad and it seemed I fainted on the sofa. Suddenly I was somewhere else. I knew my body was on the sofa and I was near a dimension never visited before. Around me, bright beings talked to each other in an unknown idiom that resounded in my consciousness in the form of thoughts. I clearly sensed that someone said that it was not my time to definitely leave my physical body, I still had things to do. I saw around me a strong white light that inspired me an immense peace never felt before, and I did not feel like coming back at all. I thought I was really dead, or it was like I was pretending, but I was not scared at all, quite the opposite, I was attracted by that threshold that I could clearly see and I recognized as origin and home. I was so immersed into that light and I could distinguish something as a bond between that light and the darkness I had left behind. I could not perceive my body anymore and, unlike when I was in lucid dreams or in ordinary experiences of astral projection, I had gone really far, where I had never been before. I began to feel more and more the urge of a force that somehow was pulling me back to that darkness.

For some moments, suspended in that threshold, I saw photograms of my physical life belonging to a foreseeable future and that actually would have carried out few months and years after. I saw life as an opportunity rich in meanings, an occasion to achieve something impossible to do without a physical body. And so I deliberately agreed, expressing the will: 'All right, I come back to my body.'

Right then, I felt pushed behind that threshold, attracted and then trapped in a terrible darkness. How hard is to explain the pain of being literally ripped from the hug of that sublime light! I found myself floating in the room, near the sofa where my body lay inert. It was not a proper awakening, because actually it was not a dream. I had been somewhere else, beyond the threshold, to live a new experience. I found my cold and stiffened body that seemed having suffered a collapse from which I luckily recovered. I knew that one day I would have crossed again that threshold, but not before the right time. So many mysteries still slipped from my awareness! The only clear thing was that, somehow, it was a gift to be in a body again." (From: Hermelinda, A Mystical Journey: Meetings with Extraordinary Masters, Magicians and Shamans)

Deathbed Visions

Death visions are a phenomenon first studied by Elisabeth Kübler-Ross, a Swiss psychiatrist, founder of psychotanatology and one of the leading exponents in this field. Kübler-Ross repeatedly listened to the different descriptions of those who were dying and found that in such situations they saw deceased relatives or friends and even disembodied spirits. Faced with these visions, the dying person perceives serenity and peace. Subsequent research confirmed the existence of these phenomena, also at an intercultural level. The studies involved not only the descriptions provided by the patients, but also their verbal and non-verbal behaviours.

Elisabeth Kübler-Ross began her near-death studies when, after the Second World War, she went to Poland to set up first aid centres. After being a field doctor in Switzerland, she moved to New York, where at the beginning she worked as a psychiatrist at Manhattan State Hospital. She then dedicated her medical career to caring for terminally ill children and the elderly. She closely observed a phenomenon that occurs in terminally ill children who, before death, acquire the awareness of having the ability to live an out-of-body experience, out-of-body journeys that help them in the transition from the material plane to the spiritual plane. During these experiences, they realize that they are not alone, but instead surrounded by beings who guide and help them.

One of the first NDEs that Kübler-Ross studied was that of Mrs. Schwartz, a dying patient of hers. She told she had seen herself out of her body and then found herself floating above her bed and looking at the resuscitation procedures. She reported details on all the words said and the actions carried out by the health personnel. When she was out of body, she had tried to communicate with them, but soon realized they could not see her. After forty-five minutes she was declared dead, but later she came back to life for another year and a half, surprising the doctors. Kübler-Ross suffered the tendency of her colleagues to classify such experiences as "hallucinations", "illusions" or "feelings of depersonalization", in a mere attempt to give them a label that could then be removed as if nothing had happened. This episode made her realize that this was not such a unique and rare event, so she analysed the collecting data on other similar cases. She participated in some important research on NDEs of people who have both come back to life naturally, and through resuscitation procedures. In the following years, more than twenty-five thousand of similar cases were collected worldwide, from different countries and cultural contexts, with patients in the 2 to 97 years age range. Kübler-Ross also participated in OBE research in collaboration with Robert Monroe, which we will discuss later, and examined both spontaneous and laboratory-induced out-of-body experiences.

Regarding the phenomena of "deathbed visions" that she witnessed, she talked about an experience that impressed her, concerning a young Native American woman who had been hit on the street and rescued by a stranger. The young woman was aware that she was dying and told the stranger that there was nothing he could do for her. She asked him to go to the Indian reservation where her mother lived, about 1,200 kilometres from there, and tell her that she was fine and happy because "she was already with her father." Then she died in the arms of the stranger, who later decided to fulfil her last wish. When the man arrived at the Indian reservation and met her mother, he found out that the girl's father had died of a heart attack an hour before his daughter's accident. The daughter did not know anything about it, yet she discovered it when she was dying and found herself welcomed on the threshold by her father. Cases like this happened many times. Dra. Kübler-Ross says:

"We have seen a lot of cases like this, in which someone was dying without being informed or knowing about the death of a family member, yet was welcomed by him. We understood that their task was not to convince or convert others to the idea that death does not exist, but simply to tell about it. If you are ready to hear and willing to maintain an open mind, you will have and find your own personal experiences."

Kübler-Ross listened several times to the descriptions of the vision of the "Light", cosmic awareness, made of unconditional love, understanding and total compassion, source of pure spiritual energy, which does not judge and does not condemn. She is aware that in the human being, born of God seen as an absolute source, there is a divine spark that makes us immortal and that the physical body is only a "cocoon", a temporary house in which we live for a certain time, and then return "free as a butterfly".

She therefore realized that we are never alone in this life, because we are surrounded by spiritual beings who love us, protect us and help us along the path of our destiny. She suggests that we can get in touch with them, asking them to make their presence known to us, asking them questions before falling asleep to have an answer in a dream. There is a deep immortal spiritual part within us that can guide us and provide help.

Kübler-Ross worked to change the attitude towards terminally ill people, formulating precise standards regarding end-of-life care, to allow people to be treated with dignity and compassion while dying. She managed to overturn the death taboo and the preconception that medical science was only about life and not death. She experienced first-hand the encounter between medicine and spirituality, the latter seen by her in a broad sense as awareness of the existence of something greater than us, of which, however, we are actively part.

Neuropsychologist Peter Fenwick, in a 2018 study on English patients, found that in 70% of cases the figures seen by the dying were of deceased relatives and friends, in 2% were religious entities, while the remaining 28% were unidentifiable. It seems to be a very frequent spiritual phenomenon, which instils comfort and reassurance to the person who knows he is about to die and who realizes the presence of someone on the other side who is watching over him and will welcome him beyond the threshold of death. It does not depend on the religious inclinations of the dying person; it happens both to those who have a religious faith and to atheists. The visions seem to be located in a point of physical space and are perceived with extreme clarity. Clear and coherent conversations are carried on between the dying person and invisible guests. It seems that the dying person is suspended between the physical dimension and another dimension that is perceived as more real than the ordinary one. Those who are dying somehow shift their awareness from one world to another for hours, or for a few days, before their final detachment from the body. These visions are caused neither by hallucinations nor by mental suggestions derived from beliefs or expectations. Raymond Moody reports that it also happened many times that those visions were also perceived by people who were in the room with the dying person.

Erlendur Haraldsson, research psychologist, member of the Institute of Parapsychology and researcher of the American Society for Psychical Research, carried out research in the field of NDEs, comparing about 500 cases reported by patients, both in the United

States and in India. He did not find any differences in their reports, despite being from different cultures. For this reason, the hypothesis that NDEs could be caused by hallucinations or suggestions induced by the religious belief was discarded. Later he focused on reincarnation studies, collecting numerous cases of children who remembered past lives, from all over the world. The information obtained from their memories was checked and, in most cases, gave a reliable result.

Together with his Latvian colleague Karlis Osis, Haraldsson carried out a study on what occur and is observed when the time of a person's death approaches. Osis had previously carried out a study-pilot investigation to analyse these phenomena. The research was intended to verify or disprove the hypothesis of survival after death. The results of this research were published in the work "What They Saw. At the Hour of Death". Haraldsson and Osis identified some assumptions regarding the type of vision, comparing two models to verify or not the hypothesis, considering in favour of survival the factors of telepathy or clairvoyance intervention, perceptions through extrasensory experiences, presence or absence of medical factors or beliefs and expectations that could determine hallucinations. Doctors and nurses collaborated in this research and, with questionnaires and interviews, witnessed the experiences lived alongside the dying and reported what they said. The questions, both closed-ended and open-ended, investigated visions of people or environments by terminally ill patients and sudden mood improvements by dying patients. Data on visions and patient information were then analysed using statistical procedures relating to the frequency of visions and patient characteristics, with particular regard to personal data referring to age, culture and religious beliefs. About half of the data concern patients who, up to four weeks before death, or more frequently within an hour of their death, reported seeing people around them, who the healthcare professionals did not perceive and seemed *"in some way suggestive of another world."*

An example is about a sixty-five-year-old man with stomach cancer who lucidly *"looked at a distant point; these things appeared to him and seemed real to him. He stared at a wall and his eyes and face lit up as if he saw a person. He talked about light and splendour, and saw people who seemed real to him. He said, 'Hi' and 'Here's my mom.' When this vision was over, he closed his eyes and seemed immersed in a great peace. He gestured, stretching out his hands. Before that hallucination he was very suffering and tormented by nausea; afterwards he was quiet and calm."* Healthcare professionals have noticed that as a result of these visions, patients had a positive transformation in both appearance and attitude, regardless of their age and pathology. There have been cases of people who considered curable by the doctors who treated them, but who instead had reported "seeing" figures, mostly of deceased family members, who had come to take them with them. In fact, these people then died, contrary to the doctors' expectations.

Several witnesses reported that during the visions it seemed that *"the patient [...] was simultaneously in two worlds"* and often found themselves witnessing dialogues between the person and the vision.

Haraldsson and Osis concluded that most of the experiences are undoubtedly attributable to an extrasensory source; that the visions' aim was to take the dying with them as a "transition to another existence," in some cases in contrast with the patient's will. From this, they deduced that there is the possibility of an existence after death, while hoping for the development of future research to confirm their conclusions.

In later research, some witnesses reported that during the visions of the dying they had actually seen well-defined figures or something like globes or luminous halos.

Lawrence and Repede in 2012 studied the visual, auditory and kinaesthetic experiences during communications at the point of death. They analysed hospice graphs during the thirty days before the death of each patient and interviewing nurses, thus detecting a significant incidence of the "deathbed communication" phenomena. According to Lawrence, during this experience the dying person is oriented in space and time, but lives an extraordinary experience of communication with a deceased person, which typically lasts from a few seconds to a few minutes.

In a 2014 study of hospice patients, Luczkiewicz, Depner, Nosek, Kerr, Woodworth and Wright involved 63 hospice patients willing to participate in the research. 82.5% of these reported a dream or end-of-life vision.

In his work "Glimpse of Eternity", Moody talks about another phenomenon, experienced by people who assisted a dying person: the "empathic NDEs", probably provoked by strong emotions when a loved one is dying. In this circumstance it is even possible to momentarily participate in the NDE of such a person, whether he or she has just died or is about to die, and this is done in a similar way to that of a classic NDE. It seems that when a person is dying, a spiritual threshold momentarily opens and it is possible for those present to glimpse the afterlife.

I personally lived this experience, without even knowing what it was at that time. In 2017, I assisted my father with terminal cancer. He had signed his discharge from the hospital, against medical advice, so that he could live his last days at home. It was as if he felt he did not have much time left. In fact, his clinical situation plummeted as soon as he returned home. Without the support of hospital care, he fell into a coma for three days before finally passing away. During those days I, his caregiver and a nurse in the night shift cared for my father. His nurse told me that, during the night before his death, my father, from his coma, had pronounced "mom" several times, referring to my grandmother who had died twenty-three years earlier. This phenomenon could be referred to as "deathbed visions", as described above. The next day my father slipped into an even deeper coma and the doctor who had come to visit him announced that he had a few hours to live and that we would find that his breaths would become increasingly rare. In the early afternoon, I walked away from my father's house for a moment, looking for a priest from the nearby church for the last rites. I had searched for him in vain in the previous two days and finally found him, just at the right time, when the caregiver called me and told me that my father was starting to have less frequent breaths. The priest and I arrived just before my father took his last breath. When I arrived, the caregiver told me that my father had not breathed for about a minute but, when I approached, he exhaled his last breath, just as if he wanted to wait for my return before leaving. The moment my father exhaled for the last time, I had a very special experience: I sensed that my hearing was muffled, as if there was a buzz in the background. I experienced sensations very similar to when an OBE is about to take place, a phenomenon that I will describe in detail later. I saw a bright fog enveloping the entire room. For a few moments I felt like I was lifted off the floor, like I was flying. I felt a very strong vibration, a movement of the air as if there were wind, and at the same time the emotion I felt was not at all the inevitable pain of what was happening but, on the contrary, an inexplicable joy, associated with a feeling of freedom. I am convinced that that joy and that freedom was what my father's soul was feeling, freed from the suffering his body was living lately. Somehow, I had empathically come into contact with such emotions. Moreover, I had been allowed to go part of the way together with him, making me glimpse that light and lightness, in a principle of detachment from the body that I then promptly blocked. I did not pay much attention to that experience, being well accustomed to "non-ordinary" spiritual phenomena. But as I read Moody's "Glimpse of Eternity" five years later, it was a considerable surprise for me: I found a remarkable comparison between my experience and what he calls "empathic NDEs". According to Moody, empathic NDEs are a phenomenon that deserves to be further explored.

Finally, there are some cases in which something unusual could happen near the dying person, as happened at the time of the death of the famous psychic Gustavo Rol:

> *"When Rol passed away, the head nurse present observed a light emanating from his mortal remains... a light that will remain for her an indelible memory."*
> **(Dr. Pierantonio Milone, Primary Emeritus of General Medicine at the Molinette Hospital in Turin)**

CHAPTER 4

YOU DO NOT JUST LIVE ONCE

> *"The emotion of feeling yourself an immortal and eternal being who has lived before and who will live again..."*
> **(Brian Weiss)**

> *"In the vast majority, memory of previous lives is not present. This is really a blessing conferred by the all-wise Being. Any contact with previous lives would seriously complicate the present life. When you attain perfection and reach the end of a cycle, all will be revealed and you will see a whole rosary of lives threaded upon the one personality."*
> **(Swami Shivananda)**

As we have already seen, reincarnation is crucial in religions such as Hinduism and Buddhism, as well as in the Sufi tradition of Islam. The belief in reincarnation existed for thousands of years in Judaism too and it was called "Gilgul". Around 1800, it was eliminated following a process of modernization to be more relevant to the Western scientific context. Even in New Testament Christianity there were clear references to reincarnation, which was eliminated by Emperor Constantine when Christianity became the official religion of the Roman Empire. On the occasion of the Second Council of Constantinople in the sixth century, reincarnation was declared a heresy. The reason was that the belief in the existence of multiple lives seriously jeopardized both political and religious power and threatened the stability of the empire. It was more convenient to let the faithful believe in a single Last Judgment at the end of time. But church fathers like Origen, Clement of Alexandria, and Saint Jerome, like all Gnostics, firmly believed in reincarnation.

References to reincarnation can also be found in Greek philosophy. Socrates in Plato's Theaetetus talks about the state of wakefulness and sleep consciousness. It also seems that Socrates is putting Theaetetus into a trance with an Ericksonian technique, saying: *"what evidence could one have to prove, if someone should ask now on these terms at the present moment, whether we're asleep and dreaming everything we're thinking, or we're awake and conversing with one another while awake?"* Later, Socrates stimulates the disciple in evocative hypnosis to a process of anamnesis-reminiscence, which allows the soul to recover knowledge and truth that have always been in the deep consciousness. In the Meno dialogue, Plato refers to past lives, when Meno asks Socrates how to obtain virtue, and the answer is: *"The soul, then, as being immortal, and having been born again many times, and having seen all things that exist, whether in this world or in the world below, has knowledge of them all; and it is no wonder that she should be able to call to remembrance all that she ever knew about virtue, and about everything;"* This is the anamnesis: it is not a teaching, but a reminiscence, that is, a recollection of knowledge already acquired in past lives. When in the tenth book of the Republic, Plato speaks about the experience lived by Er in the afterlife, as we have seen before, he reveals that the souls of the deceased meet the Lachesis Moirai and have to choose how their future life will unfold. They also choose their guiding spirit. This would happen totally in free will and responsibility, as we will see later talking about "life between lives".

Carol Bowman, an American psychotherapist and expert in past life regression therapy, is one of the most important researchers in the field of reincarnation. She focused her research on the study of the cases of many children, who reveal clear and detailed memories referring to other lives, often saying: "I remember when I was older", "I remember when I died". In several cases, the authenticity of their memories was verified through clear and irrefutable evidence. Among these cases are children who reveal memories of relatives who died before their birth.

Unfortunately, our society tends to disqualify children's stories, attributing them to childish fantasies. But they should be taken seriously, because those memories, dreams and stories seem to be connected to past lives.

The psychiatrist and head of the department of psychiatry at the University of Virginia, Ian Stevenson, is among the greatest scholars and researchers on reincarnation and has collected several testimonies related to cases that occurred in different places, cultures and social classes. He catalogued numerous stories of children, linked to different proofs that confirmed their authenticity. For example, the case of the Indian child Gopal, who from the age of three provided details about a previous life in a city about 300 kilometres from his current home. He provided precise details about his home, family and job; he reported that he had been one of the owners of a medical company and had been killed by one of his brothers, about eight years before his birth in the present life. When the child had the opportunity to meet the family of his previous incarnation, he recognized places and people and provided them with details known to them only.

Among the cases of past lives of children studied by Ian Stevenson, with the attention of Mahatma Ghandi, is a well-documented case from India: Shanti Devi was a girl born in 1926 and died in 1987, who claimed to remember details of a past life of a woman who had died ten days after giving birth. At the age of 4 she had clear memories of her home and her husband in a village about a hundred kilometres from where she lived. These memories were subsequently verified.

Stevenson's publications collect all the cases studied, some of which provide evidence such as scars and birth defects that corresponded to wounds from previous lives. Particular attention was paid to "xenoglossy", that is, the ability of a subject to speak a language never studied and never learned in present life. They were checked and analysed to exclude any risk of deception.

"It's been said that there's nothing as troubled and painful as a new idea, and I think that's especially true in science," Stevenson says. After 45 years of research, Stevenson identified several universal cross-cultural factors: the age of memories of past life is especially between 2 and 5 years; the age of discontinuous persistence of spontaneous references to past lives is 5 to 7 years; the frequency of memories of violent death or of the manner in which death occurred in another life is high.

Jim Tucker, a physician and professor of psychiatry, worked with Stevenson in the research directorate of the Division of Personality Studies at the University of Virginia, and dealt with the cases of children with past life memories. 70% of these were inherent in memories of deaths following traumatic circumstances. In his work "Life Before Life", he reports the results of ten years of research on reincarnation on subjects from all over the world.

Past Life Regression Therapy

Brian Weiss, a graduate psychiatrist at Columbia University, specialist at Yale Medical School, chair of the Department of Psychiatry at Mount Sinai Medical Center in Florida and a professor at prestigious university medical schools, published numerous scientific articles in psychopharmacology, neurochemistry, anxiety-depressive syndrome, substance-related disorders, Alzheimer's disease, and is the author of bestsellers translated worldwide. He is the pioneer of the use of regressive hypnosis for the memory of past lives, as a therapy to solve problems and traumas of the present life.

At the beginning, Weiss was somewhat sceptical of non-ordinary phenomena that referred to a more parapsychological field, a sector he initially considered absolutely unscientific.

His scepticism was challenged in 1980, when his patient Catherine began a psychotherapy path, as described in his work "Many Lives, Many Masters." Catherine did not suffer from any form of psychosis, hallucination, dissociation or multiple personalities, or substance-related disorders, and was not at all suggestible. Her problem were strong phobias, in particular related to water, darkness and asphyxiation. Weiss worked on these symptoms with traditional psychotherapy for more than a year. However, her symptoms had not only not regressed, but had exacerbated to the point of preventing her from leading a normal life. For this reason, the psychiatrist decided to change his approach and began to use the hypnosis to go deeper and possibly discover traumas that had been removed from consciousness. On the occasion of the first hypnosis session, Catherine slowly slipped into a trance state and, when Weiss asked her to recall the first time she experienced those symptoms, she told a story that did not concern her present life, but referred to a life that took place during the second half of the nineteenth century. Catherine was Aronda, a young Egyptian woman who unfortunately died young along with her little daughter, following a violent flood. Initially, Weiss thought that Catherine's memories could be the result of fantasy or have a dreamlike nature. But what happened next upset Weiss: after a week, her symptoms began to improve conspicuously, until they completely vanished. During the other hypnotic sessions, Catherine had also recalled other past lives, which had suffered several traumas that seemed to be the reason of her current life's symptoms. Weiss then came to the conclusion that no fantasy would ever be able to produce such a healing effect. But what further amazed him was that in a session of deep hypnosis, Catherine revealed insights and knowledge about private details of his life, which she could not have known: details about his father's death, which occurred nine months before the first consultation, 12,000 miles away and without any obituary being published. Catherine also revealed details about the untimely death of his eldest son Adam at just 23 days old, which occurred nine years before that moment. When Weiss, extremely upset, asked her, still in a state of hypnosis, how she knew all those things, she replied that the "Master Spirits" had told her. The Master Spirits would be highly evolved souls who transmit messages regarding the purpose of life on earth, the meaning of death and the reality of reincarnation. Through Catherine, they would have said: "*We are the ones who choose when to enter our physical state and when to leave it. And then we understand when we have accomplished what we were sent down here for. We know when time is up and you will have accepted your death. Because at that point you will have understood that you can't get anything more out of this life. When you have had a chance to rest and reorganize your soul, you will be allowed to choose whether to return to the physical state...*"

"*Our task is to learn, to become like God through knowledge. We know so little. (...). Through knowledge, we draw near to God, and then we can rest. Then we can go back and teach how to help others.*"

Weiss found out that a soul knows when to reincarnate and when its time in a life has ended. And when it will find itself in the "life between lives", it will know if and when to return to Earth. As we will see later, this will be confirmed by Michael Newton and Dolores Cannon's research.

From the Masters' teaching, it is confirmed that the path of each human being consists in learning different qualities, including love, charity, hope and faith. Among the different life lessons that human beings must learn is the development of empathy, compassion, non-violence, patience and approach to the spiritual levels.

People who in deep hypnosis became channels of transmission of the communications of master souls, described the situation as something that did not come from their subconscious or even from the super-conscious part, but from some entity present in the background. These emanated great wisdom, warmth and love.

After this experience with Catherine, Weiss acquired a new vision of psychotherapy, understanding that regression to past lives was a quick method to treat psychiatric or psychosomatic symptoms. He then began to use that method on other patients, all of different geographical origin, different socio-economic status, education, religion and beliefs. Many of them have recovered from chronic symptoms such as phobias, panic attacks, recurrent nightmares, physical pain, and various illnesses. To those who might object that this could be a placebo effect, Weiss says that his patients were not at all suggestible. They instead could clearly remember details such as places, data and people.

Weiss was convinced that what Catherine had experienced during the hypnosis sessions was something real, which gave access to a truly existing spiritual dimension. Talking about Catherine and other patients' healing, he believes that in the spiritual worlds there is an immense healing force, much more effective than any medical approach of modern conventional medicine. This becomes possible by recalling every detail of trauma suffered either by the body or the mind, all the human situations, terrible events, tragedies, catastrophes, which occurred in previous lives. Its success was undeniable.

Weiss asked himself several questions and formulated several hypotheses. He also took into account Jung's theory of the "collective unconscious", which consists of a collection of all human memories, often expressed in symbols, universal archetypes; something that, according to Jung, is inherited by every human being, leaving a trace in his brain. But Weiss's patients were able to remember in a too specific and personal way, with different details, precise people and places, while the collective unconscious reports generic images referring to cultures and traditions. These memories seem to exceed the conscious ability of each individual subject, revealing knowledge that could not have been acquired in other ways, neither during childhood nor from books nor in any other way in the course of that life.

In this way, Weiss found out that we have a soul that does not die with the death of the physical body, but continues its evolution in other lives, at different times and places. He came to this conclusion, despite being initially sceptical of everything that had to do with a parapsychological sector.

Weiss believes that in a state of deep hypnosis a person is able to let higher entities speak through him, which he identifies as "Masters". The person becomes like a channel capable of revealing knowledge from the "Other world". So there are not just past lives, but there seems to be something else. This impressed Weiss, challenging his rational-scientific mind and his initial scepticism. For this reason, his professional and personal life inevitably changed. Weiss underwent a radical transformation as a human being, beginning to perceive greater peace and joy. He finally had the feeling that there was a purpose in life and began to lose the fear of death, both his own death and that of his loved ones. In fact, he was discovering what secrets were hidden beyond the threshold of death.

During his research, Weiss's rationality was always active in analysing, evaluating and possibly criticizing any data collected. However, it was promptly refuted by the obvious nature of what was in front of him. Weiss, like other researchers in this field, found himself acquiring a real body of spiritual knowledge that proved to be consistent, despite the differences between the individuals involved in the research.

According to Weiss, hypnosis is a state of consciousness that could be experienced daily even without realizing it, as it is a state of extreme concentration, like the one we have when reading a book or watching a film. In hypnotic induction the therapist guides the induction and the hypnotic state, while the patient has full control of the entire process.

Australian psychologist Peter Ramsten created a television broadcast in 1983, "The Reincarnation Experiments". He subjected his clients to regressive hypnosis and accompanied them in their re-enactments of past lives. He discovered interesting evidence about the authenticity of these experiences.

According to Alex Raco's experience, one of the leading experts of regressive hypnosis in Europe, the hypnotic state is *"much easier to reach and experience than it is to describe it."* We continuously enter and exit a hypnotic state. Meditation can be considered as self-hypnosis, while hypnosis conducted by another person is considered as guided meditation.

After thirty years of experience with meditation, I personally realized the potential of hypnosis. In meditation the achievement of a non-ordinary state of consciousness occurs sporadically and is generally short, as you are not guided, except by your own mind that is not always collaborative. On the other hand, in hypnosis, thanks to the presence of an external guide, it is possible to maintain this state longer, remaining alert and not slipping into sleep.

In the waking state, the conscious mind predominates and the unconscious observes and records every event; in the sleeping state the opposite happens. The trance state achieved through hypnosis is in the middle, since the conscious mind and the unconscious coexist and neither of them is predominant. It is like a meditative state of hyper-consciousness. Here are Alex Raco's thoughts on this:

"Within my path I thought that the episodes involving extrasensory perceptions, coincidences and strange physical effects were invented by people with a strong sensitivity. Nothing more. However, little by little, I saw that what might appear to be imaginative experiences if told by a single subject, assumed a statistical value if confirmed dozens of times, especially by people who did not know each other and with totally different backgrounds."

In Raco's book "Non c'è vita senza amore", which means "There Is No Life Without Love", a patient, faced with the memories that quickly arose, comments, *"My conscious part witnessed as a spectator amazed and unaware of what my voice said, and the mind's eyes were visualizing. Everything happened so fast that with my logical and cognitive faculties I could not control nor invent the facts I was telling."*

According to hypnotherapist Joe Keeton, all hypnosis is self-induced, so we should overcome the view of television shows that showed us a weak mind that was manipulated by a strong mind to gain control. It is about reaching a state of consciousness accessible to everyone, in which we maintain full control of what we say, as well as the mastery of choosing whether to say something. It is a state in which we are deeply relaxed and something remains within us that watches over everything in hypervigilance.

The goal of hypnosis is to access the contents of the subconscious mind, the layer beneath our ordinary conscious mind, beneath the ceaseless flow of thoughts and sensory perceptions. It is a deep level of consciousness, which gives access to what is normally covered by the din of sensations, perceptions, incessant thoughts and un-controlled emotions. From this layer come intuition and wisdom, it is the place of our creativity. Moments of "spontaneous hypnosis" open a communication between the unconscious mind and ordinary consciousness. The subconscious collects forgotten memories: ev-erything is stored in detail and all the events of one's existence can be restored and recalled through the hypnosis. During this practice, the patient retains full awareness and manages to maintain cognitive lucidity to answer the hypnotist's questions, despite being in a state of consciousness in full access to the subconscious, a state of deep relaxation. His mind is extremely lucid, alert and aware. It is as if the patient becomes at the same time a spectator, protagonist and even critic of a film. In order to fully access subconscious content, the hypnotic technique must be able to overcome the barriers of the ordinary conscious mind.

Patients have precise knowledge of the geographical places and the time in which the memories of past lives are placed, contextu-alizing their memories in a relevant way both to the events recalled and to the present time. The revival of memories related to past lives allows overcoming the mental barriers of ordinary consciousness, to be able to tap into content that tends to affect the contingent life of the subject, causing disorders and symptoms.

In classical psychoanalytic hypnotic practice, we go back in time to bring to light traumas, often dating back to childhood, which cause psychological and even physical problems. Freud and Jung found out that our worst pains, fears and traumas are buried in the depths of our unconsciousness, without us being able to remember the origin. Conventional psychotherapy, however, only explores current life, looking for the root of traumas among past events. Otto Rank went back to birth and the gestation period. The subconscious stores and records everything, as a faithful recorder. On the other hand, the conscious mind tends to remove painful or terrifying events, as it would not be able to handle them.

Multiple psychological disorders originate from a protective circuit as a defence against trauma. These dynamics are learned from the family, teachers or through life experiences. This circuit would also be built inappropriately. It is a mechanism that tends to protect the conscious mind from reliving the real incident. Through recalling, emotions related to the trauma emerged, identifying the incident at the origin of the problem. It is like exploring the unconsciousness layer after layer.

Studies and practice of regressive hypnosis on hundreds of patients allowed Weiss to go further, uncovering memories which were not related to the patient's present life. So he discovered the past lives, considered the key to solving traumas whose origin goes back much further in time. Bringing certain memories to light has proven critical to the healing of thousands of patients. Weiss found that for almost 50% of his patients it was not enough to dig through memories related to present life. In order to fully resolve their clinical problems, they needed to find the root much further, in previous existences. This proved to be the key to therapy. This methodology digs so deep that it retrieves memory stores inaccessible to the conscious mind. It is essential that the procedure is carried out by an experienced therapist, who will be able to ask the appropriate questions and specifically enter certain critical points. Moreover, he should help the subject to integrate the thoughts, information and emotions brought by certain memories. For this reason, only a qualified therapist can practice regressive hypnosis. Unfortunately, nowadays, there also are "therapists" who, without any title or proficiency, improvise psychologists and randomly use "past life regression techniques", thus risking serious damage.

Past life regression therapy is not intended to replace conventional medical therapies, especially if there are overt physical diseases. Such a therapy does not presuppose the belief in the existence of past lives, which is not strictly demonstrable. The therapy will work in any case, even if the subject believes that those images are the result of a creative "daydream". On the other hand, those who believe in it, do not need to prove it, because they deeply feel the truth. All the doctors and psychologists who have practised the method of regressive hypnosis and analysed thousands of cases, have been forced to believe it, considering the continuous unequivocal evidence, while having to distort their previous certainties based on their scientific background.

All this explores the links between mental and physical illnesses. Past life theory intends to deeply explore this connection.

To those who object its authenticity by presenting the "Genetic Memory Theory", according to which the memories of past lives are just the result of the genetic heritage transmitted by DNA, the evidence of the testimonies reveals that there is no correlation: for example, white patients remember the lives of black people, or Spanish patients remember the lives of British soldiers in World War II, and so on.

Weiss distinguishes several regression patterns: the first is the classic one. Here the patient recalls a whole life, precisely framing all the events from birth to death. The second pattern is the "flow of the key moment". Here the subconscious mind selects the most important moments of a life as they are connected to the problem in question, even of several existences simultaneously, detecting connections between several lives and dynamics that tend to repeat themselves incessantly.

In his work "Through Time Into Healing", Weiss presents many cases that show the therapeutic potential of regressive hypnosis. In his work "Only Love Is Real", he tells the story of Pedro and Elizabeth, patients who have met from life to life and who, in the present life, have the opportunity to continue their journey together.

Angelo Bona, a specialist in anaesthesia and resuscitation, and psychotherapist, took part in a study at the Irccs, Santa Maria Nascente in Milan, on subjects in deep hypnosis, with the use of functional magnetic resonance imaging and the analysis of neurotransmitters and biochemical variants. This research showed that in a state of deep hypnosis, frontal cortical consciousness is deactivated, while visual-occipital areas are activated.

According to Bona, hypnosis can be considered as a yoga, seen as a method to free oneself from the dominance of the mind, loosening the ordinary barriers of defence mechanisms. This kind of psychotherapy does not consider only the mind-psychic, but the deep essence of soul, spirit, meanings; these, are unfortunately excluded following the birth of scientific psychology in the nineteenth century. Originally, the word "psyche" was rather connected to the meaning of "soul" in a spiritual sense; later other meanings were attributed to it, such as "reason", "judgment" and "logic". The etymology of "trance", from the Latin "transitus", leads us to the meaning of "trans", which means "beyond", and "ire" or "to go beyond". The concept linked to this word indicates the passing from the contingent rational reality to another spiritual one, which is free from the limits of mind and reason, to re-join the sphere of the unconsciousness and the divine absolute. According to Bona, the concept of "trance" can be compared to that of "ecstasy", which expresses the idea of "being outside" (the dominance of the rational mind).

In his work "Il profumo dei fiori d'acacia", Bona points out that the meaning of "going beyond the mind" is also expressed by the science of yoga. Yoga aims to integrate the individual soul with the absolute one, realizing the suspension of mental activity that obscures the spiritual faculties. According to Patanjali, yoga's aim is precisely the suspension of mental activity, to get free from the chains of duality, the illusion of Maya. But we will go into that later. You can find more details about spiritual practices in my books "Paths for the Spiritual Search" and "Oltre l'orizzonte dello spirit".

In his book "L'arte della levatrice", Bona says that during a walk, Raymond Moody revealed to him: *"We are soul transceivers and the great meditative yogis or ordinary people in deep hypnosis can cancel time by identifying themselves in entanglement with the Eternal."*

According to Weiss and other therapists' experiences, past-life memories are far from fantasies or projections of traumas experienced in the present life. Instead, they contribute to forming and determining the behaviour of an individual since childhood, presenting patterns of thoughts, emotions and actions of previous lives. In the same way, Freud assumed the origin of the mechanisms of neurosis and compulsions, which could therefore be extended not only to contingent life.

It is about accessing not the memory ordinarily stored in the brain, but a "a soul memory", although it is possible to assume that all memory has a spiritual nature, and the brain is a medium for a more "physical" storage. However, neuroscience accepts that there are different areas of the brain that store different types of visual, auditory, tactile, cognitive memory, and so on. Different types of memory, such as short- and long-term memory, have also been distinguished. All these types of assembled memories would help to provide us with a more or less stable sense of identity.

The mind is closely connected to the body and influences it also causing real disorders and symptoms. In some cases, the mind can also cause death, particularly if you surrender to an illness, and this could happen despite all medical care. On the other hand, even if from a medical point of view it seems that there is no survival, the will to survive could make miracles, as happened to Anita Moorjani and her NDE experience. This would be the power of an even deeper mind, the soul, which carries the memory and traces of a long past history and is capable of generating disorders in cases of unsolved traumas, or of healing them if such resolution has occurred.

It seems that consciousness is nothing more than a tiny part of our mental activity. Most of the mechanisms that govern our ordinary activities are not under the control of consciousness. If we really want to overcome symptoms and mental problems permanently, we need to identify those root causes that can be found in the unconscious processes. The true origin and the emotional reaction associated with these symptoms are to be sought. In this way, the subconscious mind realizes that the reaction to the original traumatic event was protective but not rational and, above all, no longer functional in the present. But ordinary medicine tends to use drugs to treat the symptom and physical manifestations. Even the psychotherapeutic approach that uses hypnosis to impart suggestions to partially manage a problem is just limited. Such a method may be fine for minor issues, such as pain control or self-esteem issues, but it does not solve inner conflicts at the bottom that seem to have more distant roots.

Past life regression therapy is effective in treating conditions such as those that impair the functioning of the immune system, headaches that do not respond to drug treatment, allergies, asthma, arthritis and ulcers. Moreover, it seems to improve tumours or cancerous lesions. A complete healing is obtained, different from that produced by the use of drugs, since it heals the roots cause underlying these disorders. When these are discovered, we have the opportunity to understand, elaborate and solve them. Precisely in this way, symptoms begin to disappear. Even in cases where a complete healing does not occur, regressive psychotherapy produces a psychological healing, making the subject realize the causes of the problem.

Many conflicts experienced by couples have their root causes in a previous life: anger, fear, hatred, jealousy and different negative emotions. Through sensations such as immediate attraction or repulsion, you can even recognize people with whom you have a connection from past lives. The improvement of inter-relational dynamics is particularly clear once people understand the real causes of conflicts. There is always a reason why certain meetings and events take place at a certain time and not before. This is because we must learn lessons, as if they prepare us before that moment. For this reason, patience is crucial: it allows destiny to unfold with balance and harmony.

Weiss says that he had the opportunity to use this practice with members of the same family. When comparing their experiences, he found out that they had retraced in hypnosis the same past life in which the other member was present. Weiss witnessed joint regressions of shared lives, in which both subjects evoked in deep hypnosis the same events experienced. This occurred in his patients Elizabeth and Pedro, as described in his work "Only Love Is Real".

In many cases, the person recalling the past life spoke the same language of those times and places, although he had never studied it.

The results of healing, peace and serenity of those who have explored in deep hypnosis what lies beyond physical life, come from the awareness of having an immortal soul. This is only temporarily united to a physical body and brain; actually it has a true nature that goes beyond all this and that is free from any type of context, even the most painful.

The goal of most therapies based on the recalling of past lives is to reach the unconscious mind without subverting the presence of the conscious mind. But not all methods use the technique of hypnosis. For example, Morris Netherton, a pioneer of past life therapy, does not use the real hypnotic state, but focuses on the sentences most used by the patient as a guide. There is a rhythmic repetition in an attempt to open the doors of the unconscious mind, gradually bringing out connections. It is as if, starting from the ordinary state of consciousness, some data were required from the unconscious mind, which therefore chooses to take part and communicate voluntarily.

Although Netherthon does not use hypnosis for past lives, he believes that it is a valid means to reach the unconscious mind, for research purposes. In one of the cases analysed by Netherton, it was possible, through the Hall of Record, to verify the existence and death by hanging of Mrs. McCullum in 1903.

> *"Responsibility is simply knowing that you are the cause of your life. You're the one who chose it. In some ways, you've been the same person for centuries. You have to know who that person is and promise yourself that you will act responsibly, understanding exactly what your strengths and weaknesses are in order to develop your potential."*
> **(Netherton)**

Changes following past life therapy also involve other people, as new behaviours will develop that will elicit different reactions in them.

Past life therapy is a problem-oriented technique, as it considers one symptom, works on it specifically, or on other problems that will gradually emerge, in order to rebuild a balance. Every memory of an event will be taken from the unconscious mind in a natural and spontaneous way. The word is a symbol, it is magic, it creates and evokes entire destinies.

Netherton does not believe that this type of therapy is miraculous, but firmly believes that the true protagonist and healer is the subject himself, fully responsible for his improvement, as long as he is open to collaborating. It is essential to leave the past behind, so that the person can be able to fully realize their human potential. It is the patient who heals himself and his healing will not be due to the therapist. The subject has the full responsibility: there is nothing the therapist can do that the patient cannot do. Each patient is unique, each life has its crucial events that mark the beginning of certain patterns.

Past life therapy is aimed at people who want to grow and go beyond the limits of their contingent psychological situation and look at themselves with honesty, ready to face a change that could affect their behaviour, relationship patterns with others and, in particular, their awareness. According to researcher Baranowski, not everyone can undertake a journey through past lives: one must be willing to let go of attachment to one's contingent personality and approach the broader awareness of one's higher self.

> *"For too long the healing of the bodies and of the mind have been considered different disciplines. Past life therapy, however, indicates that the holistic approach will again be granted the respectable status it once enjoyed."*
> **(Joel Whitton)**

Certain emotional journey would lead to physical illnesses, such as, in therapists' experience with particular clients, cancer, arthritis and ulcer. The main symptom is the clue to framing the patient's problem. Often there are aspects of behaviour that are discovered as therapy progresses. But one symptom at a time is addressed. Occasional difficulties in flowing unconscious memories may be experienced, but often it is enough to overcome a block to access deeper. Parts of oneself left in the shadows are recovered, which need to emerge and be brought to light, expressed and evolved, reconnecting the person with the true essence of an immortal soul. The recalling of past lives is cathartic, purifies the soul, gives a new balance, a new spiritual maturity and above all an awareness of one's own value.

The researcher Jim Alexander investigated the data collected from the memories of patients' past lives, with clear references to dates, places, events and, in numerous cases, he managed to find obvious correspondences in the census records, only with some occasional discrepancy. For example, a patient reported clear memories, with precise references to names of areas of the city of Leeds that at the time of her current life no longer existed. This patient had never been to Leeds and had no connection or interest in these places.

Through regressive psychotherapy, people often discover hidden talents, which had manifested in past lives but which then had remained latent. It is therefore possible to discover strength, capacity and creativity. There are many levels of the self, because we are beings living in multiple dimensions and we are not stuck at the body-mind level at all. What we experience in the ordinary world is nothing more than a small piece of the totality of our being.

Ultimately, the regression to past lives aims to dispel the fog that envelops the spirit, momentarily silencing the ordinary mind.

The result of Weiss's decades of research is that we are eternal and immortal, because our souls never die. We should therefore act aware of this and in that case our lives would benefit from it. Living the awareness and gift of immortality means developing quality relationships, the ability to love and forgive, increasing compassion, helping others and improving one's health, not only physically but psychologically and spiritually.

Letting go means having compassion, understanding and empathy, without feeding hatred, resentment, revenge or fear. Self-love is the basis of love for others and implies self-esteem and security. The latter is connected to the awareness of being a soul that has lived numerous lives and will still live others; an immortal and eternal soul, which can never be damaged by anything.

Physical life is to be considered a gift: Earth is a school where you learn to manifest spirit in matter, to enjoy the pleasures of life, but without harming others. Life is eternal, we never die and, actually, we are never properly born; we go through different stages and states, through multiple dimensions. We have the power to positively influence both the future in this life, and other lives, also influencing the future of other beings, our planet and other planets in the universe.

The question often asked by Weiss is where some of today's souls come from, considering that compared to when planet earth began, there are many more people. Actually, many souls come from other dimensions, because the Earth is by no means the only habitable place in the universe. This will be Dolores Cannon's discovery, as we will see later. According to Weiss, as a psychiatrist that believes that vocation and mission of life is healing, the human being is naturally led towards understanding, evolution and spiritual growth. The human soul is destined to evolve towards a path of health and well-being. It lives in time but also out of time: the past and the future coexist in the present and we orient ourselves towards progress and health.

There is a very mysterious horizon, which appears in Weiss's work "One Soul, Many Bodies": the "progression into the future life"; not only does the past influence the present, but both could even be influenced by future lives. Weiss found that it is possible to project patients into the dimension of future lives. This happens because it is possible to access a timeless dimension, in which the past, the present and the future seem to take place at the same time. This does not mean that the future and any future lives are already established. On the contrary, the future is variable, but for each individual different possible paths unfold, depending on how they are acting in the present life. From the data collected by the subjects that Weiss led to the progression, it seems that in 100-200 years the world will be similar to the current one. There will be traces of disasters and natural catastrophes at the local level, greater pollution and global warming and new methods of growing food. Going further, in 300-

600 years, there could be a new Middle Ages: a population decimated by a reduction in fertility, the spread of viruses and poisons, the fall of asteroids and meteors, wars and natural disasters. Not everyone will be reincarnated at that time. Many souls will live in other worlds or dimensions, as if the Earth were just the primary or secondary school, while high school and university could only be attended in other worlds. Once again, this is not an immutable future, but one of the many possible outcomes, based on the current situation of the Earth's inhabitants, with the spread of hatred, wars and misuse of the ecosystem. However, this topic would lead us very far and require a worthy in-depth study that is not possible here.

A Brief Personal Experience of Regression

From "A Mystical Journey: Meetings with Extraordinary Masters, Magicians and Shamans":

"And so, when you learn to dig inside and you keep doing it, what comes out is unforeseeable. What came out of my depths would have been inconceivable before. And it changed my lifetime, making me more sensitive before the ordinary events and making me find out new meanings. This was the period that I call 'my exile', nearby a village in Tuscia, right in front of an old building called 'God's house'.

In that stage of my life, my job at school was not so easy, as to give me new life lessons. I tried out what loneliness meant, even if I learnt to take shelter and find solace, in the air the moving music by Ludovico Einaudi. In loneliness, I found even more myself, and because of that the unconscious has opened wide some very deep trap doors: images of people and events not referable to this life started to emerge step by step. I cannot exclude that I had been temporarily destabilized by feelings of unavoidable nostalgia in regular life.

During those moments, I had to consolidate a firm balance between ordinary life and what was emerging from my deep unconscious. The images of what seemed to be "past lives" go and insert in our own present life as many little pieces that gradually come back together, acquiring sense and coherence. The problem is that in that personal situation, the mosaic with these pieces was incomplete because of important missing pieces and it was not clear the connection among them at all. But memories were so vivid and, above all, full of various emotional contents. Precisely for the suffering of certain memories, the other fragments of the plot had been strictly removed and hidden by consciousness, leaving room for a vague nostalgia and a faint and delicate melancholy, that became the constant background during those months.

In that period, I read some books by Brian Weiss and Angelo Bona left in my bookcase.

Due to my experiences, I felt that it was the right moment to investigate the experiments done by those doctors and psychotherapists that had used the past life regression on some patients, very often reaching mysterious neurosis recoveries or somatic disorders. I studied these subjects with critical thinking and, most of all, suspending judgement. Surely I had already heard of that before and I had not been sceptical, but puzzled: I believed that even if the hypnotic regression could bring back memories of previous lives, it could be dangerous without an appropriate preparation. And I had so much spiritual work to do in this life that I could not understand how useful it was to go and dig in your past, if not for mere curiosity. But in that case, after an accidental approach with this sort of experiences, I needed a direction and to give a meaning to what I had lived. My memories are not sprung up because pursued or induced by any hypnotic method; they are born by reaching a deep level of consciousness over my techniques of meditation, in a state of deep relaxation, totally lucid.

In situations of deep research, I found myself considering images and different places, without having looked for them. I visualized scenes where I walked, in the evening, in the streets of an enchanting European town. It could be the end of the Eighteenth century or the beginning of the Nineteenth century. It was cold and I wrapped in my coat while I walked towards a precise place, where I entered with the relief to seek shelter and warmth: a café, a bar of those times. And I knew who I had to meet and where I had to go, a hidden corner inside. A table of men around a man radiating a strong personal magnetism, a great power and an intense wisdom. We talked about spirit, magic, esotericism and paranormal events. Sometimes I simply listened to him, absorbed and captivating, sipping a cup of hot drink, with a magic half-light as backdrop. Were we disciples of that authoritative man? Was I part of any secret society? I definitely think so, what does it matter to know which one, where and why? It seemed that my fate in the esotericism was to go on in different forms and places, as I noticed with other images that emerged from the deepest levels of my being. In those images, I found myself in the Nineteenth century, English soil, in a temple with decorations and ceremonial tinsels, on the point of starting a magic-esoteric ceremony. It was the same image as many years before, right when, as an adolescent, I started my path. That is why I had always been deeply attracted by magic and Hermeticism: there was something inside me establishing a strong connection with these contexts.

It is difficult to regroup after living all of this in dimensions beyond time and space and then you have to come back to the dimension of the ordinary time, in the physical body. I experienced the eternity of my deepest essence, that in different times and places borrows a physical body to live precise experiences and meets again souls with whom it had already shared something, to walk together again, for a bit. Once I would have considered all of this spiritual romanticism, but at that point, it started to have a meaning, at long last."

CHAPTER 5

LIFE BETWEEN LIVES: THE SPIRITUAL WORLDS

> *"You would know the hidden realm where all souls dwell. The journey's way lies through death's misty fell. Within this timeless passage a guiding light does dance, Lost from conscious memory, but visible in trance."*
> **(Michael Newton)**

Michael Newton's Research

Among the pioneers of "life between lives" is the Canadian psychiatrist Joel Whitton. In his work, "Life Between Life: Scientific Explorations into the Void Separating One Incarnation from the Next", he shows different case studies on what happens in that state between lives, "meta-awareness", which he defines as *the threshold of experienced awareness that separates one incarnation from the other*. Andy Tomlinson is another pioneer who has written numerous books on this topic. Morris Netherton also discovered the existence of this "space between lives", when he had stumbled upon it accidentally during some sessions. However, he stated that he still did not fully understand its meaning.

Psychologist Roger Woolger founded the "Deep Memory Process", a kind of transpersonal psychotherapy that helps the client to access the afterlife, through active imagination in Jungian style, Moreno's psychodrama and Reich's bodywork.

However, the psychologist, hypnotherapist, professor and member of the American Counseling Association, Michael Newton has systematically explored this sector, creating together with Alan and Dee Chips the original certification program in "Life Between Life". In the '70s, Newton found out that it was possible to reach states of very deep hypnosis, which allowed the patient to recover not only the memories related to past lives, but also the experiences lived in the spiritual planes between one life and another.

After years of research on hundreds of cases, Newton was able to gather information on the cosmology of the spiritual worlds and on the characteristics of the spiritual life after death that anticipates the subsequent rebirth. His research leads us both beyond the states of consciousness related to the recalling of memories of past lives and, in particular, far beyond the spaces glimpsed by the subjects who have experienced NDE; beyond that threshold of non-return, as they are memories stored deeply of our soul. Like other specialists, Newton was initially sceptical and had rather begun to use hypnotic techniques to act therapeutically on patients' memories, those related to contingent life, going back to childhood, to find the origin of traumas and dysfunctions. This was until, just like Weiss, he worked on a patient suffering from chronic pain, without any objective medical cause but with immense discomfort. Una, a middle-aged woman, suffered from a state of depression, lack of energy and motivation and also complained of feeling alone and dissociated from other human beings. She reported suffering from a deep and gloomy indefinite nostalgia for "old friends". In a state of hypnosis, in the "alpha" stage where memories of past lives usually arise, she recalled some existences, but these memories did not seem directly connected to the problem.

The causes of her suffering did not seem to be linked to the present life, nor to past lives, except for some critical issues related to her death, which was caused by the wound inflicted by a bayonet, in France at the time of the First World War. Newton sensed that there was more. He refined his method of hypnotic induction leading his patient beyond the "alpha" stage, towards the "theta" state, or the state of superconsciousness. At that point, Una was able to recall the memories of the spiritual world where the soul lives in the life between lives. She was able to meet again with extreme joy and relief the group of souls connected to her. She reported seeing them "at home". *"Do you mean the home of one of your past lives?"*, Newton asked, still unaware of what Una was evoking. She replied that it was her true home in the spiritual world, where her group of souls was present. In her present life, she had found herself isolated from her spiritual group in order to learn an important karmic lesson, namely to become more independent, having the opportunity to grow spiritually without their help.

Newton understood that there was much more beyond the memories of both contingent and past lives. He began to take his patients back in time, before their last birth on earth, discovering significant connections between content that did not seem influenced by fantasy, but that appeared extremely coherent and authentic. The therapeutic potential, both physically and mentally, of recalling these memories was also important. He began his investigation, developing a methodology that employed a systematic strategy to enter and then, if necessary, exit the "life between lives". Newton discovered that the answers to the mystery of life lie within every human being's mind.

His hypnotic technique aims to reach an even deeper layer of consciousness than that achieved by both traditional hypnosis and regression to past lives. In the hypnotic state, the analytical conscious mind works with the unconscious mind to receive and respond to messages addressed to the deep memory.

We should highlight that the ordinary conscious mind, that is, the part associated with the waking state, with logical and rational thinking, uses 10% to 18% of brain capacity. The conscious mind filters the information that will enter the subconscious and is able to reset it through a process of repetition. Under the ordinary, critical and analytical conscious mind, lies the subconscious. Here the memories related to both the present existence and past lives are enclosed, with the alter-egos temporarily connected to the bodies/personalities. It makes up 90% of the mind and is linked to imagination, emotion, dreams, long-term memory and habits. It governs bodily functions, the autonomic nervous system, the immune system, and so on. The subconscious has great potential and resources: as if it contained a sophisticated computer, in which all present events and past lives are stored and complex programs are operated. We can come into contact with it when the brain reaches the "delta" waves. However, there is an even deeper state: the super-conscious, which is the centre of the Self, our real identity, a deep soul, which encloses all those experienced in the spiritual planes and can be manifested when the brain emits "Theta" waves. In the hypnotic regression to life between lives, as in that of regression to past lives, the conscious part is minimally awake; the subject can indeed speak and describe the memories that will emerge from the "Delta" and "Theta" stages.

Newton was surprised to discover that in the deepest range of the stage of Theta waves there were hidden memories that it would not be possible to recall in the most superficial stage of alpha waves. Those who had previously operated in the regression to past lives, on the other hand, thought that the memories referring to the space between one life and another represented a gap of foggy limbo and clouded by oblivion. This was due to the fact that the stage of brain emission of alpha waves cannot recall memories located in the super-conscious.

Newton noted that in the state of subconsciousness, subjects tend to see time chronologically, in moments distinctly placed in the past, present or future. On the other hand, in superconsciousness everything is "now". Coming from a physical dimension creates and sustains the illusion of time progression.

The "genetic memory" can be seen as the memory of the soul that arises from the unconscious mind. The consciousness memory is instead characterized by the contents of ordinary memories stored in the brain, in connection with the five senses; its purpose is the adaptation to the ordinary world. Therefore, it tends to be limited and subject to particular defence mechanisms. Then, there is an immortal memory, which arises from the subconscious and contains the memories of our origins and other physical lives. It is a bridge between conscious memory and super-conscious memory. From the latter spiritual memories arise: everything lived in the dimensions of the spiritual life between incarnations. It is a source of high inspirations and intuitions, evolved by a higher conceptual thought, a high intelligence, independent of the body-mind. It is therefore a trace of our experiences of immortal existence.

In 1994, Newton published his first work "Journey of Souls" and in 2000 "Destiny of Souls", which are the result of 35 years of research on hundreds of cases, which lay the foundations for the description and mapping of spiritual worlds. In 2004, he published "Life Between Lives: Hypnotherapy", a guide to the regression to life between lives, aimed at professionals in the sector.

All cases examined by Newton were carefully compared to each other to derive common patterns and exclude any construction of memories, suggestions or falsifications. It was possible to obtain a model of the spiritual worlds, which contains important universal truths about the souls that reincarnate repeatedly on Earth according to predetermined lines.

In this kind of hypnosis, the lives and moments of death are also reviewed. Patterns can be found that are identical to both the accounts of the NDEs and those of regressive hypnosis to past lives. According to Newton, a patient manifests the desire to experience spiritual regression at a particular moment in their life not by chance. At that moment, they are actually ready to explore certain meanings underlying particular events in their life.

> "O my God! I'm not actually dead! I mean, my body is dead, I can see it underneath me, but I'm floating… I can look down and see my body lying in the hospital bed. Everyone around me thinks I'm dead, but I'm not. I'd like to shout, 'I'm not really dead!' It is incredible: the nurses are putting a sheet on my head, people I know are crying. I'm supposed to be dead, but I'm still alive! [...] My wife is crying. I'm trying to contact her mind to tell her that everything is okay. She is so overwhelmed with grief. I wish she knew that my suffering is over. I am free of my body, I no longer need it. I will wait for her [...]"

From the moment of death, Newton leads the subject to recall the images of the spiritual world, that is, what happens beyond what in the NDE was a threshold of no return: from the subconscious, the subject is conducted to the super-conscious.

From the cases examined by Newton, it seems that those who have just died do not want to spend too much time near their bodies. Some, on the other hand, tend to stay for a few days near the place of death, especially if it was unexpected, to try to comfort loved ones who suffer their loss. But they do not experience pain because they have realized that there is an afterlife and that they will meet again. Similar to the NDE, in the memories emerged with this methodology, the frustration of not being able to get in touch with their loved ones was repeatedly reported by various subjects after their death, as the latter were too involved in their pain. In other cases, some souls fail to leave the earth because of unresolved issues.

Newton believes that the access to the spiritual world must take place gradually, unlike the return to physical life from the spiritual worlds, which would happen more quickly. The change from material density to spiritual lightness could be destabilizing for the soul that has just left the body.

"[…] 'Am I in the place of spirits? […] I feel the power of thought around me […] it is difficult to express it with words. I feel… thoughts of love, company, empathy and it's all combined with anticipation; as if others were waiting for me."

From the descriptions of several subjects, it seems that the spiritual worlds are "made of clouds". As in the NDE reports, there are several descriptions of a tunnel that leads further and that indicates the passage from one dimension to another.

In all subjects, the awareness of being back home is manifested; in a world that we have always known and from which we know we come. It is the same feeling you have when you return home after a long journey and feel the beauty, with the joy that gives relief to what had always been an indefinite nostalgia.

As in the NDE, subjects who recall the memories of the spiritual life between lives in hypnosis hear particular sounds and vibrations that transform into celestial music: this is the energy of the universe and it seems to have a revitalizing power on the soul.

The spiritual world has always been presented by esotericism and Eastern philosophies as divided into different dimensions that become less and less dense and far from the heavy earthly influence. However, Newton did not find this strict division of the "astral world" into seven dimension, as supported by the Eastern esoteric schools. It could be the result of an attempt to label and encode certain concepts. Newton recognizes the existence of an "astral" dimension, which is accessed through a dense atmosphere of light that is around the astral plane closest to the Earth and that would create the tunnel effect on passage.

There are different descriptions of what people first saw in the spiritual world: sunflower fields, castles, rainbows. The wonder in rediscovering the beauty of the spiritual worlds is great. A lot of people describe the encounter with friendly spiritual entities, which are identified according to parameters of an energetic-invisible type that often seem to reflect human characteristics. These souls are perceived as particularly familiar, both from the life just ended, and from previous lives. They are also perceived as guiding spirits, which we will talk about later. It seems that they were waiting for the subject, as they knew when he/she would arrive. Several persons even speak of a "party" to celebrate life just ended and the arrival at home. These souls have had many faces during the incarnations, but their true essence, which never dies, has a single face that is evident and can be easily recognized.

Death becomes a change of state. It is as if our deceased loved ones are in another invisible room, next to us. We cannot see them with physical eyes, but that does not mean they do not exist. From the earthly perspective, death is seen as painful and frightening. On the other hand, the spiritual world considers it a wonderful moment of joy and celebration.

During his investigations, Newton noted the existence of souls who intentionally choose to remain in the spiritual planes closest to earth. This is due to unsolved issues, great discomfort, non-acceptance of death, connected to a particular place, confusion, despair, unwillingness to interact with other spiritual entities and guides. This reminds us of George Ritchie's NDE, when he visited those astral dimensions together with his guide. It is widely documented by para-psychology and it would cause the manifestations of "ghosts" who try to interact with the living. It could also be just a part of the soul's energy, while the remaining part has already gained access to the higher spiritual planes. According to Newton's interpretation, it is not true that "ghosts" do not realize that they are dead and that they are trapped. This trap would consist of the confusion generated by obsessive attachment to certain people, places and events that they cannot let go. However, these suffering souls are monitored by special guides. They wait for the moment when the souls feel ready to proceed on their journey into the spiritual planes. As mentioned before, these souls are in such situations because they have suffered a traumatic or unexpected death, or because they want to stay with some person and protect them. Moreover, the "ghost" does not represent an earth shell without an animic awareness, because different portions of spiritual energy could remain in different contexts.

For example, if the living subject indulged in vices, he could take them to the other dimension, without the possibility of satisfying them. For this reason, such souls could remain on the lower astral planes in order to be closer to humans on earth and derive satisfaction from it, just as happened to the souls seen by George Ritchie. They will need the guides' help: they will show them how to overcome these limits, realizing that it is pointless to watch humans indulge in vices since these cannot be satisfied in those dimensions.

Returning to the Spiritual Worlds

The journey back to the spiritual worlds includes stages, rhythms and speeds according to the subject's level of evolution. Each journey is unique and non-replicable.

The guides pay special attention to young and inexperienced souls, who experience the transition from the physical to the spiritual plane in a more traumatic way.

On the other hand, if the soul is "old", meaning that it has already experienced many lives and deaths, it is aware of the new dimension and of its "returning home". So it does not need to be guided or reassured.

Usually, the guides appear during the transition from the physical plane to the spiritual one. According to Newton's experience, none of his patients have ever reported meeting divine figures such as Jesus or Buddha. In the NDEs' reports, divine figures can be found instead; in this case, the subject found in his guide religious traits.

Once arrived in the spiritual planes, the soul is different — it does not have the same emotions, the same humanity with its limits. Instead, it reveals a spiritual majesty typical of the spirit. It is a time of reflection, as well as energetic restoration and healing by spiritual guides and entities. It is also a moment of joy and comfort for the reunion with the companion souls with whom one may not have met during that life. Depending on the evolutionary level of the subject and the type of his life, this return can take place in different ways. However, there is a period, of variable duration – although talking about time in these dimensions is quite relative – of reorientation with the guides, before meeting their own "cluster" group of companion souls.

Newton refers to it as a "space of healing and orientation": different persons have mentioned areas, spaces, not to be understood on a physical level, but as a metaphor for the energy structure of a specific spiritual situation. They use similar definitions and metaphors to identify a context of regeneration and healing, rehabilitation, such as a "healing shower", while meeting their guide. The latter, as we will see later, is linked to a soul from multiple lives, knows deeply its strengths and weaknesses, and nothing can be hidden: in a spiritual world, based on telepathy and the power of thought, there can be no lies.

There could be influences of the previous physical human form on the soul, especially if traumas had occurred, causing disharmonies. Moreover, if these are not solved, they may persist in the soul and be transmitted to the bodies of future lives, as widely found in cases through the hypnosis of regression to past lives.

In the spiritual planes, it is possible to resolve such traumas through the art of "energy reconstruction", a kind of "remodelling" of the soul.

A patient of Newton recalls: *"They begin to examine the particles of damaged energy. These dark areas are removed and what remains — the voids — are reformed with an infusion of neo-purified light energy. It is fused into the energy for reinforcement."*

Newton's patients talked about "Guardians", custodians who seem to have no defined identity, very attentive and discreet, who assist us in restoring our energy to promote the healing processes. They use their frequencies to treat the subject's energy, repairing the damaged parts. It is like working with geometric shapes, "spirals of energy", which affect the configuration of critical points, as if the circulation of energy moved through "lines" that could be damaged, intoxicated and obstructed. Stagnant negative energy blocks the flow of positive energy.

Groups of Souls

A kind of "rest area", has been identified on several occasions, where souls transit to be directed towards their destination. It can be compared to an airport terminal: each soul will travel on a different route depending on the plane it is getting on. Here it is possible to meet other entities. Images of light, tunnels, corridors, energy filaments and points of light are described. A universal bond with other beings is perceived, in total lack of strangeness and hostility.

The arrival is its own group. Often, but not always, the soul meets a relative or companion from the life just spent.

Different subjects examined by Newton describe it with an analogy: a spiritual school led by master-guides, with different classes depending on the level of evolution and maturity of the soul. The group seems to be in a classroom or gathered around the steps of a temple or in a garden. The soul could also meet other groups who will notice it, even with greetings.

The wonder of the spiritual worlds, as described by different subjects, consists in the fact that all souls have the same value, because everyone is on the way to a process of evolution and transformation into something greater. We are in a structure based on the values of ethics, compassion, harmony, extreme kindness, patience, tolerance and unconditional love.

Once the souls reach their groups, they are summoned together with the guide before the "Council of Elders" — they examine the activities of the soul. Several names are given to the members of this council: "sacred teachers", "venerable", "examiners", "committee", but the most frequent is "Elders". Here is what a Newton's patient recalls:

"There are always the same six Elders in front of me, wearing long white robes. Their faces are sweet. They evaluate my perceptions of the life just lived and how I could have done better with my talents and if my actions have been beneficial. I am allowed to freely express my frustrations and desires. All the Elders are familiar to me, especially two of them who speak to me more and look younger than the others [...] They are honest and authentic and I am always treated with respect. I cannot hide anything, but sometimes I get lost when their thoughts are relayed to each other in quick communication. When it is beyond what I can handle, Veronica [the guide] translates to me what they are saying, even if I feel that she does not tell me everything. Before I return to Earth, they want to see me again."

The Elders almost always wear white-purple clothes that give them a particular dignity. Typically, seven council members are displayed. An advanced soul can see from seven to twelve of them. The more evolved it is, the more specialization the Elders need to have. The Elders represent the authority, they are high souls. They do not seem to be at the top of divine authority, however they are in a high position, as responsible for souls still incarnating on earth. They express extreme patience and compassion towards human weaknesses, defects and limitations. They are always ready to grant second chances for future lives in order to promote our learning and spiritual growth. The guides accompany and assist the subject during the session in front of this council, often helping them to interpret what may not be clear. When the soul is particularly evolved, the guide sits together with the members of the Council.

The Elders' aim is not to punish the subject, but to interview him and make him reflect in order to help him achieve his goals in future lives. They approach the subject with firmness, goodwill and indulgence, without criticizing him. Encouraged by the most sincere respect, they tend to give advice. The soul can only perceive reverence towards them. They are able to highlight his progress, making him consider his life events from new points of view, providing alternative interpretations. Nothing can be hidden from them, not even our innermost thoughts — they have a deep and powerful telepathy. There is no truth to be proved and no need to have a defence attorney as is the case in our courtrooms. The Elders ask us about how we felt during the main episodes of our life. They ask us if our physical body helped us or if it was an obstacle and how we feel before the prospect of another future life. They want to understand whether the deep essence of our soul has preserved its ideals and values during its life, despite the cumbersome presence of the brain and body. The Elders do not care how many times we fell, but how we got up and how we used our potential. Everything matters in life, even small and maybe insignificant actions. They did not seem to be important, however they were significant and decisive for other people.

Behind this council a high force can be perceived, *"This is what is closest to God"*, as described in more cases. It is a "Presence", which assists the work of the council. They do not want to call him "God", as the idea linked to this word has been excessively personified. They define him as "Source", "Origin", "Super-soul".

Between the two meetings with the Elders, the soul can interaction with other souls. Here there are no trials, joy, pain or anger. In this way, it is possible to work on future connections in different forms in life.

According to the different testimonies, it is possible to see the existence of high spiritual beings. They are not deities, but advanced souls who have completed the cycle of their physical incarnations and help human beings who still live on Earth and face karmic trials.

When the souls are with their groups, they feel they are at home. It is similar to a school class. The group of souls is structured and organized, according to the evolutionary level and level of consciousness, as if it put together close friends. It is a small unit of entities, ranging from three to 25, that have frequent contacts, as if it were a family. These primary groups would be subsets of secondary groups of souls, enclosing thousands of souls, as a large community. It is possible to meet different groups, depending on the lessons to be learned, following existential connections or particular personality traits. A network of connection is created that involves different souls, based on their similarities reported in shared earthly experiences.

According to descriptions of Newton's patients, the souls would have a colour: from white-grey to red, yellow and blue. It is an energy field influenced by vibratory qualities, with densities, forms of light and colours radiated in proportion to their level of awareness, wisdom and evolution. Newton identified six evolutionary levels of souls, which have different shades of colours. The first level is the one of the beginner soul in white; the second one is low-intermediate, white with red shades. The third level of the intermediate stage soul is yellow, while the intermediate-advanced level is golden-yellow. The advanced fifth level has light blue tones. Finally there is a highly advanced dark blue/purple sixth level. From the fourth level, there is the opportunity to start being a "junior" guide, and then become a "senior" and "master" guide in the following levels. In some cases, they reported souls beyond the sixth level, characterized by an even more purple hue. These seem to be very close to the origin of creation. They are mysterious, unreachable and extremely venerated. From the fourth level, the colour change becomes less evident. Each colour corresponds to certain qualities. White represents purity, clarity; silver shades indicate confidence, flexibility; red is linked to passion, intensity, sensitivity. Orange represents impulsiveness, openness, exuberance; yellow is strength, courage, protectiveness; green is connected to healing and compassion. Brown represents tolerance, grounding and industriousness; blue expresses revelation and knowledge, while purple is the colour of wisdom, truth and divinity.

Some souls are able to evolve more quickly, while others need more time. The interactions and combinations that bring out the peculiarities and unique characteristics of each soul will be very lively and endless.

Newton also identified four categories of souls. The first category consists of souls who are not made to be on an individual level: they tend to be reborn in the spiritual worlds in group contexts. Then there are souls who choose not to incarnate in the physical worlds and remain in the spiritual worlds, moving between different dimensions. In the third category, they choose to incarnate only in physical worlds, having no inclination for interdimensional travel or living in spiritual worlds. Finally, there are souls who can and want to be in different contexts, both material and spiritual.

Souls with an "intermediate" evolutionary level always remain in contact with their primary group. However, after hundreds of incarnations (about fifty thousand years for some souls or five thousand for others), they often move towards another more specialised group. Here they meet souls similar in level of evolution, inclinations, skills, objectives and abilities that they will learn. Based on his patients' experiences, Newton identified several areas of specialization: masters of the dream, redeemers of "lost souls", "guardians of neutrality", "masters of reconstruction", "archivist-souls", "musical directors", "guardians of young souls" (the latter are guardians of child souls who have not yet begin their cycle of incarnations on Earth and could be disoriented). The "masters of design" work on the creation of animate or inanimate objects that form the environments of the planets, through energy and thought, manipulating the cellular and molecular structures of living matter. This means that behind the worlds' physical nature, there is an immaterial and invisible spiritual origin.

The resources of a group of souls in the spiritual planes are very important, due to the great healing power that the interaction with their fellow souls has — a source of support and inspiration. Newton attributes human characteristics to entities that are nonetheless spiritual, as on Earth they expressed human characteristics. They are peer groups and any form of hatred, suspicion, rivalry or competitiveness is absent among them — there is great respect and compassion.

Therefore, the soul is reunited with his spiritual friends, in the name of the purest ideals of brotherhood and solidarity. Each journey in the post-mortem purifies the lower nature and develops wisdom. This will make a difference in later lives, as well as in the future of humanity in general. Relationships with similar souls are even closer and more authentic, because the lower waste has been burned and the highest part of association and communion remains. The same state of consciousness is shared.

In some cases, groups include subgroups made up of entities that are united by the same types of issues that block their evolution, despite having different characteristics. Members of these groups have worked together for so long that they have a deep familiarity and a deep group identity, developing a strong sense of belonging. Both solitude and belonging with the group are necessary for the soul's evolution: solitude as a moment of reflection and an opportunity for learning; socialization as an opportunity for support, comfort and sharing. Newton's patients report that during moments of solitude, a soul learns to produce energy, putting together geometric shapes: *"We must learn to intensify our energy to focus on what is disordered and mixed, to give it some kind of basic form."*

In addition, these moments can mentally help loved ones, through an "interdimensional blue-silver" energy field. It is possible to release positive vibrations aimed at certain people and geographical places, in order to produce transformative effects. Christian purgatory can represent a state of isolation and solitude needed in particular circumstances. However, it would not be a punishment or damnation, but a stage of transition.

Recreational contexts are also described, with open spaces where souls of different levels of learning gather. These are less formal contexts, which seem to follow the terrestrial activities of which they feel most nostalgic: exploring landscapes, swimming in the sea and spiritual food tasting. It is as if the soul recreates in those worlds an image of their previous body. It is the rest from more work-related and structured activities, moments that can also become long periods. It is also possible to recreate environments and contexts of one's beloved places, freezing certain eras, situations and family contexts. There are also souls who choose to have a period of "holiday".

They visit the Earth, just remaining spiritually close to old familiar places:

> *"My wife Erika and I loved the little house we had built in the Bavarian Alps. After our death, we wanted it back; so we built it with the help of our energy master. He thought this would be good practice for us. The pattern was in my mind, but he saw it perfectly before we started transmitting energy. Other adjustments of the exterior came from our friends Hans and Elfie, who were our neighbours in Germany and are with us now. Erika and I chose the interior decoration. I created my old library and my wife created her kitchen just as it was. It's wonderful to be me and her alone again like this."*

All the possibilities of the soul are explored, which can become an object, both animate and inanimate, merging with the elements air, fire and water, changing its form and substance.

The astral plane seems to be a co-construction: each soul brings a scenario, perceptible by others, so each contributes to the creation of different scenarios and contexts that will be shared. The scenario of each plane is produced by the fusion of the mental images of those who inhabit it. For example, the Native American Indian clairvoyant shamans visualize the celestial world, penetrating the lower planes of the astral through the "shamanic journey". In this way, the religious teachings of tribes and peoples originate.

There are also disembodied souls who explore the earth without ever having incarnated in a body. Folklore and mythology identified them as beings of light, friendly, peaceful and helpful, and more distant, irritating and quarrelsome darker beings. No demonic spirits are perceived, but the negative emotions of fear, hatred, anger that pervade the Earth and create incessant disharmony would cause turmoil. According to Newton, there are unhappy spirits that roam the astral dimensions closest to the material planes, but they do not invade people's minds, as some parapsychological theories believe. Evil seem rather to exist in the human mind.

Behind beliefs and dogmas, there is a human intuition of truth. Interpretations change, as they are conditioned by the mind and the contingency of space-time. The human mind has always imagined the existence of a higher power, of which there is a spark, a reflection in our deepest inner being. In the spiritual planes, the soul never escapes the judgment of its own conscience. It is as if its best examines and judges everything that is below that limit. It is as if seeds were planted that will blossom towards progress, and in the astral planes we can receive the energies, stimuli and resources that will make the soul express with a new potential in the following lives. As if during sleep, the information of waking life is reworked and connected in a new way, correcting errors and seeing everything from a new perspective, or even welcoming new brilliant insights. It is the same thing, but on a more super-conscious level: life in the astral planes in post-mortem seems to be a period of study and exercise that will then be put into practice in future physical life. Philosophers, scientists and artists will find "books of knowledge" that will reveal what they could not know, with a new creative power, always aimed at building, improving and transforming incessantly. New models are created of what will later be brought into the material world. Even on Earth, every creation has a mental origin: what is created externally first exists as an image in its creator's mind.

There are different descriptions of lives in other worlds, other galaxies, other planets; and Newton asked many questions to different subjects, in an attempt to learn the atmospheric composition, topography and gravitation. As one of his patients says:

"From the spiritual to a physical world, it seems that a door opens and you see the walls, or it seems to be a corridor that rotates on an etheric side. Then another portal opens and you're there. When I step into another dimension

*to a mental world, I am like a piece of static flow through the screen of a
television into magnetic zones structured by pure thought. The voids are made
of large energy button fields. I feel the power of this energy more than in a
material universe."*

*"I have come to the conclusion that everything on Earth and in the universe
is apparently connected by thought waves to and from the spiritual world."*

Some souls travel on an interdimensional level and describe their
movements between spheres connected at the vibrational level. They
learn to orient themselves along paths of points, lines, surfaces and
energy zones that connect dimensions and universes,

*"These dimensions are mixed with each other. I do not have the perception
of boundaries, except for two elements — sound and colour. With sound, I
must learn to tune my energy to the vibrational frequency of each dimension,
and some are so complex that I can't go there yet. On the other hand, colours
like purple, blue, yellow, red and white are manifestations of light and
density for those energy particles in the dimensions where I travel."*

The Guides and the Book of Life

As mentioned before, many of Newton's patients affirm that, after
reunification with their group of souls, they found themselves in a
kind of library, which contains a systematic collection of "books of
life", where it is possible to study and reflect. Its structure is rectan-
gular; the books are arranged on walls and other souls are studying
there. The "archivist-souls", who seem calm and peaceful monks
who co-assist souls together with their respective guides, handle all
those books. Every experience, event, word and thought of every life
is recorded in these books that represent the symbol of the Akashic
records, the essence of all universal memory. They register every
slightest movement and vibration of the living energy in the uni-

verse, past, present and future. Everything can therefore be recovered in this spiritual context.

It is a real book of life: a photographic book without texts, with multidimensional images that change. The "Akashic records" have the same concept, as described by Eastern philosophies and by Edgar Cayce, a clairvoyant, who was able to access the Akashic memory of his clients: the spiritual book of life.

According to several subjects, these books are like multidimensional screens; it is possible to select different moments from each timeline and to choose particular sequences of events. It seems that just with your thought, you can interact with the book, scanning at will, as if your light waves resonate with the lines on the screens, focusing on certain images. All waves run along the timeline, from the point of view of a dimension of spiritual time that is the "here and now", in which past, present and future seem to take place at the same time.

What human beings build on Earth seems to be an imitation of what they remember of the spiritual dimensions from which they come.

Newton states that all his patients had a guide: this is perceived as a disembodied figure, displayed as an image and heard as a voice. Guides are master entities who guide us through wise instructions, both during our physical incarnation, — often however unheard due to excessive mental noise—, and when we return to the spiritual planes. They support during difficult times, challenges and existential pains. The guide has been assigned to us since the creation of the soul. During life, it is possible to acquire other "junior" secondary guides, which are souls of a lower evolutionary level and still in the phase of intermediate apprenticeship, therefore a "level three" soul according to the classification made by Newton. In some cases two guides work together on a soul, each with their own teaching method. There is a constant guiding of each other, up to great master guides who lead entire groups.

They want the best for the soul they follow and strive to leave them free in their choices. They could not prevent sufferings, which, however, have the function of making the person grow and mature. The guides assist us constantly and accompany us throughout our evolution, through the changes and transformations that will come when we are ready. Especially in most difficult moments, we may feel the mysterious presence of someone invisible who is watching us. They have a particular way of guiding the soul, through clues, showing in small steps the direction to take. A guide is empathetic, almost parental, not authoritarian or dictatorial, and is very compassionate.

Souls from the spiritual planes can have contact with people still incarnated on Earth. Subjects often describe a "shower" of energy, or a protective cloak-cloud wrapped around the person they want to protect, identifying weak points where energy is blocked or does not flow properly. Projections of rays of light or images animated by love are also described, which are powerful for any type of physical or emotional trauma. The soul coordinates its vibrational resonance with the body of the physical person, tuning in with his soul and his physical organs.

The soul can often interact with familiar physical objects. In this case, energy is tuned to elements such as fire, using them as conductors of intention and will. The energy of the soul is liquid and can be directed through concentration and practice to achieve certain goals. Energy has electromagnetic properties that can affect objects in mysterious ways. Rays, beams of light, lines are created that interact with the corporeal world, with the physical, magnetic and electrochemical forces. Several subjects have also reported the creation of "balls" of positive and healing energy thrown on the Earth in order to balance its negative energy. With the guides' help, the souls can learn real spiritual faculties.

According to Newton's patients, in the life between lives souls are not sad for leaving the physical life, although at times they may feel nostalgic for it. In those dimensions, the soul of the deceased is at peace, as it is no longer influenced by the character and biochemistry of the body-brain. They acquire new energy with the contact with guides and fellow souls and can also recover the energy left behind in those planes before incarnating in the life just spent. There is a feeling of being complete again.

The Ring of Destiny and Return to Earth

According to Newton's research, different subjects visualized the "Ring of Destiny": a circular domed theatre, with panoramic floor-to-ceiling screens that completely surround them, who are in an observation point, as on an elevated bridge. The subject sees the future life in different scenes based on how it will unfold, from childhood to adulthood, without defined time categories. There is something like control panels to scan the timelines. It is like watching a film on a video-player, thus having the opportunity to dwell on a certain scene and scroll back or forward. However, it is not allowed to see all scenes and epilogues; it is focused on the period ranging from eight to twenty years. The soul seems to be alone in this theatre, but with the presence of a "projector" entity in the background. Someone who handles this presentation of people and events: the master souls of time, who are not directly perceived. This happens once the subject has developed, with the help of the Elders, the awareness of the fundamental stages that will be faced in the next life with the objectives to be achieved. On these premises, the choice between different possibilities and alternatives of life paths will be made.

The alternatives of a future are many but not unlimited. However, they guarantee different possibilities for learning and evolution. Every small detail and decision could change an entire destiny, but one's free will is essential, in different opportunities and occasions. The background here is a time that is manipulated by compressing and stretching particles of energy, thought and vibration. What this Ring shows will subsequently be veiled by amnesia, so as to preserve free will and self-determination, without being influenced by what we saw there.

The type of information that dominates the mind could be different from the goals of the soul, as the mind is more influenced by the sensory world, society, the chaos of emotions and passions, and so on. The challenge is listening to the voice of your soul, despite the obstacle of the mind.

The experiences in the next life will depend on the evolutionary project established before birth, the path that involves the groups of Souls to which you are spiritually linked and the evolutionary path of all mankind. However, one's own soul will have much influence because with its free will, one can make important changes with respect to what has already been established.

The life project can be accepted or rejected; the subject could also postpone the moment of reincarnation, or even reincarnate on another planet other than Earth.

The soul could decide to leave the body before its natural death, for example if the mind blocks the free flow of information from the soul, producing irreversible damage; or when the soul has already carried out all possible experiences with that body and mind, and is ready for new experiences in different contexts. Or this happens when its physical death could induce an evolutionary leap in the souls with whom it is spiritually connected. Sometimes a soul can achieve its goals easier from the spiritual planes; for example, it can protect and support its loved ones more effectively than if it had remained in a physical body.

The time spent in the spiritual planes varies depending on the personal evolutionary path. The force of the "Dharma" leads to a new incarnation, which indicates the call of the Divine, towards the awareness that our true nature is divine and this realization is the purpose of life. Creation took place because God wanted to know himself through his creation, in the wake of the thought "May I become the many."

We are also called to earthly life by karma that has not been completed, in order to finish the evolutionary path. The path is clear and the soul builds its evolutionary program, carefully choosing the circumstances of life that will allow it to follow its own personal path and face its own karma, including free will. The soul that reincarnates is made up of all the energies that will create a new body-mind complex, and the memories of past lives will be buried by oblivion.

Therefore, the transition from the astral planes to reincarnation takes place, which some esotericists refer to as the "second sleep of the soul". After all it has accomplished in the spiritual planes of the post-mortem, the soul needs to process it and manifests a desire for rest. It was able to satisfy desires, ideals and ambitions and feels that that phase is finished. It therefore manifests the need for new experiences in a new life, to realize the developments achieved in the spiritual plans. It will be changed, different from when it entered those levels. It is now heading towards a current that will gradually lead it to rebirth. This spiritual lethargy will continue even after birth: the awakening will occur very slowly and gradually throughout childhood, culminating in adolescence and early adulthood. However, in some cases, the awakening occurs early, especially in particularly evolved souls.

Those who return to a new physical life are not reborn by punishment, but always following their will and desires, which can only be fulfilled with a material body. The soul will be directed towards the contexts most suited to the type of inclinations and objectives. It is only after many lives that it realizes that all earthly desires are vain and illusory. However, before this realization, there will be distractions such as desires of a different type, even if not material, but in any case achievable only in a physical life. The energies involved in a desire can be of different kinds, expressing different types of situations connected not only to having but also to doing, in particular, to being and becoming. As for the choice of the conditions of the future life, the younger and less evolved the soul, the less conscious the choice, which will be more instinctive. On the other hand, the more the soul is evolved, the greater the understanding and conscious participation in the choice.

When returning to Earth through the new incarnation, the union of the Soul-Self with the ego-body-brain takes place: the soul joins this organism in the foetus and the union between soul and body will begin. This process is unique because the soul, together with a particular mind in a particular body, will create a unique personality that, although partly temporary for an entire lifetime, will leave an indelible mark on our eternal essence. It will be a unique opportunity for the soul to experience the Earth in that particular "here and now", with those particular and unique combinations.

The passage is quick, but it involves traumas and difficulties too. There is a fusion between spirit and body. However, the immortal soul remains the seat of everything that will unfold the development of the human ego. Spiritual strength will always be present, the result of infinite awareness and multiple life experiences. The soul is not trapped, but it is limited. It can always contact the spiritual levels during sleep, in deep meditation and on the occasion of particular existential situations, such as undergoing total anaesthesia for surgery.

Part of the soul remains in the spiritual planes even when reincarnated, which is why it is possible to meet a relative who died thirty years earlier and at that time already reincarnated in another existence. In fact, not all the soul energy can be carried in an incarnation, otherwise the impact of the soul-body connection would be so intense as to burn the circuits of the brain. Following death, with the transition to the spiritual world one begins to gradually recover that energy, together with the healing procedures to which one is subjected.

For a young soul, a "beginner", its first earthly incarnations will inevitably be difficult, since it is accustomed to the harmony of the spiritual dimensions. It will feel disoriented when facing the complexity and contradictions of human society. It will be more influenced by social conventions and dominant power and will lack in independent thinking. The possibility of learning certain lessons will depend on your inclinations, your motivation and your cultural background. In physical life, what matters most is how we have lived and how we behaved with other people, the compassion developed and the ability to accept others for who they are.

According to Newton's experience, it often takes months to understand and integrate the memories recovered during regressive hypnosis sessions into one's ordinary life. Their lives have been positively transformed because they have had the opportunity to align themselves with the purposes of their soul.

Reliving life between lives reconnects us to the deep intelligence of the soul and to the spiritual beings who constantly support us. A deep love is reported that is emanated by the guides and all spiritual beings. Some subjects report a real telepathic contact with their guides even during the ordinary state of consciousness. You are aware that you have chosen life situations and therefore you are not a victim of situations and other people.

You are now aware that there is no separation: everything material and non-material is part of an "all that is", eternal divine origin.

Each soul has a specific extra-physical dimension where it has spent the periods between lives, as an extra-physical home.

The soul, whether incarnated or not, could be in two places at the same time. A terrestrial and a celestial part coexist in us. Our spiritual part is not bound to the boundaries of the body, space and time. We all have the gift of intuition, the instinct, something that takes us beyond the material plane.

"The spiritual world is a place of rest. You learn, teach, re-evaluate, but then you have to test what you've learned. You test yourself living different lives, to see if this has really and truly become part of your essence. It's like when they hurt you: do you have a deep instinct to forgive? Do you have an instinct deep inside to show compassion? Do you have unconditional love without demands? All this is put to the test in a lifetime."

The Law of Karma

To better understand "life between lives" and what the next life will prepare, we need to briefly focus on "karma". Karma is not related to punishment, but to a law of cause and effect: a cycle in which the one who was an executioner in a past life will become the victim in a future life. The reward/punishment do not matter, but the understanding implied by role changes. Karma means "action", which generates consequences, creating an inevitable cause-effect mechanism. Our destiny is determined by causes related to the actions we have done both in the present and in the past lives. Nothing happens by chance; instead it depends on a precise law. There are karmic links also with regard to diseases; the search for such connections guides regressive psychotherapy, which starts from a specific initial question, following a common thread, along a path that will lead to the dynamics that have generated a problem. The therapist should focus on a limited topic in order to optimize psychotherapeutic work.

Patanjali, Indian philosopher, father of yoga and author of the "Yoga Sutras", teaches us that karma has five "klesha" roots. The first klesha is Avidya, ignorance, lack of spiritual awareness, inability to perceive the divine in and out of oneself, conviction that ordinary physical reality is all that exists. The second klasha is Asmita, namely selfishness, self-worship: the tendency to identify oneself with the body and mind. The belief that the self is closely identified with the body-mind complex. The third klesha is the desire for what causes pleasure, power, fame, money, the desire for possession, jealousy. The fourth klesha is Dvesa, or the repulsion towards what is a source of unhappiness. The last klesha is Abhinivesa, that is, the desire to live, which manifests itself as attachment to earthly existence; it is an instinct of life opposed to the "death drive".

We produce karma continuously, with every thought, emotion and action. Everything we have produced imprints on our deep part of the soul that contains all memories, of all samskaras. These traces create the character and personality of an individual. This is at the base of the mind, which is animated by instincts reflecting the vasanas, that is, the unconscious tendencies that incessantly move the deep recesses of the psyche. Karma generates these samskara, which then produce the vasanas that influence the subject, leading him towards certain actions, reactions and behaviours. An effect always has a cause that originates from a samskara imprinted in the unconscious. Psychotherapeutic work aims at understanding these imprints, carefully analysing the symbolic language of the mind. We try to find the basis of the conflicts. Then it will be difficult to untie that knot in depth, allowing deep meanings to be translated into words by the patient.

The cause of what we like is linked to experiences with favourable results; on the contrary, what we dislike is linked to negative results. The individual characteristics, namely the different dreams, aspirations, desires, fantasies and impulses, are not inherited. For example, twins with the same genetic heritage are characterized by uniqueness and differ in many aspects. If certain desires have been intense and have not been fulfilled, the soul does not let them go in the process of purification and carries them as "karma" into the next life as an innate tendency. We therefore find ourselves repeatedly in certain situations, despite the efforts to avoid them, because we bring them as they are attracted by unresolved knots. These will continue to promptly lead us back into the same dynamics, until we recognize their origin. You will understand the connection of your conscious and unconscious thoughts, your emotions and behaviours to events. There are traumas so deeply rooted that when evoked in some situations they produce fear and anguish, forcing unnatural and compulsive behaviours that lead to escape and avoidance. In these situations, unresolved traumas have imprinted themselves as dense matter in the deepest layers of the soul.

In life, there is a preparatory phase in order to develop the necessary skills to carry out the existential program or remember them from previous lives. You live non-random situations, which are connected to your karmic dynamics. There could be momentary deviations from the evolutionary path, following emotional disorders or passionate impulses that reduce the lucidity of consciousness. They still have a meaning and a learning function.

It is always possible to identify activities, situations or relationships that are not necessary, or that would have been better avoided, or decisions to be taken with more consciousness.

The evolution of consciousness is the most important aspect and purpose of physical life.

Karma is a real system of justice. The law of karma explains the inequalities in the world: poverty, suffering, violence, murder and wars. Life events are not random: they seem to follow a plan governed by a universal mind. Everything creates karma, even a simple thought or desire, so all this creates great responsibility in the subject who becomes at the same time the judge and the jury of himself. Even people who caused us problems have contributed to our spiritual progress. The difference lies in how we react, how we are able to let go of the past, purifying negative emotions of anger, resentment, revenge, hatred and fear. Pain, adversity, suffering are an opportunity to connect to who you really are and discover your potential.

The most difficult karmic trials take place in romantic relationships. Newton rejects the existence of the "Twin soul"; according to this new-age concept, two souls would be parts of a single unit. He instead argues that each part of energy is unique and is created as a single entity. Newton highlights the importance of primary companion souls, for example partners or family members, who enrich life with meanings and values, providing help to achieve our goals. There are also "companion" souls: they are close companions in our cluster group, who support us. Then there are "associated" souls who belong to members of secondary groups that include from one to a thousand souls, who work with us from several lives, some in limited periods, others to bring us important karmic lessons.

According to the testimonies collected by Newton, it happens that members of the same group of souls return in subsequent incarnations in the same genetic human family. It is important that experiences are made in different ethnic and cultural contexts. However, the return to the same family takes place to resolve certain karmic issues left unresolved. Newton brings the example of cases involving difficulties with a parent and always finds the answer to the question: "What did I learn through this person, who gave me the wisdom that I would not have had if he or she had never been in my life?"

We are masters of our destiny and we can change our choices and actions, changing the course of our destiny.

COSMIC CRADLE: CHILDREN BEFORE BIRTH

> *"Paradigms that only describe the development of the physical body have not solved the mystery of life and the secrets of the mind. Subatomic particles, biochemistry, family, society, the stars, consciousness and spiritual forces, all contribute to the human incorporation of a soul that is incarnating."*
> **(Carista Luminare-Rosen)**

The psychologist Elizabeth Carman and the biologist Neil Carman interviewed children and their parents and studied children's memories regarding their birth, their intra-uterine life, the period before birth, conception, pre-conception, in some cases they also analysed clues of past lives. In most cases, these memories are retained in full consciousness and not obtained through hypnotic procedures. They generally have been revealed from 2 to 5 years old and then tend to fade from 6. Therefore, the younger the child is, the closer he is to the spiritual dimensions from which he comes.

Ian Stevenson, David Chamberlain and Akira Ikegawa conducted research on thousands of subjects from different parts of the world and they all seem to reveal a multidimensional nature.

This field of research developed in the 1990s and aimed at discovering the true nature of awareness and the potential of different states of consciousness. They revealed that children are not a tabula rasa, as the philosopher Locke said in 1690, but have a state of awareness that brings remarkable memories and learning that dates back before physical birth.

Studying a child from the point of view of psychology and academic medicine is different from living him in everyday life.

This contradicts Freud's theory of "Infantile Amnesia", coined in 1966, according to which it would be impossible to recover memories dating back to the first years of life, before the age of three.

Chamberlain rejects this theory, considering it naive and not supported by sufficient data. Among the studies that deal with childhood memory, doctor Carolyn Rovee Collier analysed childhood memory and the ability to learn and remember that increases with age. Very often, children can remember an event during the period before the age of 3 and, if exposed to non-verbal reminders, they can recall and use memories in different contexts, contrary to what the dominant academic theories state.

In 1986 Chamberlain studied birth and pre-birth memories; Akira Ikegawa reported on memories related to birth, intra-uterine life, conception and pre-conception, and did the same thing in 2015 with Masayuki Ohkado. The outcome contradicts the official paradigm according to which it would be impossible for a newborn or unborn child to see, feel pain, learn and remember what has been done in his presence; moreover, certain procedures do cause damage or trauma in the developing child. Therefore, children before birth can see, feel and learn, reacting with behaviours and perceiving the emotions of people in the surrounding environment.

Their memories appear in states of life in which the brain does not yet exist, or it is just developing. Therefore, the existence of a spiritual essence before conception is theorized, which is conscious during pregnancy and at birth. From the work "Cosmic Cradle" by Elizabeth and Neil Carman: *"Imagine all your senses just rolled up into one sense of being [...] All my senses were connected [...] I was like a bullet of light."*

Memory therefore transcends physical cells; it begins well before the age of three, even before birth. Chamberlain writes, *"Consciousness reflects an innate and permanent endowment of intelligent awareness that has a similar meaning to the word 'soul'."*

These memories are spontaneous, consistent over time, without change. These are not fantasies, otherwise they would change over time and in the different accounts. The story is told through direct eye contact, common patterns, with a serious tone of voice that, although coming from a child, seems almost adult. The content is perceived as truthful and the listener perceives a deep intuition of authenticity and has no doubt about it. Researches were carried out in different countries and continents, revealing analogies and deep coherence of structure. The patterns are the same among thousands of children from different geographical and socio-cultural contexts and their testimonies are characterised by a consistency over time, credibility and veracity.

Ohkado's investigations reveal that 42% of 21 cases of pre-conception memories, 70% of 215 cases of intra-uterine life memories, 86% of 156 cases of memories of the moment of birth were considered true, therefore with confirmed evidence.

A first type of memories are those related to the period before conception, which describe existence in non-physical dimensions, real spiritual worlds. As described in the testimonies reported in "Babies are Cosmic", the most frequent statement among children in the very first years of life is: *"I chose you as a mother", "Mom we met before, when we were in Heaven with God."*

Isaac said to his mother: *"I have chosen you as a mother. I have looked down on the Earth, from the world of 'Half children'."* Diego said: *"We all come from there, but most children forget this from the age of six."*

In several testimonies collected by Elizabeth and Neil Carman, the process of perceiving totally all the terrestrial situations is described, having the possibility of "zooming" the precise location of the selected parents. Some children claim to have chosen a mother to promote important changes in her existence, her healing from any physical or psychological problems, to impart life lessons, to take care of her and give her love. Merille *said, "Mom, I chose you because you needed me."*

In some stories, children have observed their mother from the sky for several years prior to their birth, waiting for the right moment, as was later confirmed by circumstances. In other cases, there was even a participation of the child's soul to influence the events that would lead to their birth. Casper, 3, told his mother that he was "up in space", where Evelyn, his maternal grandmother, lived, who guided him to be born at the most appropriate time. Faced with this revelation, his mother Aimee was amazed: the son did not know his grandmother's name and certain details such as her nickname and that she hated being called "Grandma". Aimee noted this story down on her computer and when Casper was 9 years old she let him read it. Unfortunately, Casper did not remember saying such a thing.

Another example is Jen, who stated, *"I remember being with authoritative spiritual entities who showed us a timeline, depicting the course of my future life on Earth. We had to choose between a variety of parents among different*

*places, age, socio-cultural status, strengths and weaknesses and what their learn-
ing was [...]"*

They remember having lived, before being born on Earth, in another dimension, defined as "sky", or "above the clouds" or "city
of clouds". In a context from which they have the perception of
observing the Earth from above, they need to choose their parents.
In these situations, they describe interactions with spiritual beings,
or "angels", and also other children souls waiting to incarnate. For
this reason, some children during their first years of life, as soon as
they can speak, feel a kind of "homesickness", which concerns the
spiritual dimension from which they remember to come. This clearly
confuses their parents.

These preconception memoirs, together with the NDE accounts
described above, suggest that prenatal life and life after death coin-
cide, as they both take place in the same dimension of the non-physical spiritual worlds. These testimonies are in line with the information collected by Newton regarding life between lives, especially with
regard to the planning of the future life on Earth. Our true essence
is deeper and more complex than the awareness that works through
the physical mind-brain and cellular processes associated with the
body. Our body is only a tiny fragment of our true essence. The
consciousness that incarnates in a body already has a sense of "I
am". Our human self is clearly multidimensional and seems to exist
from before birth.

Then there are the memories related to conception: the memory
of the moment of conception and the movements of sperm and
ovum, or even references to in vitro fertilization.

In "Cosmic Cradle", Brian recalls his spiritual life before conception and reports that he was a light sphere that lived in a spiritual world together with other spheres with which he communicated
telepathically. He tells of being guided by an angel who pointed out

to him the prospect of choosing between two different families. Brian was drawn to a woman in distress because of her husband's abuse. He clearly remembers an argument in which his future siblings were involved. His sister Jan and his older brother ran to the bathroom saying, "Let's start bathing, so we don't get in trouble." Years later, his sister confirmed to him that it actually happened. His mother believes that Brian's memories refer precisely to the day on which his conception took place.

According to Paramahansa Yogananda, at the moment of conception, and therefore of the union of ovum and sperm, a flash of light occurs in the astral-spiritual dimension. This glow, which reflects the parents' state of awareness and, in particular, how they felt at the time of their union, will attract a soul with a vibration compatible with this energy.

Memories related to intra-uterine life are very frequent: a simple foetus seems to have a lucid and sentient consciousness. During gestation, there is no real presence of the conscious mind, which will only be present from the moment of birth onwards. So the soul unconscious mind works on its own, without its interference. The unconscious mind of the foetus records everything: all his mother's thoughts and words and everything that happens around her. There are many visual and auditory perceptions related to events that take place in the surrounding environment. The testimonies reported have remarkable analogies in the type of perceptions: the colour perceived in the environment, a red-pink shade. The movements are similar to swimming and the foetus is aware of the positions taken from time to time. Sometimes the temperature is hot and sometimes colder. There is the awareness of looking from the outside through the maternal navel. Deep and changing emotions are experienced that can range from discomfort to fun, as well as the clear perception of the mother's moods. According to current medical-scientific perspectives, it would be impossible for a foetus to live this kind of experience, since its physical senses are not yet developed.

Octavia, 2 and half years old, said: *"I always wanted you to be my mother when I was in your belly. Do you remember I was in your belly? It was dark there. There was no light. I wasn't scared, but my legs were crushed. I didn't like being in your belly, because you were crying and you were sad."* Her feelings were consistent with reality: her mother suffered because of her husband's abuse.

Memories of different flavours of maternal nutrition, introduced through amniotic fluid, have also been reported.

It seems clear that there is a psychic complex already during gestation, regardless of brain development. This psyche can accumulate experiences through an innate learning and memory process.

Ririko said, *"I know this place. I saw it from inside Mom's belly."* That was where she used to walk during her pregnancy.

A two-and-a-half-year-old boy remembered having attended a family party and the names of all the guests, and that in that circumstance his mother's well-being favoured the growth of his fingers.

There is evidence related to the foetus' pain following medical procedures such as amniocentesis and foetal surgery, as if its environment had been violated. For this reason it is a real trauma: *"Mom, why did you do this? I saw a needle while I was in your belly. It was terrifying,"* said Kaku, recalling the amniocentesis when the foetus was just 10 weeks old. Sarah, 3, talking about her intrauterine life with her twin sister, said: *"It was dark there, Mom. Hannah's feet kept kicking my head in, and I was looking at her."* Sarah did not know that she was child A, at the bottom, while her sister Hannah was child B, right at the top.

Intrauterine memories are just an example of prenatal intelligence. Official theories are proven wrong. According to these, during pregnancy, the baby has his mother's awareness, has no sense of self, does not have developed senses, so he is blind, deaf and inert, as if he were in a dreamless sleep state or even in a coma. However, it seems that children are able to hear even without developed ears, see without eyes, and this leads to think that consciousness is independent from the physical support. They also consider impossible for the foetus to experience emotions. However, it has been found that not only can the foetus experience emotions and implement movements related to them, but that these patterns tend to recur even after birth. In intrauterine life, the foetus already develops a relationship with the mother, is inclined to learning and recognizes the mother's voice among others. According to Chamberlain, learning and memory are connected, as learning depends on memory and is evidence of it.

Pregnancy is influenced by the soul that is coming. As described in "Cosmic Cradle", Leslie confirmed the pre-birth memories of her daughter Elisabeth, with regard to medical examinations, the first pregnancy then ended in an abortion that took place in the shower, the fights of the parents, the caesarean delivery, the return to the womb as a second pregnancy.

Finally, memories of the moment of birth were also reported: different perceptions and emotions, feelings of pain, disorientation, often difficulty breathing. Different rotational movements have been described, often to accommodate exit manoeuvres from the uterine canal. Many subjects recall a sensation of cold, as opposed to the heat previously perceived in the womb, and the consequent sense of vulnerability. They also describe a strong sense of blindness towards the new external light and an extreme sensitivity to noise. In several cases, precise memories have been reported, regarding the instruments used, the umbilical cord, specific surgical procedures, even in the case of caesarean section, and any neonatal therapies, in addition to the physical characteristics of the doctor, the midwives and other people. If at that moment the situation is complicated, people do not express calm and confidence, there is a sense of rejection, panic or discomfort, that stress will be part of the newborn's life.

According to medical knowledge, when the baby is born and takes his first breath, its ductus arteriosus of the heart closes. At the moment of death, when the last breath is exhaled, that same duct instead will open for the last time, and then close forever. Perhaps this means that the soul enters the body at birth and leaves it when the body dies.

Gerard reports detailed memories of his intrauterine life: the noises, his mom's breath, her heartbeat, the temperature and different shades of light. He remembers the moment of birth: at first he had been pushed back towards the cervix, because he risked being strangled by the umbilical cord, and then being repositioned to get out.

In the books "Cosmic Cradle" and "The Babies are Cosmic", we can find cases recalling past lives, specific and detailed memories referring to parents, places, life situations and sometimes circumstances of death relating to an existence different from the present one. In some cases, these memories relate to intrauterine lives with spontaneous or induced abortion.

"Mom, before you were my mom, I had two brothers and a dad, but you weren't my mom."

Yui remembers her previous gestation, which unfortunately ended in abortion, and reveals to her mother: *"I flew to heaven because your heart, soul and spirit had to be cleansed."*

Although children's bodies are small, their spirit is the bearer of a deep history and great wisdom. A human being is by no means limited to a single life.

There is different evidence that reincarnation often takes place within the same family. For example, Peter Junior has many behaviours, characteristics, passions and habits in common with his grandfather who died three years before his birth. He was extremely familiar with his grandmother already in their first meeting, when he was 2 years old and exclaimed: *"I missed you so much. I liked your black hair better."* In fact, after her husband died, she had stopped dyeing her hair and left it white. When Peter found the picture of his grandfather in the military band, he recognized himself. Over the years he told many stories lived in that previous life, despite not having been told much about his grandfather. One day, he found a hat belonging to his grandfather in the attic: he recognized it as his own, remembering that he had worn it for a long time.

Memories are also revealed through drawings, analysed by experts in prenatal development. They revealed deep connections to the stages of embryonic and foetal development.

In some cases, brothers/sisters were the first to know about their mother's pregnancy, even before she herself was aware of it. Corinne, about her daughter Alia: *"She was the first to know that I was expecting my third child. At the supermarket, she stopped and said, 'We have to get the baby food for the baby in your belly.' [...] Once back home, the pregnancy test was positive. I was only two days late. How could she know I was pregnant? Both of my daughters knew it was a girl. I kept saying it was a boy. When I was 12 weeks pregnant, Alia started talking about how babies choose their mom before they come down to Earth. They choose who they want as a mom. 'Ava and I chose you'."*

There are many cases in which children appear to parents, relatives or dear friends before conception, through visions, apparitions and dreams.

I happened to have a similar experience. Two years ago, I dreamed of Violetta's son, a dear friend of mine with whom I have a special bond of spiritual brotherhood: a beautiful lively and athletic young man who ran along the shore of a beach. I was aware that he was Violetta's son and I thought he had become a really handsome boy! When I told Violetta about it, she laughed: she had no children and, in fact, she was convinced that she was sterile. Two months later she was surprised to find out that she was pregnant. She had a beautiful boy! It seems that the soul of those who are about to be conceived wants to announce their arrival on Earth. Dreams are a way to get in touch with the spiritual planes, as we will see later.

Research shows that many of the children who remember previous lives, memories related to gestation, birth and the first months of their life, have an above-average IQ and do not show any signs of psychic pathology.

Awareness does not need a developed brain to manifest. Contrary to academic dogmatic theories, our life does not begin at birth — it seems to have more distant roots. The unborn child is already extremely aware.

Behind the scenes of the soul's journey to human birth there is great planning.

CHAPTER 7

IN SEARCH OF LOST KNOWLEDGE

> *"Through the process of reincarnation we have ALL lived on other planets and in other dimensions, and we will continue to do so after our lessons on Earth have been completed. Earth is merely a school — one of many in our long education."*
> **(Dolores Cannon)**

Dolores Cannon began her work as a hypnotherapist specializing in past life regression, in order to achieve the healing of her patients through the recollection of traumas that originated both in the present life and in past lives. In many cases, such healings were instantaneous and incredible. However, her research led her where she had never thought to go.

Cannon initially discovered that all knowledge is hidden in the recesses of the human subconscious and that it is necessary to recover the contents of memories, putting the subject in a non-ordinary state of consciousness: here the defences of the ordinary rational mind cease to exist. She discovered that most of the ordinary problems have very distant roots, linked to events that took place in past lives. After several failures, trying to find an explanation and a cure for a problem of a physical or psychological nature, and after numerous medical examinations, analyses and consultations of different kinds, one usually turns to this type of unconventional psychotherapy.

But how is it possible that a problem related to the soul-field can even cause symptoms, often limiting or even disabling? The reason is that the subconscious, which contains all the memories and emotions, both of this and other lives, is that part of the mind directly connected to the body; it regulates its functions as it is in direct connection with the neurovegetative system, therefore with what regulates vital functions, the heartbeat and breathing. Contact with the subconscious was something natural and immediate for primitive man, it was vital for their survival, it made them more sensitive and receptive and made them perceive any dangers. Nowadays, there is a greater predominance of the conscious part that wants to control everything and often comes into conflict with its own deep part.

The subconscious can be reached through deep hypnosis and it turns out to be detached, independent of problems, endowed with an impersonal and objective point of view towards different existential situations. The system of hypnosis developed by Cannon addresses the heart of the subconscious' power to heal the mind and body.

Among the clinical cases encountered during her research, Cannon reports the examples of physical disorders suffered by her patients and tries to generalize their origin. However, each situation is unique and the result of different combinations of existential events. For example, some cases of migraine would originate from head injury by humans, animals or weapons; overweight problems would often be related to people who starved to death in a previous life. In particular, gain weight would be a protection or a way to be less attractive and keep people away, in order to avoid being hurt. Cases of fears and phobias seem to be related to the ways in which people died in a past life; for example, those who died from suffocation could suffer from claustrophobia and wake up every hour during night-time sleep. Cannon's method makes the subject explore a past life in order to find the answers to current problems.

When healing occurs, once discovered the causes of the problem, the person believes now that the symptom is no longer necessary, as it belongs to a body that has long ceased to exist. Nothing is lost: everything is stored in our subconscious, and can be recovered and used in the present life.

Cannon's hypnotic method, later taught to specialized operators, reaches the deepest layer of trance, an almost "somnambulistic" level. Other methods tend instead to remain at a more superficial layer where the ordinary conscious mind could still interfere. It is similar to Michael Newton's method, but it seems to have reached even deeper states of consciousness. In these levels, the subject could communicate directly with the greatest source of power and healing, the origin of all consciousness, something she calls "subconscious." This is what Michael Newton called "super-conscious," Higher Self, high and immense Awareness, which contains the answers to any question. It is that mysterious point in the human being where the individual meets the universal. There is something wonderful within us that knows everything, what the conscious mind usually fails to grasp, if not sporadically. The super-conscious keeps all the knowledge and, before the hypnotic session ends, always conveys important advice to the person.

In her work "Between Death and Life," Cannon talks about the first time she made her patient relive his death. She was not fully aware of what was actually happening. From her patient's account, she discovered that after his recalled death, in subsequent memories his personality had remained intact, despite the temporary confusion due to the new state of being. At that point, she investigated the spiritual life between physical lives, just as Newton had done.

From her investigations, she collected data and compared them, managing to rebuild a coherent framework. This is full of information corresponding to data collected in recent decades both about NDEs, past lives and life between lives, and, unexpectedly, about the origins of the Earth and other non-human civilizations, as we will see later. She collected pieces of history, not only relating to individuals but also situations of a cosmic and universal nature; she put them together, deriving entire chapters of history of the origins of the Earth and humanity, with data relating to the existence of other civilizations and planets, and the possible outcomes of the future of human existence. Cannon did not think she had the complete picture, but she managed to go beyond the surface and venture into the deep unknown of the recesses of human consciousness, also to understand the meaning of the existence not only of an individual, but of human beings in general. The subjects involved in her research were normal people, united by the search for answers and solutions to doubts and existential problems, always asking: "Where am I from? Why am I here? Where am I going?" We all have this information inside us and we could recover it with a digging process through different means.

Cannon said that she had particular experiences with the recordings of the sessions: strange noises, sudden accelerations and decelerations, overlapping voices, phenomena that should not happen in electronics. She was aware that interference from the conscious mind could often occur, which could distract and confuse the subject.

Cannon gives an explanation to the meaning of forgetting our multiple lives, similar to what has been discovered by other researchers: if there were no forgetfulness of past lives, it would not be possible to focus on the lessons to be learned in our present life, as memories would not leave room for anything new. All memories are still stored deep in the subconscious and will never be lost. All things, even thoughts and actions, produce energy, which remains in the aether of Akasha. Some people may end up serving their karma in one life-time, others will need more existences. There are also lives of "rest" that might be seen as an insignificant life. But every life is unique and unrepeatable, precious and important. What is important in karmic dynamics is to learn something from experiences, otherwise these will be relived, until their meaning is realized. The ability to let go and forgive what we have suffered is also fundamental. Death is nec-essary to progress, because when learning certain lessons, it is nec-essary to put aside the experiences that have served such learning, in order to leave room for new content, with a new mental framework without previous conditioning.

We have accumulated debts that need to be settled, then progress can be made. Not everyone evolves in the same way and at the same speed, although time is relative to the lessons learned. We determine how to pay our karma debts, even if we cannot consciously remem-ber them. We learn the value of patience, the wisdom of balance, not to judge others, to forgive and to trust our intuitions. We are born with a dominant trait, which often marks an element to work on to rebalance karma. Therefore, we learn to work on our limits and weaknesses. We are carrying a burden from which we need to be lightened.

What matters is not whether a life is "easy" or "difficult", or the experiences themselves, but what we have learned. We need to live multiple lives because we cannot learn everything in one life. Dif-ferent lives are necessary to deeply understand the lessons that have been assigned for our own learning path. All beings arrive at the same destination, but through different paths, depending on the dif-ferent combinations of destiny.

Spiritual contacts with people remain unchanged and continue even when they leave the body and pass over the threshold. Karmic connections can produce alternating roles, with connections that can reappear in different lives and can be intensified or weakened depending on the circumstances.

There are shared plans between souls, so that a person will remind the other of who they are. A kind of "promise" is made in the spiritual planes, so that each one brings a piece of memory of their authentic essence and the spiritual worlds from which they come.

Cannon became familiar with the concept of "energy": everything is made of it and it never dies. It only changes shape according to its vibration and frequency. We are surrounded by countless dimensions with vibrations so high that they are invisible to our eyes.

Karma unfolds according to the energies' interactions, sometimes as a cause, sometimes as an effect, in a dynamic way in which everything is connected to each other. One's own individual karma is connected to that of the universe. We have to do our best to work on our past karma in order to create positive existential conditions in the future.

Cannon, like the other researchers, believes that we are masters of our destiny, because we have chosen, together with the guides and higher spiritual entities, the experiences we wanted to live and we can always choose, maybe taking a different direction. We should also be aware of our power to influence the people around us. We often choose difficult challenges in order to accomplish in one life what could otherwise be done in multiple existences. However, nowadays, it is even more difficult to evolve due to the materialism of the contemporary world. Lives must be considered from the perspective of love and learning, instead of punishment and pain.

With her hypnosis method, Cannon's patients talked about the guides and the Elders, the agreements for goals and projects concerning the next life, as Newton's patients stated. In addition, they confirmed the existence of groups of souls united to perform certain tasks. We can have multiple guides throughout our lives or in the same lifetime and they are crucial: they provide assistance with their experience and wisdom, but the choice is up to the subject with his free will. Fate is really in our hands.

For this reason, Cannon confirms everything Newton discovered in his research from deep trance patient reports, the same patterns also identified by other researchers. Several subjects evoked the Council of Elders in a room with an energy field of an intense purple and circular shape; there was an empty space in the centre and a row of chairs on steps like an amphitheatre, or like an oval court surrounded by golden columns and curtains. It is perceived that in that spiritual place the purest beauty is manifested. Entities emit beams of light and those sitting in the Council seem to have evolved in a superior way. Their energy radiates and interacts, expressing extreme respect and compassion. Just as Newton described, the Elders reveal how much influence we have had on Earth and on what we might have in the future. In addition, it is also analysed how we have related to things, how our individual destiny has interacted with the evolution of the universe, and what is our path towards enlightenment.

One of Cannon's patients, speaking of the Council of Elders, recalls:

> *"It's like a dome that retracts and opens. The soul travels through this portal. It opens when they choose to travel out of their world. Now I'm in a big room. There's a table and spiritual beings around it. I'm in front of a council. There are twelve chairs and they say it is 'the council of light' [...] It's not a governing body, but a spiritual council. They follow the Law of One. These come directly from the Origin."*

According to the information collected by Cannon, there are different types of Councils, in the solar system, the galaxy, the universe, and a specific council for the Earth, which collects information and knowledge. There are rules and hierarchies and nothing is left to chance. She also mentions other councils above the general councils: these are universal councils that manage entire universes, and councils at the level of creation, co-created with God.

One continues to work on one's karma even between lives. The work done in the spiritual planes between one life and another is crucial to process the learnings from the life just spent and to prepare for the next life. This happens with the guides' support, with whom one has an agreement. The guides need to do their work. They can help make decisions, but the responsibility lies with the subject who must make choices, using thoughts and concepts. In addition to what Newton found, Cannon reveals more details regarding the relationship between the guide and the subject. During physical life, it may happen to feels the presence of our guide, perceiving a sensation of heat, tingling, a light, feeling an intuition or a sudden certainty. The guide can speak through the subject's mind and even influence events in order to head in the right direction. They do not influence, but help, advise and try to project light on the path, so that the persons can create their own path without putting pressure on them. Their relationship is special, variable, from life to life, without being bound by strict rules.

The data collected by Cannon show souls who can become "first level" guides and help other souls who are at a lower evolutionary level. They can also influence the events in their lives, in order to limit any damage that would reflect negatively on other people. The guides are followed by a council and guided in turn. Helping a soul seems to be a complex process involving multiple guides of different levels. For example, the most critical moment is the transition from physical to spiritual life. It involves a period of adaptation in which they try to help the soul, understanding its needs. With this information we can understand what happens beyond that threshold that people who lived an NDE could not cross: the point of "no return" beyond the great light is like entering another body and world, and it is the beginning of a great change. Cannon also reveals the function of NDEs, stating that they often happen because people were in a dead end on their existential path, with consolidated patterns that their true spiritual essence could not fully emerge. The NDE is a way to upset this situation and to take a new turn that will open up new horizons.

In the spiritual planes we consult and help each other, we interact with souls who offer advice, share their experiences, and the help is mutual. There are many schools in the spiritual dimensions, the most advanced ones are in the "Temple of Wisdom," surrounded by mountains, where the "Palace of Learning" is located and here everything can be learned. There is the Temple of Healing, the "mosaic" room and the library, with a bright round space, where the spiritual body is healed of all the possible discomforts and diseases it suffered in life, before meeting with the guides. The Temple of Healing is also a place of transformation.

Places of healing are also accessible to those who are still incarnated in earthly life. It is a place of the spirit, described as wonderful, made of coloured precious stones: a light radiates from the gems, bounces off the centre of a round space and transmits energy. Rays of that light purify and eliminate all negativity, before the soul can continue its journey.

The "mosaic" room is like a museum of great beauty, with intense vibrations and full of energy. There is an entity that guides you to understand the deep meanings of this spiritual architecture. You have the sensation of smelling garden scents, although without the physical sense of smell. There is a ceiling with the shape of a church dome, windows from which so much light enters and walls that look like they are made of marble. This spiritual place looks just like a museum where everything shines. Every life is connected like a thread in this mosaic: here all lives threads of human souls connect with each other. Each life is interconnected with those of all other souls. The mosaic represents the precious uniqueness of humanity, which is one but made of several connected parts influencing each other. Each part is necessary and could not live without the others.

Many subjects say that the "Temple of Wisdom" is made of precious, radiant stones, with a library inside and a great light that illuminates the entire place. The same library was mentioned by Newton with his research, where a guardian helps in the search for knowledge. Everything reflects light, and that is where all knowledge is stored through living thought.

The spiritual worlds are wonderful and are among enchanting scenery and cities that seem made of jewels. It seems that these wonders are a prototype of the most beautiful places on Earth.

A patient says: *"Everything, the fountains, the temple, the mountains and the landscape, is perfect and eternal. The colour intensity is breath-taking. It is impossible to describe the beauty of this place."*

It is like an energy flow that flows from life to life depending on your personal path, stage, projects and learning objectives. This energy flow will guide the return to the physical plane, although a portion of the soul's energy must remain in the spiritual planes, as Newton's research showed. This flow is conditioned by universal laws, according to which once the energy has embarked on a certain path, it must complete it before being turned in other directions. The energy pathways determine the events.

The events that take place on Earth and seem to be inexplicable according to the laws of ordinary physics, are indeed determined by spiritual entities operating on other levels and frequencies of energy and that can interact with the dense energy level of the physical plane, since everything is connected. On each plane there are different rules, but sometimes overlaps could occur, as the spiritual planes coexist with the physical material plane. Therefore, "coincidences" produced by thoughts become possible, which are just energies that subtly influence things.

Cannon tracks the soul's journey after physical death, noting that the white light at the end of the tunnel is the boundary between our physical world and the spiritual one. Once the threshold is crossed, we meet the souls with whom we had a strong karmic connection in previous lives. Memories will resurface and the dead person will rebuild his entire karmic picture of past lives, understanding their connections and discovering what there is still to work on.

Beyond the threshold of death, at the beginning the mind is still immersed in projections closer to what is familiar. However, the next step will begin to show things for what they really are.

In the spiritual worlds after death everything is energy. It is a perfect land, without destruction and decay. Cannon also notes that there are different levels of existence, for example, she interacted with a woman who belonged to the "seventh" level, the plane from where inventions, music, everything that is creative and that is spread through dreams come from.

Human beings can move through the different levels of existence. These levels are in the same place but have different frequencies, based on the state of consciousness. According to Cannon, in the sixth level there are spirits who do not want to leave the Earth; in the ninth level, instead, there are masters such as Jesus Christ, avatars, semi-gods, great masters and bodhisattvas as described in Buddhism. The level of the Earth is the fifth level and below there are the elementary spirits as the first level, composed of basic energies; these do not have individual personalities, but express collective life. However, they have great potential that should not be underestimated.

In the spiritual planes there are no physical boundaries, but transitions in consciousness from one level to another. These are different energy vibrations. Cannon brings the example of an airplane taking off: it progressively heads over several layers of the atmosphere, with a gradual transition without seeing those levels, as studied by scientists, but noticing that things change as it goes up. The ideas of "Heaven" and "Hell" would indicate a different way of perceiving the energy. These are nothing more than ways of describing the spiritual energies perceived around the subject while crossing the threshold. However, these projections do not yet express the true reality of the spiritual planes.

The "Plan" is therefore seen as a state or condition of activity of the energy of the spirit. Each plane indicates a different degree of energy vibration. The soul is on the plane where *"the best and the highest of oneself can develop and expand,"* says William Atkinson, also known as Yogi Ramacharaka. Once you are freed from everything that stands in your way, you develop the best within you.

Cannon notes the existence of an "intermediate astral plane": here the soul recalls particularly important situations lived on Earth, such as beautiful houses, pleasant people, as if it were a residential area. And then there is a "higher astral plane" with prototypes of all the earthly natural beauties but even more enchanting with ineffable colours: gardens, mountains, oceans, waterfalls, rivers, lakes, cities of jewels and temples. From this higher astral plane come evolved souls who choose to incarnate on Earth to assist humans in their evolution. *"This is the world. It's the real world,"* says a subject while recalling these memories.

The universe is made of well-defined energy. According to Cannon's patients, there is no single universe: each universe has its own God, however there is a single underlying divine essence common to all universes. Each of these considers God as the superior creative power, whose reality is absolute and constant in all universes.

Cannon derives a new concept: God is not one, but is everything and we individually are part of Him. God is all that is and is perfect, so everything is perfect; for this reason, what we perceive as imperfect is due to our limited perceptions. What is called "bad" would be nothing more than misdirected energy. There are many types of negative energies: these are not "spirits", but misdirected energies due to contact with human beings. Cannon believes that the best form of protection consists in visualizing a white light surrounding oneself, so as to keep negative energies away.

Cannon talks about cases in which before physical life, an "imprinting" is made, taken from the Akasha. This happens in particular for souls who are on Earth for the first time, but also for already incarnated souls, who may need certain knowledge to achieve particular objectives. With this process, knowledge and skills will be infused to orient them in the new life and to have points of reference. When the soul intentionally chooses which life it wants to live, it also chooses whether to receive an imprinting or not.

All information Cannon received was obtained from people who did not know each other, had different backgrounds, occupations and religions. It seems similar, almost as if it had been reported by a single person. Similarly to what happened to Newton's research, from this information it was possible to draw the map of the spiritual dimensions of the afterlife, with precise rules and hierarchies that maintain the order. Cannon understands that it is not easy to accept a way of thinking different from what we have been used to believing since birth:

"I think it would be impossible to expect our mortal minds to grasp or comprehend even a piece of what all of this really is. But it's fascinating to realize that there's more to this than we ever dreamed possible. [...] My research was like reading a geography book about a foreign and exotic country that is far away, on the other side of the sea. It is a real place and we know it exists because the book describes it and shows us photos of it; it tells us about the activities of the

inhabitants there. But until we actually go there and see it, the information will remain just words and photos in a book."

It is indeed similar to when we take a trip to another country and see the place described by the tour guide, perhaps ending up finding different things than those we had read.

We human beings live on the physical plane, but at the same time on the spiritual one, vibrating on different frequencies. The spiritual world is here and now, but on a different frequency than we are ordinarily tuned to when we are in our body during the waking state.

The Three Waves of Volunteers and Extraterrestrial Beings

During Dra. Cannon's research, something incredible and unexpected emerged: on several occasions, numerous subjects evoked strange and unusual environments and contexts, which did not resemble the Earth at all. She found that certain historical periods coincided. So she had the opportunity to explore past times, planets, unknown dimensions and civilizations. Cannon often checked information she had already received on other occasions, asking subjects questions as if she knew nothing in relation to the topics addressed. Different subjects provided the same types of information without contradictions, therefore the data collected seemed to be consistent and its validity could be hypothesized. During these searches, she also came across testimonies regarding UFOs and aliens.

She had always been interested and curious about these phenomena, as she was convinced that not everything could be explained by logical thought and sceptical dogmatism. She was introduced in the field of UFO research in 1985, on the occasion of a meeting with the members of Mufon, a large UFO research organization that included representatives from different scientific sectors and countries. Walt Andrus, at that time International Director of Mufon, believed that hypnosis could be a valid tool, but it was necessary to abandon established certainties and conventional methods, and be willing to approach the unknown without being disturbed by what could have unfolded, something that for most ordinary dogmatic psychologists and psychiatrists would have been unacceptable. Cannon was asked to apply her hypnosis method to investigate phenomena related to UFOs: contacts, abductions and missing time. In this way, she discovered constant patterns: subjects taken on spacecraft, who underwent medical tests, short grey beings with large eyes or beings similar to strange insects, books or maps shown and the following erasure of memories. Many subjects have come into contact with these alien beings since childhood. Cannon adapted her hypnosis technique in order to communicate directly with the subconscious and avoid the emotional load of the conscious mind that usually brings memories distorted by fear and emotions.

In her book "The Keepers of the Garden", Cannon lays out the theory that extraterrestrials have been watching over humans since the beginning of life on Earth and are keeping an eye on our development. Until then, researchers in the field of ufology had limited to a sectoral study, or addressed abductions or sightings, while Cannon discovered individual fragments of a larger picture involving our origins as human beings and the origins of our planet. In order to understand the reasons for tests and medical examinations carried out by such alien beings, the researchers had interpreted the phenomena in different ways, including genetic manipulation carried out by them for selfish purposes. Cannon believes that there is instead a project for the benefit of human beings, since extraterrestrials may have produced life on our planet several eons ago to create a perfect species, endowed with evolved psychic abilities. Genetic manipulation has been constant since the beginning of our species: our physical and mental development has been positively influenced, allowing us to achieve thinking and intuition skills far beyond those of animals. These extraterrestrial beings have not only turned out to be "gardeners" but above all Custodians, hence the title of Cannon's work "The Custodians". The so-called "genetic manipulation" would have the purpose of protection and to guarantee the survival of the human race, making it capable of resisting an environment that becomes increasingly polluted and contaminated, with diseases but also catastrophes, collisions, earthquakes, volcanic eruptions, tsunamis and other disasters. So the theory that Cannon developed based on the information received in the hypnotic sessions is that extraterrestrials care about our development, so we should not be afraid of them, but welcome them as our ancestors and guardians.

Among the different information regarding the beginning of life on our planet, Cannon discovered that several eons ago there was no life on Earth, as the atmosphere was full of ammonia.

There is a system of high spiritual intelligences, "councils", that manage the creation of life in the universe and preside over galaxies and the universe. There comes a time when a planet can support life and some groups of ancient evolved beings are responsible for starting life on that planet. The origin of material life is spiritual: it was spiritual beings who fostered the evolution of unicellular and multicellular organisms. It is as if spiritual beings plant seeds of life and let life sprout, occasionally monitoring the situation. It is not easy to establish life on a planet: the life of a living organism is really fragile, even if it is endowed with an intrinsic strength that makes it endure critical conditions. Spiritual intelligences underlie the formation of air and water, and all essential resources. Human life was therefore created by spiritual entities who took care of it as if it were a garden, from here the title of the book "Keepers of the Garden". This is traced in myths and legends of ancient civilizations as the "culture bearers": beings considered as divine, who for example brought fire or taught agriculture. In order for the human being to be different from animals, a genetic manipulation was necessary, mixing cells and genes from other living species in the universe; precisely for this reason the human species was able to make a very rapid evolutionary leap. These divine entities still assist us, often in imperceptible ways, transmitting new ideas, intuitions and inventions that help us in our existence and promote our evolution. The characteristic that distinguishes human beings from other beings is their free will. Spiritual beings do not interfere in our choices and decisions. They only help and give us knowledge. If the knowledge received were misused, for example for negative purposes contrary to evolution, spiritual entities would not act, respecting free will and letting human beings learn the lesson independently. An exception would be in the event that human actions could cause the destruction of the planet, as it would also affect nearby galaxies and compromise the life of other planets and dimensions: everything in the universe is closely connected with each other.

Humans could be compared to children who for thousands of years have played inside a box, watched by adults without interfering. However, if they risked damaging the box, then the adults could intervene and clean up the box in order to avoid surrounding damage. Similarly, if the humans risked damaging Earth leading to destruction, the spiritual beings could act to avoid damage to the entire universe. Earth is small and isolated, in a small corner of the solar system. Human beings are under special surveillance, perhaps a little feared.

The spiritual entities wanted to create a perfect species, without disease and death, as if Earth were a garden of Eden. But circumstances did not follow their plan and, at the beginning of the development of life, the Earth was hit by a meteorite that brought bacteria that were at the origin of diseases. What to do now? Should they have destroyed everything and started over, or let life continue despite the new problems? The Council decided to continue, since much effort had been spent for the formation of life on Earth, hoping that the human being would have evolved into a perfect being without diseases. Spiritual entities continued to monitor life on Earth until now, but there was one event that alarmed them: the atomic bomb explosion in Hiroshima in 1945 during World War II. Atomic energy, which could have been used for constructive purposes such as the production of energy and electricity, had instead been used as a weapon of destruction. After the end of World War II, sightings in the sky and unidentified objects began to be detected, as they were there to monitor the situation. High spiritual entities could not interfere from the outside, but they could provide help from within, sending souls to help the planet and human beings trapped by lives in the cycle of rebirths, in the "wheel of karma." These souls had never been on Earth before, so they were not involved in the dynamics of karma — they incarnated for the first time. These tens of thousands of souls had previously lived on other planets or dimensions. They were so pure that seemed to come directly from the creative source unknown to the human being: immense light in which everything is united without any separation. These brave souls, who lived in deep harmony, chose to incarnate on Earth, such a complex and chaotic planet, full of negative emotions, assuming a physical body and finding themselves without memory of their life in the universe, so as to be put to the test. Their arrival promoted an energetic change on Earth and in human beings, to help them raise their vibrations and to change their dimension. By analysing the cases and comparing the data, Cannon described three different "waves" of soul-volunteers. The first wave are people who are now between 60 and 70 years of age (in 2011, when Cannon released her book "The Three Waves of Volunteers", they were between 50 and 60 years old). These are souls animated by pure love and desire for peace, who have had difficulties adapting to the low energies of hatred, anger and violence on Earth. They have always been animated by the desire to "return home," despite having no conscious memory of their spiritual home. Despite their apparently happy and serene lives, they suffer from a deep discomfort without rational causes.

The second wave of volunteers, who are currently between 40 and 50 years old, have had greater opportunities for adaptation and are endowed with a unique energy that influences others without them noticing, just because they are there. They have an instinct to help others, although they often prefer to be alone. Some of them have chosen not to have children to avoid karmic ties that bind them to the Earth. They are observers and even without engaging in particular activities, they facilitate change, as they are like energy channels.

Finally, there is a third wave of children born in the early years of the new century and who seem to have an altered DNA. Some of them reported serious adaptation problems at school and have been diagnosed with ADHD. These are very advanced souls, but they struggle to adapt to the low and dense vibrations of humanity, as they operate on a higher frequency, proving to have rare intelligence. The souls from the first and second wave must overcome the feeling of not wanting to be on Earth, otherwise they would fail without fulfilling their mission due to serious psychological blocks. These souls have indeed a mission to carry out: first of all, they need to find themselves, facing all the obstacles and challenges of life like all other human beings, until their memories and awareness return to the level of consciousness.

> *"I feel like I've been more in space than in a body for most of my life. It is almost an alien feeling to feel 'myself' and not be united with everything else. I'm used to total freedom, to flow freely. I don't understand how to go out of nowhere and feel spacious and having the surrounding outside, feeling alone in a body and having to be somewhere."*

A patient of Cannon let us understand the discomfort of such a soul, who voluntarily arrived with his first incarnation on Earth, but who feels limited and blocked without understanding why. This condition could often worsen, causing diseases, as if you had the unconscious instinct to leave the body and return to the spiritual worlds from which you come: a dimension full of light, beautiful colours and where you can live in full happiness. However, their mission is to teach people to love, care for others, have faith, create peace and live in harmony with nature, overcoming diseases.

> *"They wanted me to come here to help change the planet. And they put these things in my body so I could do it. They wanted someone to come and influence ordinary people's lives. If I had another position, being for example the President of the United States, I would not influence such numbers of people as I am doing now. I'm reaching everyday people. The President of the United States influences only a smaller group of people on the planet. [...] With this energy in my aura, I can transform the people around me. The people I talk to are transformed. Using the phone, the energies can go through the lines. It is just like that. They're all being transformed."*

There are many people of this type, of different levels and from different backgrounds: these souls are on Earth to observe, but without accumulating karma and therefore being stuck in the circle of rebirths.

Several cases show that these pure souls, who voluntarily came to Earth for the first time and who suffered from loneliness, received visits from extraterrestrial beings through "contact" or "abductions" in order to re-establish contact with their people and feel comforted. Volunteers often expressed a desire to stay with them, rather than return to Earth, but were encouraged to continue their mission, even receiving suggestions. When returning to Earth, their memories of such interactions are removed, so as not to interfere with other planes.

Cannon also received information regarding the "alien plants" inserted into the body of the "abductees" during the abductions. These plants allow communication and localization, as they gather the information that the subject receives in the brain. This information would then be "downloaded" and stored in archives, in which the history of civilizations and the planet is recorded. Some plants release medicines or devices to help in case of illness.

As mentioned before, Earth is a complex planet, to be considered as a school where we learn lessons, but it is by no means the only planet existing in the universe. From her research, Cannon found that many subjects have lived different lives on other planets, some with a thin layer of energy that makes them immaterial and etheric. Cannon initially thought that it would be impossible for a person to experience life on Earth in the current historical period, as adaptation to Earth should be gradual. However, she then discovered that currently several souls incarnate for the first time on Earth after having lived previous lives on other planets and dimensions. They received an imprint, as mentioned before, through a "Library" that holds the knowledge, the chronicles of the Akash and the record of every life since creation, in order to get a preparation and be able to live in such a chaotic and complex way.

Cannon also points out the existence of beings that are not spiritually evolved, which should not be considered in a negative way, since from an absolute point of view there is neither positive nor negative — there is only the beauty of One. Reference is made to extraterrestrials who work with some governments and are on Earth to procure metals, chemical elements and minerals. They often take more than they should, but that does not mean they are negative, as many researchers believe. They are evolving and provide technology, giving and taking.

There are also extraterrestrial beings that operate on multiple dimensions, even on materials ones, manifesting themselves with their vehicles. They have the ability to influence other beings, often with their mere presence. Their frequency and awareness protect the planet.

Cannon came to the conclusion that there is a deep connection between the three waves of volunteers and extraterrestrials. Many of her patients did not want to explore past lives, but obtain an explanation relating to strange events that occurred in their lives, which had challenged their rationality, from typical "alien encounters" to something more complex.

Nowadays, aliens usually attract disbelief, distrust and humour, or anguish and fear. Cannon has discovered something different from what has been documented by researchers in the field of ufology: it is possible to affirm that the human being has an extraterrestrial nature. In a sense, the extraterrestrials created the human race. We are extraterrestrials because our essence is the same. There is a deep connection; however, the human being has lost track at a conscious level, due to the eradication of memories, which are destined to re-emerge when the subject is ready. Fear is the natural reaction to not being able to understand something on a rational level. Cannon's method sets the ordinary mind aside to make room for the subconscious, which knows what information can be released and accepted by the subject's conscious mind. From the transcripts of her sessions, it seems that a special relationship is created between Cannon and the subject's subconscious, which talks about the subject in the third person. In some cases, the guide or another entity has manifested itself, but the subconscious has full access to a greater range of information, being in direct contact with the origin.

In her book "The Custodians," Cannon reports the results of 25 years of research on cases of "alien abductions." However, she then discovered more with the connection between the three waves of volunteers and their role on Earth, which overturns the concept of "aliens:" these are just protectors of the volunteers who are part of their own people. Volunteers would be observed, protected and helped, even if they are not aware of it.

For this reason, encounters with aliens help to keep track of those brave souls who arrived on Earth, who had never been abandoned, but always treated with care and attention. Such encounters are described in a positive way: the alien is kind, compassionate and reassuring. There are also grey aliens who have a certain job, as if they were programmed robots, described as quite busy and focused, apparently without emotions. Scenarios are described in which the subject is taken in a ship and finds himself on a table. Here he is subjected to medical procedures or analyses.

Aliens are capable of breaking the molecular structure of the body, so that it goes through solid objects such as walls, ceilings or roofs. They do not have a linear time. Unlike human beings they are not accustomed to measuring something that does not really exist, which is just an illusion and a human invention. It is difficult for the human mind to accept this, because our life is marked by time. They can travel instead, precisely because they are not bound by any space-time limit. There is nothing paranormal about it: UFOs actually seem to follow physical laws that we have not discovered yet. They can reveal themselves and then disappear from radar; they can travel light years away changing their vibrational state. What is material vibrates slowly, while other dimensions have faster and higher vibrations. To reveal themselves on the material plane, aliens must lower their vibrational level. Many of them are made of pure energy, they do not have a material body, however they can manifest with bodies if they interact with human beings. We cannot see them because their vibrations make them invisible on the material plane.

Extraterrestrials developed life on Earth, taught primitive humans the basic skills to survive and to learn how to develop a civilization. They were treated like deities, as they seemed immortal; they could actually decide if and when to die, leaving the Earth at will. They had a lot of advanced technological knowledge. They promoted the construction of temples and stone circles, which were systems for monitoring the stars and planets and the alternation of the seasons. Hence, the Egyptians' sophisticated astronomy. Their structures also served as landmarks from space.

Extraterrestrials communicate through symbols, which are blocks of telepathically transferable concepts and information. Such symbols reveal information that is transmitted to the subconscious mind. Just looking at a symbol, it is possible to transfer the information that will be stored in the subconscious mind, without the need for the message to be understood by the conscious mind, as it penetrates the cellular structure of the brain and is ready to come to light when we need it. Symbols, as in the "crop circles", are a system of communication with the human species of messages of peace, harmony, light and beauty. These messages do not need to be grasped by the rational mind, because the subconscious will receive them and understand them, as communication that takes place at a deep soul level.

They invested time and energy in the development of the human race and do not want its self-destruction. They can travel through time and space without limits. They actually do not even know the concept of time. They use spacecraft similar to those we see in the skies, which travel fast from one dimension to another. Some of these dimensions seem to be those of probable futures. There are many testimonies relating to space-time portals, which were used for example in Egypt. Through such portals, travellers from the future would be able to go back in time and gather information.

There are countless dimensions that surround us all the time, but we cannot see them with our physical eyes. Extraterrestrial beings travel through the vibrational raising and lowering of their craft, as described in Cannon's book "The Legend of Starcrash." We do not see alien spacecraft because they are different dimensions, unless they come into our dimension. In the future, technologies will be developed to detect the presence of these spacecraft in the atmosphere and determine their position. Groups of UFOs travel regularly on Earth and with their dimensions they can be seen; others are not perceptible, as they seem to travel quickly through a temporal distortion.

There are beings and life forms that can materialize at will. They can see what they want on Earth and integrate information remotely, and then go back to their base, as if they had a GPS system. They can help humans, including by sending thought forms. They are aware of the alternation between light and dark, peace and war, and their purpose is to try to raise general awareness.

Planet Earth, unlike other planets, is a place full of challenges, as human nature finds it difficult to live in peace and tends to war and discord. The world is currently going through a major irreversible change and its frequency and vibrations are rising. The Earth is characterized by the material slowness, while other dimensions are speedier and make thought materialize instantly. There is life on other planets, which are monitored just like the Earth, with several experiments underway. The Earth is one of the most recent planets and the human being is an innovative being, since it is awareness, in a fusion of emotions and feelings, everything hosted in a physical body. The great experiment consists in the fusion of the spirit with biology, physicality.

In other dimensions, there are gaseous worlds, populated by beings who have a light body with just energy and without blood and organs. They exist at a high spiritual level and can move through time and space, unseen by humans. There are so many beings in the universe with different aspects, abilities, cultures, ways of living and conceiving existence. There are countless forms of expression in the universe, of which the human being is not aware. The universe is subject to different forms of expansion, contraction and implosion, with subsequent explosions. The main element of our system is the sun, which is a source of energy, an expression of the thoughts that derive from the inhabitants of the universe. It stores and projects thoughts into the universe, especially those related to the Earth. Energy never dies, it just changes its form. There are different universes that are connected and vibrate in harmony. We clearly are not the only living species in the universe. There are many scenarios of life. For example, a patient of Cannon evoked a planet with a purple sun. Planets made by thoughts produced by different group minds have also been described: here one creates, travels and explores through thought.

We record and collect knowledge and information, which is a very important element, as the NDEs' testimonies have shown. In the next chapter we will delve into the mystery of extraterrestrials and their relationship with the spiritual dimensions that we access after death.

Lost History and Possible Futures

From the memories evoked by Cannon's patients, it appears that the destruction of civilizations often occurred because they had reached the peak of intellectual and technological knowledge and had slipped into an abuse of power, due to greed and ego. A real upheaval against the laws of nature had taken place, due to experiments in genetic manipulation between humans and animals or experiments with dark matter, thus risking the planet's destruction. For this reason, a cataclysm was necessary in order to sweep everything away and rebuild it on new foundations. The volunteers' intervention on Earth would represent an attempt to avoid a new tragedy. Those catastrophes would have been the consequences of the energy misuse, to the point of breaking the natural protection of the planet. It takes a long time to restore its balance. Indeed, following serious disasters, for a long period the Earth was uninhabitable and only after thousands of years it was able to host life again. Other planets also disappeared, for example a planet that was between Mars and Jupiter and whose explosion left an asteroid belt.

There are subjects who, throughout their history, have witnessed the destruction of their planet, either as witnesses while this was happening, or when they came back and saw that everything had been destroyed. It was a traumatic experience that is still present today, in the form of undefined and unmotivated sadness. Their soul knows why, but their mind does not. Those souls have voluntarily chosen to come to Earth, to save it from destruction, avoiding the scenario they had lived before.

On the other hand, there are civilizations that seem to have disappeared into thin air, such as the Maya or some American Indian tribes that, after reaching an advanced level of development, have modified their spiritual vibrations, until they made a "mass dimensional change."

Some subjects in deep hypnosis recalled events related to the ancient civilization of Atlantis. The inhabitants of Atlantis were able to teleport heavy structures and huge rocks, using the light energy of crystals. This civilization had different shadows and it would have helped to drain the planet Earth of its energy. They derived energy from crystals, which generate energy and were strategically positioned based on the results they wanted to achieve. Crystals relax, purify, heal and also accumulate and release both information and energy. Their properties seem to be remarkable. There were worlds made of crystals, connected telepathically, as if they interacted with the crystals in a perennial exchange of information. Crystals were used for ceremonies, for landing aircraft from other planets, or they could be used to predict the future. They were powerful tools that stored knowledge and released it to those who knew how to access and retrieve it.

The inhabitants of Atlantis learned how to manipulate energy, but they often used it for different purposes, other than balancing and healing.

Several subjects described a "grid", namely an energy grid on Earth, which would have been damaged due to the destruction of Atlantis. This grid would have some devices, with seals and keys to defuse them. It seems that crystals contain knowledge that could be revealed. The grid would be protected by thousands of keepers.

Some subjects confirm that before Atlantis there was Lemuria, which did not have the same material consistency as the Earth, but was more gaseous and could change shape more quickly. In the last period, the inhabitants of Lemuria became more solid, more similar to current human beings.

Other interesting information obtained from the memories of the subjects involved in Cannon's research concerns the civilization of Ancient Egypt. The first pharaohs may have been non-human beings who had come to Earth to help the human race transmit information. The pyramids were built as portals to travel the universe. Under the Great Pyramid there would be many undiscovered rooms, with tunnels intentionally kept secret. Some rooms under the Sphinx would have been sealed off for protection. The same happened to its gadgets to prevent them from being used improperly.

Egyptian temples were centres of energy and learning. Energy could be amplified and transmitted, forming real energy fields. The original temples were not built by humans but by extraterrestrial beings, who knew how to create and lift solid forms through the power of their mind. This knowledge was transmitted to the inhabitants of Atlantis and was later handed down to Egypt. Temples were important for the development of civilizations, as a place of protection and storage of secrets and mysteries.

There are therefore many lost fragments of a history that should be recovered if we want to shed light on the true origin of humanity and the meaning of the experience on Earth.

People who asked for Dra. Cannon's help, wanted to know their purpose in life and why they are here. The answer they have generally found was that, as human beings, we are like a blank sheet and equipped with a brush and a colour palette, and we are free to create. We are able to manipulate energy, for this reason we could create the reality we want. The human being can be the master and creator of his destiny. The power of the mind is extremely important: it can create and change circumstances. This applies both to an individual mind and to multiple minds in a group.

The purpose of physical life is to know oneself, recovering the awareness of who we really are: the awareness that we have chosen to live all the experiences we have lived. From Cannon's research exposed in her book series "The Convoluted Universe," it seems we are part of a greater soul, our true Self, which however does not fit in a body. As the soul accumulates knowledge and learning, it can put together the different pieces. Individual aspects will develop that will come together with the whole soul forming a unique picture.

Human beings have many resources and potential in their thinking and intuitions that, if used differently, would make their existence more peaceful and meaningful. However, they usually only use a tiny part of their brain.

The human body is made of "fragments" that resonate at a specific sound level, and this involves DNA, the cellular structure. The energy can change the structure of the DNA, so that it is possible to obtain qualities typical of other living beings in order to survive and adapt to new types of environments.

Human beings must change because they need to learn to live in peace and be in balance. The spiritual entities send light to Earth, which will help to collapse the currently existing structures: the planet seems to be constantly bombarded by a light that affects people's consciousness, even causing a change in the genetic structure. These powerful energies constantly transform the body and the DNA, also causing a change in consciousness. The energy vibration and frequency is changed to induce a passage to another dimension. A change is expected that will consist of ascending to higher dimensions, but only those who have been able to raise their awareness will face it. It is as if a spiritual New Earth will be created, coexisting with the old Earth, still characterized by more material and negative vibrations. The whole planet changes its frequency and vibration, something that would never have occurred in the history of the universe. It is a gradual "dimensional shift" and the human body is gradually beginning to get used to it with some difficulty. The rise of vibrations will be felt in a physical way, as the physical bodies will change. Physical and psychic blocks will be brought to light, linked to karmic issues, which otherwise would have remained dormant, as if forced by the energies to release negative energy and resume its flow. This process could manifest with worrying symptoms, such as anxiety, depression, headache, drowsiness, muscle aches, tinnitus and arrhythmias. The high vibrations affect the DNA, awakening it in the areas where it sleeps. The energy will modify the genetic structure of the DNA to bring it to a greater state of perfection, where there are no disease and decay. The future genetic structure must be a faithful expression of the spirit. Once the vibrations reach the right frequency, they will automatically go to the next level, because it is not possible to fall behind. The physical body will adapt to the increase in energy — however, this will be imperceptible on a physical and a mental-rational level, even if the subconscious is deeply aware of it. Rising to another dimension means raising the level of consciousness, vibrations and frequency of the physical body, which will then dissolve into light: each cell will vibrate so quickly that it will transform into light. The body temperature will rise beyond the third dimension. The body made of pure light energy will not get sick, will not grow old and will never die, which the Bible describes as "eternal life." It is the same concept of the light body for alchemists or the rainbow body for Tibetan Buddhists, as we will see later. At that point, there will be no need to return to Earth, since the karma and lessons to be learned will be exhausted. We will return to the eternal dimension from which we come, always considering that we are a unique, individual and unrepeatable imprint on the universe, and this is the real wonder.

Physical reality still exists, as it is fuelled by the support that gave it shape and solidity. It is like a dream created by mass consciousness. The universe is a highly complex organism, living in different dimensions at the same time, created by the different intentions and perceptions shared by the beings that populate it. It is like taking part in a play: everyone follows a script and play a character that can be changed at any time. However, there are many other dimensions that can be perceived. Aboriginal people say that creation was dreamed: in one's first dream, one dreamed the four elements. We have been caught up in this dream so many times, that we have forgotten why we are in this world and where we came from. The true reality is the spiritual world and, in comparison to it, ordinary life seems to be a dream. The birth process eradicates the memories of life between lives in the spiritual worlds. The soul lives life in the spiritual worlds between one physical life and another, and is individualized until it has accumulated so much knowledge that it will then be incorporated into the universal Consciousness.

All the different multidimensional realities must be integrated. We are like a point of light. We were created like this — eternal. There is no reason to fear death, which is unpredictable and we do not know when and how it will happen.

We know at an unconscious level what awaits us beyond the threshold, because we have been there and we have died countless times. However, death still is the greatest unsolved trauma, especially if we leave something unfinished. For this reason, in the present life we tend to solve problems related to situations in past lives. Prolonged agony creates waves of bitterness and resentment that will tend to persist as a deep trace, ready to re-emerge in subsequent deaths.

According to the memories of the subjects involved in this research, dying is natural, painless and pleasant and is something not to be feared at all. Memories remain intact, you feel the same, because life goes on. Once something exists, the energy of that existence cannot be destroyed.

Dra. Cannon considers the interesting information received with her research just small glimpses of what is in the other worlds from which we come and to which we will return.

We have to remember our true origin and real nature that has only been obfuscated. We can remember who we really are and expand our awareness.

We are not a body, but we possess a body. Our true essence is our soul, which gives life to the body. Without the soul, the body would have no life and would just be an inanimate shell. Our soul is eternal and comes directly from the creative source.

Cannon was optimistic, believing that science will confirm the existence of other universes, dimensions and planes of existence that coexist with our own, and that travelling through these planes is both possible and desirable. However, she believed that the true boundary was not space, but our deep soul, which can make us experience the perception of these dimensions.

"I found in death the celebration of life. I am not afraid to travel into the bright light that marks the boundary between this world and the next. I know I'm not going into a dark and menacing unknown. I'm just coming home."
(Dolores Cannon)

CHAPTER 8

A TRIP TO MYSTERY, AMONG UFOS AND ALIENS

Sightings of Unidentified Objects

The links between the UFOs/aliens, as analysed by Dolores Cannon, and the issues we are facing are much deeper than it seems at first glance. It is not only about UFO, which can be an interesting and fascinating topic, but the most important aspect is that we live in a multidimensional world.

There are different approaches to ufology. There is a purely quantitative and scientific approach, and a qualitative approach. The latter analyses individual cases and wants to understand what individuals have experienced when they came into contact with extraterrestrial beings.

The UFO story begins in 1947 with pilot Kenneth Arnold who, during a recovery of a wreck of a crashed C-46 aircraft, witnessed nine strange aircraft flying at a remarkable speed, unlike any type of aircraft ordinarily known. In the same year, a press release was issued from Roswell Army Air Field stating that a flying saucer had been taken over. However, the press release was soon denied with a cover story about an atmospheric balloon.

According to ufological studies, a "close encounter" occurs when a person witnesses the presence of an unidentified object. Joseph Allen Hynek, astrophysicist, director of the Lindhemeimer Astronomical Research Center at Northwestern University in Illinois and director of the UFO study group "Project Blue Book," identifies three different encounters: the first one occurs with a visual sighting of an unidentified object, at a distance of less than 500 feet, which shows a significant angular extension. The second type includes a UFO sighting accompanied by certain physical phenomena, such as an interference in the operation of a vehicle or electronic device, animal reactions, modification of vegetation, signs in the ground and chemical traces or a physiological effect in the witness, which could manifest as a sensation of heat, paralysis or strong discomfort. In the third type, there is a living animate creature, humanoid or robotic. Jacques Valleh, Hynek's assistant, added a fourth type of close encounter: a UFO event in which the witness experiences a transformation of his sense of reality, a situation later explored and framed in the phenomenon of "abductions" or "alien abductions." Hynek says,

> *"I would not spend a minute more to the UFOs topic if I were not convinced that the problem is real, and that the efforts to investigate it, understand it and, finally, solve it, can have far-reaching consequences, even representing the beginning of a revolution in the vision that the Human has of himself and his place in the Universe. It is absolutely false to assert that UFOs have never been seen by scientifically trained people; some of the best reports I have examined, at the time of the 'Blue Book', and lately, and the most consistent in fact, come from such witnesses."*

In 1955, the Comet Report was formulated: a 90-page study written by a group of former officers and experts in various fields. "Ufo and Defense: What must we be prepared for?"

Those who were studying it for the first time believed that one could not be certain that the UFO phenomenon was a threat until it became known what those objects really were. There have been military encounters with the UFO not only in the US but everywhere: Russia, Britain, Europe, Australia, South America and South Africa. Different alien objects have been found, supported by reliable testimonials. These unknown flying objects were characterized by great flight performance and no noise. When the UFO phenomenon began to spread, the American government authorities decided to obscure the information for several reasons: first of all, to keep the situation under control and also to prevent foreign powers from manipulating it. What other way to keep public opinion under control than to divert public attention by adopting strategies to reduce their credulity and stimulate denial? The UFO issue is definitely a matter of national security and everything possible has been done to hide what was really going on.

Faced with such a phenomenon, we tend to react in different ways. Either we deny it totally, considering it a hallucination and fraud, or we think that it is something that needs to be proved somehow. It can be considered a complex matter, to be left to the secret services or we may believe that we should think about something else.

Michael Salla, a scholar of international politics and American foreign policy, with several recognitions of his academic career, is the founder of the Institute of Exopolitics. With "Exopolitics" we mean the study of key political actors, institutions and processes associated with the UFO phenomenon, and extraterrestrial hypotheses, therefore the study of the political implications of the undisclosed extraterrestrial presence. If the anthropological sciences in studying otherness believes that there is a fear of the "other," let alone a non-human "other"!

Exopolitics helps us to disclose information to which we have been denied access. Banning extraterrestrials as mere fantasy and science fiction or ridiculing them is the most effective strategy.

As defined at the Wyoming Conference in 2000 by Alfred Lambremont Webre, a lawyer, peace, environment, and space activist, Exopolitics is the science of the relationship between our human civilization and other intelligent civilizations. Webre has always believed that human beings are isolated in the middle of a multidimensional and intergalactic universe, made up of planets that create a spiritually evolved society, from which the Earth is instead excluded due to its tendency to self-destruction and war. Only now could there be the conditions to get out of this isolation and become part of the rest of the galactic society. This is the same information that Dolores Cannon came into contact with through her research.

Exopolitics is a first step in overcoming the scientific canon of the twentieth century that states that intelligent life can only be on Earth. Going against this line had always meant to risk the exclusion from the scientific community. Exopolitics affirms that we live in a densely populated universe, full of evolved and intelligent civilizations.

On May 9, 2001, at the press conference of the disclosure project in Washington, over one hundred government witnesses, military, secret services, confirmed testimonies about the presence of extraterrestrial civilizations on Earth. In 2004, the Mexican Department of Defense released documents related to the sighting of extraterrestrial aircraft on Earth. The next year, the Brazilian Air Force also released secret reports on extraterrestrials and UFOs.

The aerospace engineer Joseph Zeromski revealed the possibility that aircraft can travel from one galaxy to another through space-time tunnels.

Clifford Stone, a former sergeant in the US Air Force, participated in top-secret missions to recover crashed alien aircraft. In 1969, while serving in the Nuclear-biological-chemical unit of Civil Affairs and participating in an training in Pennsylvania, he witnessed an aircraft crash. When he and his team arrived at the impact site, they saw a huge light. Stone went near the aircraft with a Geiger counter — a device that measures ionizing radiation —, whose scale went abruptly up, thus detecting a strong radioactivity beyond the limits. Inside the cockpit, they found four dead pilots who were not human, had large heads and smaller bodies. Stone stated that he later saw one of those beings still alive and he helped him escape, risking his superior officers' punishment. From that day on, Stone understood that it was forbidden to even talk about those entities. Only after several years, he finally decided to reveal his testimony, first to his family and then to the public taking part in conferences and interviews, while still fearing the consequences. In 2011, he attended the Disclosure Project Conference in Washington. On that occasion, he spoke of the existence of UFOs crashed to the ground and their crews, describing them as: *"thinking beings, very similar to us, with their own culture, life and family, able to feel pleasures and sorrow."*

In an interview Stone talked about sightings in Vietnam:

"One actually had a real life in the army. A real mission. These situations only occurred when they had an ongoing UFO incident and we were in close proximity. In 1965, in Vietnam, there was a base camp and an attempt was made to open fire on a UFO. They tried, but their weapons did not work. There was no electricity, until the UFO left. I can tell you having been in Vietnam for 4 years. Yes, it was for 4 years. The documents show 37 months, but if we add the TDY — which stands for Temporary Service —,

then it is 4 years. Having no power over anything, it is terrifying and those were very tense moments."

"They were called helicopters. Being in the war zone, you just go there and use a small razor to reduce everything to powder. UFOs must not exist. Let me repeat it differently. UFO is not a correct term. Interplanetary Convoys cannot exist, therefore, it must be something very terrestrial. The NSA called them UFOs when we were monitoring our communications with the Soviet Union. They qualified them as such in the hope that with the Sunshine Act, which later became the Freedom of Information Act, they would not be subject to it, saying that 7 UFOs had been sighted in such a place and so on, but they could then put in brackets: probably balloons. But, in one of the documents I'm talking about, they said the 7 UFOs were travelling at 1700 miles per hour. And balloons can't do this."

"The truth may not be what you think, but it is the truth that I know. That's all the truth I can confirm. [...] We are part of something great, very vast and we are on an adventure. We're part of this adventure."

"UFOs are a reality. UFOs exist. They are detected and recorded on radar. Fighter jet pilots try to intercept them, indeed there are cases of missiles shot down, not destroyed, but rendered harmless. There are cases of fighter jets trying to open fire on UFOs, but their weapons didn't work."

According to different accounts relating to some war events in Vietnam, an aircraft had crashed, remaining intact. Some grey non-humans were spotted on the side of the airplane, who were able to stop bullets and even stop time. When the plane was about to crash, the aliens had lifted it and brought it to the ground intact.

Stone argued that military rules dictated that "you don't talk about what you see." Why this secret? What would happen if people knew that we are not alone in the universe and that intelligent entities have visited and still visit our planet? Moreover, there seems to be considerable concern to keep the technology for military application as secret as possible. However, Stone thinks that this should not be a secret and that people who have had UFO sightings or closer contacts should not be ridiculed. Indeed, the whole world should be informed of this truth. *"How many of them were found? Who knows. But they are living, breathing creatures."* Stone wanted to draw attention to the cleverness of these living creatures, who have thoughts, emotions and, in particular, a strong spirituality.

Why do UFO aircraft suddenly disappear? There seems to be an invisible door: a space-time tunnel would allow their passage from one dimension to another, with a change of resonance in their vibrations, raising their frequency. Alien beings seem to move through time and space, moving through different dimensions, which are close to the supreme source.

The doctor and ufologist Steven Greer talks about the implications for humanity and the type of energy used in alien aircraft: an antigravity propulsion system, capable of accessing the electromagnetic environment and generate a large amount of energy without any pollution. Energy is generated by the "quantum vacuum" state. This energy flows through certain electromagnetic currents, without the need for any type of fuel. Greer makes a distinction between ETVs, Extraterrestrial Vehicles, and ARVs, Alien Reproduction Vehicles made by men. Both are equipped with an alien technology based on antigravity and electromagnetism.

But how do these aircraft travel across the interstellar space and time? According to Greer, they access a "zero-energy" field and employ a high voltage and electromagnetic flux that allows an object to become weightless and move as if it had no mass. A kind of "space shift" takes place inside and outside the material aspect of space-time, not subject to the laws of mass, inertia and gravity. When the aircraft is on our side of space-time, it behaves like any other material object; however, when it is on the other side, it seems to disappear and that is why it can move at many multiples of the speed of light. These aircraft actually cross different dimensions.

Maybe we just should think out of the box. The basis of life is something alive, conscious, omnipresent in time and space, not limited by matter, not subject to change. It is an idea present everywhere and is the non-physical basis of matter. What is unique is that extraterrestrial movement devices and communication systems can interface with the mind, thought and consciousness. It is a spectrum of non-material energy, which is outside the laws of space and time. Through this system, it would be possible to transmit instantaneously through millions of light-years. This aspect of energy reveals a type of creation that is both around and within us. It is not something supernatural, but something that has not yet been adequately studied and understood by modern science. Greer defines it as "CAT", i.e. "Technology-Assisted Consciousness" and vice versa "Consciousness-Assisted Technology."

Greer hopes there will be a multidimensional approach to understanding the UFO phenomenon. He believes that science fiction related to this field obscured the research, as there is an open intention to do it. Ordinary physics cannot be applied inside a black hole, where the matter of a body and ordinary velocity tend to infinity.

According to testimonies and evidence, the American Government is profiting from alien engineering technology, first and foremost for military interests. For example, in the Indian Town Gap in Pennsylvania there would be a military drill centre with non-radiation emitting aircraft, as they do not have propulsion systems like ordinary vehicles. Alien technologies are weapons that can produce not only physical, but also psychic and mental effects.

Paul Hellyer, former Canadian Minister of National Defense, says UFOs are real, as are airplanes flying overhead, and reveals that the

U.S. government and military are hiding this. When the news that extraterrestrial life exists spreads, a paradigm shift will inevitably take place.

Philip J. Corso, an American Army officer, participated in World War II and the Korean War and joined the National Security Council under Eisenhower, later becoming head of the foreign Technology division of the Research and Development Department, under the command of General A. Trudeau. In his work "The Day After Roswell," published in 1997, he claims that he managed the alien materials collected following the mysterious Roswell incident in 1947. Those materials were studied in the context of a technical retro-engineering project. According to him, some portions of those materials were provided to research laboratories for research and development purposes. According to conspiracy theories, from these studies modern generation technological objects were born, such as transistors, lasers, optical fibres, infrared rays, integrated microcircuits, etc. Among the statements made by Corso during the presentation of his book in Rome, in 1997, we read,

"On the night of July 4, 1947, an alien spacecraft crashed in Roswell, New Mexico. A series of blips appeared on the radar of the nearby military base followed by an explosion; then they found the rests of the flying saucer and the corpses of the aliens. That night, I was in charge of security at Fort Riley in Kansas. 2 days later, one of my sergeants asked me to open one of the wooden crates from Roswell. I was shocked: there was something in a gelatinous and bluish liquid, a soft and shiny shape like the belly of a fish. At first, I thought of a child's corpse. But it was a humanoid figure one meter long, with long and thin arms and legs, hands and feet with 4 fingers and a huge bulbous head. I touched that being: its greyish skin was like fabric. The body was destined for the military morgue for autopsy. This had no consequences and the Pentagon kept the secret for 15 years. I became head of the army's Foreign Technology Division in 1961. General Trudeau entrusted me with the study of a special archive: The Roswell files. I realized

that they decided to study that extraordinary discovery. During the Cold War, the Pentagon was convinced that the government was full of Soviet spies and that the CIA itself worked with the Kremlin: that documentation should not end up in the wrong hands! I had to act with great caution: I selected 25 local industries loyal to the homeland and entrusted them first only with technical information and then with disaggregated pieces of the materials recovered in the space crash, so that none knew the entire piece. Alien technology has been extraordinarily useful to us. We have developed devices such as integrated circuits, transistors and particle accelerators. In the spacecraft, there were very strong fibres, impossible to cut or burn, similar to a spider web: we made Kevlar from it. There was a thin and unbreakable piece of metal: by analysing its molecular composition, we discovered the fibre optic networks. I found a kind of flashlight: it didn't work and I thought it had no batteries. Instead, the object turned on once under the radiation: it was laser. The beings in the disc had no vocal cords; they were in telepathic contact with each other, with 4 brain lobes instead of 2, and with lymph instead of blood. The autopsy revealed that they were clones, humanoids created by alien intelligences to cross space."

John Schwesler, former NASA engineer and co-founder of Muton (Mutual Ufo Network), presented at a conference different documents related to all knowledge about UFOs and extraterrestrials.

Guy Andronick was part of a group of geophysicists in French Polynesia and, on the occasion of a nuclear test, saw three bright flying objects at high speed on the Fantaganga base. The veterans of the French nuclear experts, without precautions, suffered several misfortunes and health problems. Other colleagues also reported UFO sightings. According to Andronick, UFOs are a reality and military personnel would be guilty of denying everything in the name of "national security."

In Brookhaven, New York, an aircraft was found and subjected to research. They particularly analysed its collision-acceleration system of particles and a quark-gluon plasma beam released by the collision, a phenomenon in which a change in the direction of the atoms is manifested.

Edgar Mitchell's record, Apollo astronaut, reported in the interview by James Fox and published by Steven Greer, confirmed that there have been multiple visits by extraterrestrials, and that bodies and materials were recovered from crashed aircraft. There have been many attempts to keep all this secret and even to create misinformation to divert people's attention, thus hiding the truth. During the Apollo moon landing, Neil Armstrong said, "They're here. And they look at the size of those spacecrafts. And of course, they don't like our presence [...]" The part of the recording in which "You are right, they are already here" is reported, was removed from public broadcasts. There would also be allusions to a base behind the moon. Donna Hare, a NASA official in the 1970s, revealed that NASA systematically edited photos of the moon and removed UFO images. Karl Wolff of the US Air Force said that he saw images portraying structures on the moon. Many evidences, therefore, would suggest that a secret space program exists. Of course, those involved in the secret are afraid and would like to reveal the truth.

Several churchmen have mentioned the possible existence of extraterrestrial creatures. José Gabriel Funes in 2008 stated to believe that extraterrestrial life exists, however this does not contradict belief in God. Even if there is no evidence, such hypothesis cannot be ruled out. Monsignor Balducci, who has been studying the UFO phenomenon for years, believes that everything is possible and that God can be known by a variety of beings. The Catholic faith itself is based on eyewitness accounts, for this reason we should consider those who have witnessed UFOs. According to him, human testimonies should be taken into consideration and it is illogical to believe that we are the only intelligent beings in the universe. He manages to find a point of contact between the possibility of the existence of extraterrestrials and the principles of the Catholic faith. We do not know who these aliens are, could they be angels? But there is the possibility that they are more evolved than humans. Other churchmen have also supported the existence of extraterrestrials: Padre Pio and the Salesian priest Andrea Beltrami.

There are numerous stories of missing archives, inventions of antigravity tools, aliens who can walk on the street in human guise. So they could walk among us, or work and live on Earth. All this causes science to wince, as it is the case when it comes to telepathic or spiritual contacts.

According to UFO researcher Richard Dolan, ETs come from far away, from another larger reality that we still cannot understand with our ordinary tools. However, we know that these extraterrestrial beings have access to a very advanced technology: aircraft that can change shape, accelerate, go at supersonic speeds and disappear. If space-time is manipulated, this makes it possible to travel interstellar distances.

These beings would know physical laws we do not yet know: they can manipulate space and time, they are connected like a network and are not influenced by the gravitational force. Moreover, they use telepathic communication.

Dolan talks about a reality consisting of five layers. First of all, the mass reality, on which all attention is focused: the culture of mass media and images that constantly bombard us. Then there is the academic reality: they believe they see beyond the mass reality which, while possessing an extra critical attitude towards culture and society, is still far from the truth. After that, there is the "classified" reality, that is, the CIA and the world of intelligence, whose work is not known and no document is available. Then there is the "breakaway" reality, the UFO reality, which is a limited part of the "classified" world. Finally, there is the reality of the ETs: something completely unimaginable, beyond what can even be conceived by the breakaway reality.

The interesting aspect is the "insider disclosure," i.e. prominent insiders who have leaked information about UFOs. For example, in 1974 the French Minister of Defense, Robert Galley, stated that the French gendarmerie has studied UFOs for 20 years with a very large reliable report of UFO sightings. General Carlos Castro Cavero in an interview in 1976 stated that he believed that UFOs are extraterrestrial aircraft and that the nations are working together in research on this phenomenon.

According to scholars, the influence of the US in the world and the control of the NSA and CIA is remarkable. It depends on the US whether there will be disclosure or not. The CIA and the NSA have incredible control over different aspects, a real structure not only on the US, but also on other nations. Other countries would not dare to overtake America, also because the United States is in possession of a greater amount of data. However, Russia and China represent an exception: Russia has a long history of UFO encounters and of crashed UFOs. During the last decades of the 1900s, many UFO files came to light, including those of the KGB. Moreover, government officials made different statements, for example Dimitri Medveded in 2012 and Pavel Popovich, who spoke openly about the UFO reality. In 1990, Igor Matzev reported a UFO encounter near Moscow and on that occasion the fighter jets attempted to intercept and chase the flying object, but were in turn chased by it. It flew in a different and unconventional way, making movements that no currently known human technology could make. That event was witnessed by hundreds of people, including military personnel. Photos were taken but then disappeared.

Different reports state that both the Russian and Chinese authorities have made different efforts to understand the UAP/UFO topic, analysing and measuring the bodies. China has a strong Ufological community. Researcher Dong exposed several cases, while researcher Dr. Sun Shi Li testified that China has experience of a large amount of UFO activity. He talks about an accident that occurred in 1999, a recovery of a UFO crash in 1951, with evidence that Chinese UFO research believes that this phenomenon is real and that those are real aircraft.

These are phenomena that go beyond what we call reality, to the boundaries of a reality that would seem three-dimensional. The psychological aspect of technology is studied, how thought makes us communicate with aliens and their technologies.

Physicist Paul LaViolette, in his work "Secrets of Antigravity Propulsion," reveals that antigravity research is feasible for the aeronautical industry, as crucial for the development of a new generation of aircraft: flying discs with a speed of 1.5 Mach — which means 1.5 times the speed of sound — in the atmosphere, and 2.5 Mach in the upper layers of the atmosphere. Those who have worked on these projects independently have a problem. Instead, the secret military projects continued their research until the development of Bomber B-2s, which used advanced technology, deploying a high voltage and adopting the combination of traditional air engines, along with secret antigravity technologies.

In 2002, an internal Boeing project was launched called "Grasp" - Gravity Research for Advanced Space Propulsion, for the creation of other types of aircraft. How many things are classified and maybe "declassified" after 50 years? So many discoveries, so many secrets!

One cannot fail to mention the much-discussed Area 51, which had been chosen under the authority of the CIA, with two bases, one of which at Groom Lake, for its sand suitable for testing secret spy planes. However, at a distance of 12 miles there would be another lake, Papoose Lake, home to a base called S-4, where highly secret aerospace projects would be tested and developed.

Edgar Bouche has spent 30 years in the aviation industry working in different secret programs. He wrote a book based on real events and collected testimonies of people at Groom Lake. It emerges that an Aurora project involves a group of extraterrestrial aircraft of Mach speed 5 up to Mach 18, — 5-18 times the speed of sound —, reaching the height of over 120,000 feet, about 3,300 miles per hour. Some of these aircraft use a combination of conventional propulsion systems and electrogravity. The new technology, "magnet field disrupter," creates a swirling magnetic field, which neutralizes the effect of gravity on the mass by 89%. In this way, the vehicle becomes extremely light and with greater performance and silence.

After all, the physicist Bob Lazar had already explained how to generate gravity fields to be applied to spacecraft: the weight and inertia of both the vehicle and the occupants are reduced, so that the latter can survive at such a speed. Lazar is an American nuclear physicist, a controversial and crucial figure in the UFO discussion. He claimed to have worked at Los Alamos, in the federal laboratories, as a physicist and laboratory expert for the US Navy's S4 base. He carried out retro-engineering work on the unknown technology of an "antimatter reactor," that is, a disc with a sphere that contains an "element 115" and inside it a strong gravitational field would be created, with the expulsion of gravitational waves. This nuclear reactor would transform matter into 100% energy, producing a huge source of electricity and gravitational waves channelled towards the bottom of the generator, then increased in intensity by three gravity amplifiers. Generators produce a gravitational ray that is aimed at the destination one wants to reach. It is as if space were pulled towards that point by the power of the generators, at an infinite speed, involving a particular "temporal distortion:" when time is distorted, there is no longer a normal reference to time itself. Gravity is believed to be a wave that can produce a gravitational field capable of distorting time and space, bringing the destination to itself, without even moving.

The first official evidence released by the US government, that UFOs — now called UAP "unidentified anomalous phenomena", which seems to be less trivialized —, are real, dates back to September 2019. At that time, an article documented the authenticity of the videos made by the US Navy in 2015 and released at the end of December 2017 by the US Defense, relating to unknown objects with unexplained aerodynamic behaviour, off the coast of California. On that occasion, the fighter pilots recorded aircraft without wings and engines, at considerable speed, with lightning turns, such as to exceed the speed of the fighter jets. It must also be considered that a pilot could not sustain such a type and amount of physical stresses required by such rapid and sudden evolutions. Joseph Gradishen, spokesman for the U.S. Navy's deputy chief of naval operations, said that the footage had not been authorized to be shown to the public.

Kidnappings or Encounters?

Flight safety inspector George Van Tassell claims to have travelled on a flying saucer and even back in time.

Daniel Fry worked in the White Sands missile control system and claimed to have encountered a gigantic UFO and an alien who warned him not to touch the hull because it was hot. He was invited to see the flying saucer, where he learned about the propulsion system. On that occasion, Fry discovered the entities descended from survivors of a war between Atlantis and Lemuria, who migrated to space after the war. Orfeo Angelucci claims to have flown on a flying saucer and to have learned that aliens live on Earth and cannot be distinguished from humans. One night, Antonio Villas Boas was driving a tractor, when he suddenly saw a bright light, with several rays. The tractor was captured by four aliens, who carried Boas on board. Boas said he underwent organic sampling and was then guided to a tour. He reports that he later tried to steal a device, but was discovered.

After a holiday in Canada, Betty and Barney Hill decided to come back home earlier than expected to New Hampshire. Along the way from Colebrook to Portsmouth, they lived the experience of two hours of missing time, a phenomenon that indicates a total gap in memory relating to a certain period of time. They saw an object that was getting bigger and brighter and hovering in the air. Barney had a close encounter with aliens. Only with a session of hypnosis, they both had the opportunity to recall what had happened during that missing time. Both had undergone medical examinations and were later shown a star map that included the Zeta reticular, in a binary star system.

In 1972 in Australia, Maureen Puddy testified that following the sighting of a luminous UFO she lived an experience of kidnapping, which seemed to take place in another dimension.

In 1978 in Mississippi, C. Hickson and C. Parker were fishing, when suddenly they heard a buzz and saw an aircraft and a beam of blue-white light. Grey creatures took them to the aircraft, where they underwent medical examinations. When they returned, they told their experience to a sheriff, who verified that what they told was true. The sheriff, indeed, had inserted a hidden microphone that recorded what the two had said to each other when they had been left alone.

The story of Travis Walton in Arizona in 1975 begins with a glow in the trees and the vision of a flying saucer. Walton headed toward the object and was stopped by a beam of light, literally hurled backwards. When his companions looked for him, they did not find him but saw that the spacecraft was going upwards. After a few days, Walton contacted his friends to be picked up. He reported being taken into the aircraft and described the grey beings. At first, frightened and upset, he tried to fight, but in vain.

In 1967 Betty Andreasson, during a blackout, found four alien entities at her home, who subjected her to medical examinations, inside a capsule filled with a strange liquid.

In the "Aveley abductions case", John and Susan Day spotted a UFO with a blue light following them. They detected a radio malfunction and saw a fog. They lived a missing time of a few hours. Following regressive hypnosis, they remembered tall humanoids with Nordic features. They learned that aliens have done genetic engineering on humans and for this reason they monitor them.

In 1978 Elsi Oakensen noticed a green light while he was driving. The car had a strange reaction and stopped. There were other witnesses as well. He lived 15 minutes of missing time. In hypnosis, he then recalled that during that time he met two ghost-like creatures. This influenced his life leading him to develop healing faculties.

Lynda Jones, while walking, saw an object and suffered a missing time, during which she was kidnapped by three tall humanoids and taken to a room.

In 1980 Alan Godfrey was checking on livestock, when he came across a diamond-shaped UFO. He reported it to the police, who noticed that the ground was much drier where the aircraft was. Godfrey had lived a missing time and, following hypnosis, he was able to recall what he had experienced: after a blinding light coming from the aircraft, his car no longer started and he felt stuck, as if he were being recalled by the aircraft, where he met some humanoids and robots. He found himself lying on a table, surrounded by machinery. He underwent medical examinations.

A particular case is that of Linda Cortile who, following a moment of paralysis, saw grey aliens in her room. She underwent medical procedures and was carried through a blue ray in an oval-shaped aircraft. In this case, two police officers saw a huge UFO near the

Brooklyn Bridge, a ray of blue light and a woman in white pyjamas who was attracted by the ray in the aircraft, accompanied by three figures. There was also another witness, a woman who was driving along the Brooklyn Bridge.

The experience of those who had a close encounter with aliens seems to touch schizophrenia. In that situation, it is difficult to distinguish between "reality" and "fantasy", yet perceived as real, as actually happens in schizophrenia. But from their point of view, such experiences are real, even more real than what we commonly consider "reality." We must reflect on the concept of reality, which is not as clearly defined as many believe it to be. The concept of reality depends on the mind that perceives, on the perceptual categories, any alterations of consciousness and on the specificity of the sense organs. A diagnosis of schizophrenia cannot be made on an abduction experience. A psychological approach could be useful if these subjects suffer from emotional and mental problems that may or may not be related to the abduction experience — considering that ufologists do not have the therapeutic tools required to distinguish the experience from any personal problems. In most cases, however, it is important to look for the memory through hypnotic regression.

The experiences of abductions seem to be objective realities, however the stories could often be distorted and the experiences are mainly psychological in nature.

Psychiatrist John Mack believes that the abductees' experiences are authentic. He studied several cases and recognized their reality and genuineness. Some of these are enlightening experiences that have led to profound inner transformations. He found no evidence of psychiatric disorders in those who had experienced abductions. According to Mack, we are in contact with other intelligences and we must be open to a greater awareness of the universe.

The characteristics of traditional "contact" experiences are similar in some particular dynamics. First of all, the person does not know anything about the meeting. The communication is telepathic, it will continue even later at a distance and benevolence is perceived by the aliens. The recurring theme is concern about the dangers of Earth technology, so these subjects feel they have a message to communicate to the world.

Several scholars have used regressive hypnosis to analyse these phenomena. Leo Sprinkle, a psychologist at the University of Wyoming, was among the first ufologists to use it and created post-traumatic mutual aid groups. Dr. James Harder used the method of psychiatrist Benjamin Simon, an expert in therapeutic hypnosis, which consisted of letting the subject focus on periods of missing time. Of course, the technique should be done by qualified persons. Anthropologist Richard Boylan says, "Their experience is not a strange thing: it happened to millions of people." There are several reservations regarding the hypnotic method, but its reliability depends on the training received and the correct application.

In hypnosis, people can make mistakes about what they remember, just as it happens ordinarily when we try to recall something. The hypnotist could influence and lead the witness; however, he becomes crucial in the awareness of the hypnotized subject. Often the information could be influenced by other inputs. For this reason, qualified hypnotherapists are essential, since hypnosis is something that cannot be improvised.

Alvin Lawson wanted to try regressive hypnosis as a technique; his contribution was essential in grafting a scientific methodology in the field of ufology. His research showed that it is important to verify the physical and psychological state of the witness, and one cannot rely only on the data emerged from the interview. However, an ufology researcher, despite having deep technical knowledge, does not have the necessary skills to investigate reports of abductions, much less to provide guidance and support to abductees.

Budd Hopkins became interested in the UFO phenomenon when he researched a wave of UFO sightings in Cape Cod. He managed to build a bridge between ufologists and mental health professionals. In 1975, he examined the abduction case of George O' Bansky in North Hudson Park, with the same script as the other cases: UFO landing and alien beings exiting the aircraft, as witnessed by other people. O' Bansky's report shows a missing time phase of about half an hour. Hopkins worked with psychiatrist Robert Naiman on O' Bansky's regressive hypnosis procedure, studying several trends regarding the description of those beings and noting that abductions do not always follow sightings or vice versa. The presence in the subject's life of a series of events on a regular basis, from early childhood, is recurrent. The subject has scratches and abnormal signs, but does not remember the cause. Some have typical signs of when tissue samples are taken. In 1981 Hopkins and the psychotherapist Clamar, Naiman's colleague, published his first book "Missing Time," collecting from that moment a wide range of cases. Among these, we can find Kathis Davis' case, to whom Hopkins will dedicate his second book "Intruders:" this talks about artificial insemination that gave birth to strange hybrid creatures, with medical-gynaecological procedures. This is how the possible nature of a long-term genetic project in which humans provide biological material would unfold. It would explain the deeply traumatic nature of the experiences of those who have undergone all this.

Robert Bigelow's short questionnaire, with the collaboration of Hopkins and Jacobs, highlighted the issues of paralysis, the feeling of flying through the air, or experiencing a time when one felt apparently lost, but without remembering why and where one has been, or seeing unusual balls of light in a room, without knowing how they were caused and where they come from.

David Jacob, professor of history, with a doctoral thesis on the history of UFO mysteries, began his research on alien abductions following his meeting with Budd Hopkins. He learned the regressive hypnosis' technique and began to collect a large number of cases from which solid patterns emerged. They describe grey aliens, capable of passing through walls, materializing and dematerializing, communicating telepathically, leading into the spaceship through beams of light. They seem to have a program and to be interested in human emotions. The research shows forty-five examples of the same symbols drawn by different subjects.

Cases of abductions began to spread in different parts of the world. The researcher Ken Philips, together with Alex Eul from the University of Salzburg in Austria, analysed more than 100 cases of witnesses of close encounters, noting common features in the background and lives of the abductees. He discovered interesting patterns: intelligence, skill, development of extrasensory and artistic faculties. They moved their focus to the witness, rather than the one who conducts the hypnosis. Ultimately, alien abductions all over the world surprisingly had similar dynamics.

The hypnotherapist Boylan studied victims of abductions and "starseeds," i.e. children with psychic abilities and so-called "indigo children." He carried out field research, visiting the secret bases in the southwest of the USA. He believes that a possible public revelation would not be through the government, but private researchers.

They studied road abductions: before the event no other cars are seen, even in usually busy roads. Aliens seem to exert control over the surrounding environment. Interference with radios occurs and electrical structures interfere with cars, which could be a magnetic interference from the UFO propulsion system. In addition, as reported form different experiences, there is a missing time, with memories that are removed but can be brought to light in the future, especially through hypnosis procedures. "Missing time" experiences occur because it is not possible to locate interactions with beings from other dimensions in ordinary time. Whitley Strieber defined "memory screen" the memory of an event altered by the mind, interpreting it as a way to protect the psyche from memories that could be considered negative. Hypnosis is the only tool that can reveal the truth of events, giving voice to the subconscious part.

Aliens are described with large eyes, from whose gaze one has the feeling of being hypnotized. The subjects have strange scratches. They cannot remember the exact moment they entered the spacecraft. They often see a blue light and undergo medical procedures. They communicate telepathically, the subject does not resist and is instead reassured. Implants are also described — the same found in Dolores Cannon's research —, which localize the subject. These implants are not from our world and several of them have even been removed by doctors.

The subject is shown apocalyptic images of Earth, because aliens try to educate mankind. If there are other people in the room, they are "turned off." The abductees suffer from dizziness and are afraid of height.

The American doctor David Pritchard says that alien abductions are a serious and scientific study material. However, we must beware of swindlers. He believes that the phenomenon needs a new scientific paradigm. In 1992, the first scientific conference on abductions took place. Every scientist in their specific field put their skills to use to analyze the phenomenon: psychologists, psychiatrists, doctors, sociologists, physicists and astronomers.

Nick Pope, a UFO researcher, who as a former employee of the UK Ministry of Defence had access to confidential details regarding the UFO phenomenon, wonders if alien abductions possibly pose a threat, because they are unwanted and take place without any consent, or if they can even be considered as criminal offences. Indeed, an abductee wrote to the Minister of Defence, with references to the legislation on offences concerning the person. It is also possible that some "kidnapped" never returned. Pope wonders if the USA has any secret agreements with extraterrestrials, or if they have authorized them to conduct a kidnapping program in exchange for assistance and technological development.

The testimonies show that the aliens take people against their will and conduct procedures not approved by them. But what other theories might explain what is going on? He does not believe in only one solution to the problem, but in a concatenation of situations happening at the same time. According to Leo Sprinkle, when people deal with aliens, they actually come into contact with their soul's blueprint, and humanity's earthly blueprint with all the related changes. This research involves both the external senses and the intellectual and intuitive faculties: abduction is a physical, biological, psychological and spiritual experience. It is like a test that lead the individual out of his daily life, and after having lived that experience he is disoriented.

Many testimonies of abductees reveal that they have been trained to understand a three-dimensional language, supplemented by symbols. Jim Sparks in his book "The Keepers" argues that it is not an alien language, but just between the alien telepathic and technological language and our linear and verbal.

According to Michael Wolf, we need to transcend limited paradigms of our established systems of thought.

"And you finally discover, with immense amazement, that the planet you are on is not your home. What human logic can there be to those who know for sure that they are not from this planet?"

Doctor Wolf worked for the Majestic 12 project, which for decades had secretly managed the UFO issue, and had the opportunity to communicate with aliens and collect data about the "extraterrestrial biological entities" that come to visit Earth. These are beings with superior psychic faculties and experts in "psychobiophysics", capable of repairing defective genetic codes. He published part of the testimonies in the fascinating work "The Catchers of Heaven." In telling the truth, Wolf violated the provisions of the National Security Act. He was a truth-seeker and felt like a "foreigner in another land."

In the ufological landscape, people like Robert Dean and Michael Wolf have been erased, not only in the collaboration on secret projects, but in their qualifications and documents. After Michael Wolf's death, for example, his flat was cleaned of any testimony and his second manuscript was erased.

Wolf suggests that consciousness is the key: it links space and time or divides into other dimensions. The state of alteration of consciousness is crucial, in a universe where the mental part seems to be fundamental.

Moving into the unknown, we discover the multiple dimensions of the universe, whose relationships are not fully understood in our ordinary dimension of reality. The ordinary worldview imposed by science must fall. The researcher is not separated from the investigated phenomenon.

The abductions could therefore be an attempt to educate and produce subtle changes in the human being. It could turn out to be a transformative experience, or lead to the development of psychic abilities. Is it a crime against humanity or an attempt to save us from ourselves?

During this research, mistakes have been made and swindlers have polluted it, risking undermining its credibility. Pope says, *"The real crime against humanity that originates from alien abduction may not be what extraterrestrial intelligence inflicts on us, but rather the unconcern that leaves the phenomenon undisturbed."*

Captain Edward Ruppelt, a U.S. military officer and member of the Blue Book Project, wondered, "How can we convince others that aliens are not hostile when we don't know ourselves?"

Erich Von Danikhen, writer of mysterious archaeology, believes that the civilizations developed on Earth emerged not because of their evolution, but because of projects of multiple alien races: the Maya, with their concept of omnipresent time, the Egyptians with solar genetics, the Babylonians with a binary writing system, commonly called "cuneiform," the South American civilizations of the Aztecs, Toltecs and Olmecs. Other writers have dealt with these issues, such as Zecharia Sitchin, Walter Raymond Drake and Peter Kolosimo, whose works include interesting insights that cannot be dealt with here.

Those who have experienced the "contact" received information that was accepted. It seems they have the responsibility to convey particular messages. They do not seek notoriety or money, since being a witness could be considered as something negative. They faced the cultural barriers that deny what they have experienced and must find in themselves the strength to develop the messages and information received.

But what is the relationship between the UFO phenomenon and our consciousness that continues after death? From the testimonies collected and research carried out, it seems that extraterrestrial beings can access the frequency in which the soul lives after the death of the physical body. Moreover, the UFO phenomenon seems to cause electromagnetic and electric fields that, already during physical life, tend to influence us and can cause temporary paralysis, change of state of consciousness, out-of-body travel or real spiritual awakenings. There are sites on Earth with energy vortices that produce magnetic fields and a convergence of energy lines that lead to un-conscious thoughts and open the mental passage into the spiritual realms.

Neil Gould, director of the exopolitics institute, suggests that con-sciousness observes the hyperspatial and multidimensional universe: it fills our being and comes from hyperspatial dimensions, creating a quantum reality. As long as one stays connected to the Earth and the body, one cannot improve one's awareness. Spirituality is the basis for understanding the enigmas of the universe and developing psy-chic abilities. The aim is awareness.

CHAPTER 9

SPIRITUALISM AND MEDIUMSHIP

Among the sectors that have dealt with the afterlife, mediumship anticipated the discovery of NDEs and the method of regressive hypnosis. I never wanted to delve into in this field's practice, because in my personal spiritual path, I had always been discouraged from approaching this kind of phenomenon. Among the scholars of Western esotericism, Julius Evola, in his work "The Mask and Face of Contemporary Spiritualism," warned the spiritual researcher against approaching the practices of spiritualism and mediumship, which he considered not without risks.

However, I believe it is appropriate to dedicate a chapter to this topic with extreme respect, because the data collected by those who practiced mediumship contributes to providing further confirmation of the existence of the afterlife and confirms what was then discovered through other methods.

Spiritualism, also called "secret doctrine," arises as an experimental science and moral philosophy, cosmology, a body of knowledge that opens new perspectives and intends to provide an answer to the great existential questions. It believes that the only permanent reality is the spirit and that life is just its evolution. Matter is an expression of spirit, similar to the theories of quantum physics, as we will see later, according to which matter is energy at a denser vibrational state.

God is conceived as the origin of everything, life, substance, essence. The soul is immortal and is an expression of the absolute, to which it must return following an evolutionary path consisting of several lives, both terrestrial and spiritual. As the philosophy of Hermeticism states, the soul is the microcosm of the macrocosm, therefore it contains all the properties of the macrocosm-Everything. This is why it is possible to find God in the depths of one's being, following a path of spiritual search and introspection. It is not a religion, since it considers religions as partial aspects and temporal manifestations of Truth, conditioned by times and societies, dogmatism in a limiting and not at all constructive way. The ideal solution would be a religion that meets science and humanity's needs. On the other hand, science should embrace the ideals and insights of religions and spirituality.

The secret doctrine lays its foundations in the ancient philosophies and wisdoms of India, Egypt, Greece, the Alexandrian school, early Christianity, the Jewish Kabbalah, medieval philosophies and Hermeticism, and reveals a perennial tradition, of which these have only been expressions in space-time and which continues to live in the invisible. This wisdom was then handed down by the Templars, the Alchemists and the Rosicrucians.

Spiritualists say nothing different from what has been handed down by different religious and esoteric traditions: the soul is considered the principle of life, an invisible force that animates the organism and keeps it alive, unites all the faculties, the individual's intellectual and moral characteristics, maintains the agreement between the different parts of matter. Over the course of lifetimes, the soul evolves between different contexts, progressing and perfecting itself in the knowledge and development of greater awareness and wisdom.

There is a spiritual dimension that governs what exists, contributing to the execution of the divine plan. After its multiple incarnations, the soul can take part in all this. There is an Eternal Law, intelligence to which all living beings are subject.

Mediums are characterized by a sensitivity of the nervous system, and act as intermediaries between this physical world and the spiritual one, drawing from it information, inspirations, insights and encouragement both for them and for other people. With the mediums' help, many disembodied spirits had the opportunity to let their loved ones know that they are still alive in another dimension and are always present. Mediums can spontaneously go into a trance state, without being induced by any external hypnotist, and are capable of catalysing phenomena in which the materialization of spirits takes place. In order for such phenomena to occur, an amount of etheric-vital fluid of the medium is employed, so that the spirit fluid can be condensed until it becomes temporarily tangible. The risk of mediumship is that the medium could be depleted of his etheric-vital fluid, which is the basis of good health of body and mind.

The information on the post-mortem and the spiritual dimensions of the afterlife are the same as those emerged with NDEs and hypnosis of regression to life between lives. Once the soul leaves the body, there is a period of disorientation, which can last depending on the person's evolutionary level. Allan Kardec calls the astral body "perispirit" or "spiritual body," the one already seen as the protagonist of out-of-body experiences in NDEs. The astral-perispirit body is like a mediator between body and soul and communicates sensory perceptions to the soul and the experience and impressions of the soul to the body. It is bound to matter by the nervous-vital fluid of the etheric body.

For some souls, the perispirit becomes like a second physical body with the same habits, almost physical sensations, as those they had in life. The soul is in an intermediate state between the physical life just left and the new spiritual one. According to spiritualists' investigations, after death, the soul recalls the life just with a particular emphasis on the ethical-moral aspect: memories are conceived as shadows that are brought to light and the soul weighs the good and evil it has achieved, analysing all the thoughts, words and actions carried out since birth.

In 1848 in the United States, the phenomena of spiritual manifestations began to attract considerable interest from the public. Several scientists began to study them and, following a strict examination managed by the Supreme Court of New York and the Senate, they acknowledged the reality of the phenomena. In 1869 the London Dialectical Society established a commission with members expert in different fields of knowledge to investigate spiritist phenomena, thinking that it was just fantasy. After almost two years of studies and research, the commission ruled in favour of the reality of spiritist phenomena. A. Russel Wallace, a scientist of that commission, representative of Darwinian evolutionary theory, continued the research, collecting the results in his work "Miracles and Modern Spiritualism," saying, *"When I began this research I was a convinced materialist, and I did not accept, in any way, the possibility of a spiritual existence. Nevertheless, the facts have persisted and have won me over, forcing me to admit a long time before I can be convinced of their supernatural character."*

The Society for Psychical Research, founded in 1882, was the first scientific organization aimed at the study of paranormal phenomena and spiritual apparitions, which brought together exponents of different fields of knowledge including physics, medicine, philosophy, psychology, with twelve Nobel Prizes. Among these, the distinguished psychologist William James, the philosopher Henri Bergson, and the British Prime Minister Arthur Balfour.

"The state that psychic research attracts only fools and gullible could not be further from the truth."
(Arthur J.Ellison)

THE SOUL NEVER DIES

The chemist and physicist William Crookes, one of the presidents of the Society for Psychical Research and discoverer of the element thallium, together with other scientists, studied spiritist phenomena in a laboratory equipped with precise instruments, examining the movements of heavy bodies, direct writing, the appearance of forms and the sound of non-contact musical instruments. He studied the materialization phenomena of the medium Florence Cook, who was able to materialize disembodied entities through "ectoplasm," a particular substance that seemed to flow out from her body, giving rise to incredible phenomena. Among the manifestations, there was the spirit of Katie King, who appeared every night with a human body that then disappeared as a fog. The studies were carried out with strict controls and precautions to avoid any risk of fraud.

Spiritist phenomena, as well as paranormal ones, have therefore been studied scientifically. The first parapsychology laboratory was founded in 1920 by J.B. Rhine at Duke University in North Carolina, and gathered evidence related to telepathy, clairvoyance, precognition and psychokinesis, as well as thousands of reports of spontaneous parapsychological experiences, using methodologies of high scientific rigour.

In 1957, the Parapsychological Association was established and expanded internationally, bringing together professional researchers who studied parapsychological phenomena. This association has been recognized and affiliated with the American Association for the Advancement of Science.

In 1983, the first chair of parapsychology was established in the psychology department of the University of Edinburgh, thanks to Arthur Koestler. The first parapsychology professor was Robert Morris.

William Barret, English physicist and founder of the British and American Society for Psychical Research, devoted himself to research in the field of spiritualism, in particular telepathy. He found out that paranormal phenomena are much more than mere "hallucinations." He studied the mediumship and the automatic writing, finding multiple clear evidence of the survival of the soul. He also investigated the phenomenon of Death Bed Visions which, as we have seen before, indicates the dying person's ability to live between two dimensions, perceiving what in the material world is not accessible to our senses.

Gary Schwartz investigated following rigorous scientific protocols on the most famous American mediums, to test the communications they received. The experiments were conducted in a laboratory under strict observation, in some cases avoiding bringing the consultant into contact with the medium.

In Italy, Professor Ercole Chiaia studied the manifestations of the medium Eusapia Palladino, through experiments involving materialization, levitation and contributions, which were assisted by the well-known criminologist Cesare Lombroso and a team of professors from the University of Naples. They had to acknowledge that the spiritist phenomena are real. Lombroso interpreted mediumship as "externalization of the forces of the medium," but could not provide further details.

Different mediums have been scientifically examined and the results show that a part of the phenomena can be considered true.

Several scientists from all over the world have witnessed the phenomena of different sessions held in Milan, acknowledging the existence of phenomena such as lifting tables, mechanical movements of different kinds that took place without human contact, spontaneous movement of objects, blows and reproduction of sounds in the table. They had found that these had not been caused by humans. There was no fraud and this was defined as *"the triumph of a truth that was wrongly opposed."*

In France, Allan Kardec meticulously studied the phenomenon of spiritualism, participating directly in mediumistic sessions and accumulating numerous communications from the afterlife. In thirty years of research, he collected all the lessons learned from the "spirits" in different groups and from all the reports of those who had worked or assisted during the various séances. He was therefore able to assume the fundamental principles, which were clearly and logically stated and supported by precise facts and solid testimonies. Experts in different fields throughout Europe took part in congresses of spiritualism in Paris at the end of the 1800s, affirming the principles of the immortality of the soul and the persistence of a conscious self after death, as well as the possibility of authentic communication between the living and the dead.

Kardec distinguishes between "lower spirits" and "higher spirits:" the former take to the other world their material concerns, habits, needs, passions, vices typical of earthly life and therefore remain in the astral planes close to the Earth and in contact with human beings, but they often suffer for no longer being a physical body and not being perceived by other humans. They are tormented souls that communicate with physical manifestations. As we have seen, Michael Newton did not have the opportunity to live such situations in his cases of regression to life between lives. Instead, the "higher spirits" are satisfied, because they find beauty, wisdom, art, culture and all the noblest ideals in the afterlife. These higher souls feel wonderful emotions when they perceive the celestial harmonies of the spiritual hierarchies, the melody of the universe, the voice of the infinite, the origin of everything, in a spiritual place of rest. It seems to be a holiday from the hustle of life, in which it is possible to collaborate with a spiritual civilization based on deep ethical and moral laws, respect, friendship, brotherhood, without rivalry, wars, hatred or material interests.

From dialogues with spiritual entities, spiritualists have learned that, at the end of the cycle of incarnations and trials, there will be an eternal spiritual life, characterized by peace and serenity. The soul will be able to retain forever all the memories of its life between different times and places: it will seem like a long pilgrimage that has finally brought it home with a new awareness. On the other hand, those who are reincarnated live a process of gradual rapprochement of the perispirit with matter, which condenses to form a new body. The perispirit is like a fluid mould that imprints its characteristics, qualities and defects on the future physical body. Reincarnation is not easy and will unfold as a slow fall into torpor, a gradual loss of memory, as a gradual falling asleep.

A higher soul is animated by gentleness, patience, charity, capacity for forgiveness: it cannot feel hatred or resentment, because it can see things from a higher perspective, realizing that damages are caused by ignorance, as Jesus says in the Gospel of Luke, *"Father, forgive them, for they have not known what they do."* This soul is detached from earthly frivolities, but still cares about humanity and the importance of its peers' work, of family and affections, the interdependence of all human beings.

According to spiritualists, praying for suffering spirits, even if only by sending a thought or an affectionate memory, is important to help their detachment from the body and everything that still binds them to matter.

Everything evolves in the universe and tends to a higher level, everything is transformed. Life is destined to reach ever more perfect forms. The human soul is immortal and retains its identity, changing and renewing itself from life to life, towards perfection. With this evolution, it will develop high faculties.

Life on Earth is a difficult school where the soul completes its path of perfection with free will, manifesting the tendencies developed in itself, collecting the consequences of past actions, according to a cause-effect law. The evolution of the soul is accomplished by evolving spiritually, gradually detaching from material needs, developing higher interests, cultivating ideals of truth, justice, being animated by charity and benevolence towards humanity. All beings are like a big family since they share the same origin, so it is important to develop solidarity and brotherhood in life. The supreme law of the universe is based on doing good, which is the ultimate purpose to which the evolution of beings must tend. Evil is a state of temporary inferiority, which has no existence of its own.

Spiritualism brings the ideals of progress and growth, inspires values and transmits important lessons for personal improvement.

> *"Recollect that the material is invariably ephemeral. Like the ocean waves, generations roll by, empires crumble, worlds even perish and suns are dissolved: everything disappears, everything vanishes. But there are three things which come from God and which like Him are eternal, three things that radiate beyond the flicker of mortal glory, and these three are: Wisdom, Virtue and Love! Conquer them by your efforts, and having once acquired them you will rise above what is momentary and transitory, to enter into possession of that which is eternal."*
> **(Leon Denis)**

However, scholars of esoteric traditions have encountered some critical issues regarding some aspects of spiritualism. Through their sessions, indeed, one can come into contact not only with the souls that actually manifest themselves to people on Earth from the higher astral planes, but also unfortunately with animated astral sheaths, that is what remains of the astral body, now without the soul, during the process of its disintegration. The medium can galvanize an astral envelope, materializing it with its vital energy. However, this is not a spirit but only remains, like a moving shadow. The medium will animate it and make it even speak, even if this will happen in an unconnected way.

On the other hand, the higher souls no longer deal with earthly things, but there is still a spiritual bond, a kind of transcendent form of telepathy and psychic closeness, a continuation of feelings of affection and love. If the incarnated soul thinks constantly of the deceased loved one, the latter will feel a call; similarly, if the deceased thinks of his loved one on Earth, a sense of physical closeness will be felt.

The practice of spiritualism done out of curiosity or exhibition is condemned since the disembodied soul in such contexts is disoriented, distracted and its development in the spiritual planes would risk being slowed down. Even if the séance were held in order to give comfort to the people on Earth, the soul of the deceased could still be disturbed or confused, as if in a state of partial sleep. That is why in several cases the conversation with the spirit during the session brought to confused answers.

In other cases, however, the souls of the deceased could express the will to manifest themselves to people on Earth, even managing to "materialize," i.e. to assume a perceptible form to the physical senses, through a strong telepathic impression. This has happened many times without causing any disturbance, managing to give comfort to the loved one or to settle any unresolved issues.

Rather than seeking active contact with the deceased, it would be appropriate to send thoughts of love to help their development on higher planes. It is desirable to develop a higher form of communication, based on silence, because souls speak to each other without words and without physical presence. Atkinson and other esotericists therefore do not criticize spiritualism itself, rather they know it brought many people closer to spiritual truths, as it is a doctrine that seeks the truth of life, as expressed by Kardec and others. But it is wise to be warned of the pitfalls of the lower astral planes.

CHAPTER 10:

RESPONDING
TO GRIEF

"The passing of a loved one who has been important in one's life is a radical event that aims at undermining ordinary certainties, because one lives the border of death in such a direct way. One realizes that precisely death bring us closer to a spiritual path. If we were eternal, what would be the point of following a spiritual path? The mystery of death gives meaning to the Spirit, because by "spiritual" we mean everything that is beyond physical life. Therefore, when one loses someone important, one is forced before that threshold and the big words, philosophies, theorems, myths discussed about spirituality and theories about life and death are no longer valid. At that moment, instead, one faces the reality and destiny that awaits everyone indiscriminately, as a decisive threshold between the physical and what has been theorized as 'spiritual'."
(Hermelinda - Oltre l'orizzonte dello spirito)

Embracing Death

Dra. Kubler Ross, an expert in "Death Bed Visions" as we have seen before, was among the founders of psychotanatology. This is the systematic study, from both a scientific and philosophical point of view, of the phenomena that affect death. In order to assist those who are dying, it is essential to work on oneself, that is, on one's thoughts and emotions towards death. In particular, one must have worked on the fear of death, overcoming it, in order to be able to transmit certainties and authentic compassion.

Kubler Ross says in this regard, *"I want to emphasize that, for me as for anyone who has ventured on this path, it is not a matter of believing in something, but in knowing that what we call death is nothing more than the transition to another dimension, which is happier and richer than this one. There is a fundamental difference."*

Cesare Boni, professor of life cycle psychology and expert in Eastern traditions, points out that when we are at the bedside of a dying person, we must not assist them but accompany them: a living and becoming, with extreme respect and authentic compassion, rather than a mere assisting and participating.

When we are near a person who is about to die, we do not need words, but a silence that transmits what we have achieved inside us. One will manifest a kind and loving behaviour with a look, a smile, a touch, and will be a silent presence able to defeat loneliness and disorientation experienced by the dying person. More than talking, it is important to know how to listen to the other person, to allow them to freely express their experience. Death must be conceived as a positive moment, full of great opportunities and possibilities for great achievements. One should be able to communicate certainties, without any trace of doubt or fear. One becomes a channel through which the divine energy of life flows to the person who is approaching the threshold between life and death, in order to illuminate their passage from this to the other world. In this way, one will give protection and help the dying person to manage his fear. It is about trying to focus more on the present moment, expressing a quality presence, characterized by peace and silence.

Kubler Ross studied the path that people begin to face as soon as they realize that their death is inevitable. This path unfolds in five phases, later confirmed by other scholars. The first phase is characterized by shock: the person becomes aware of the severity of his illness and realizes that he is approaching death. He therefore experiences both amazement and disbelief. During the next phase, there is denial: he denies reality and refuses to believe in his illness, thinking of the possibilities that may have led to an error in the diagnosis. At this point, there is a subsequent phase of anger towards doctors or relatives, or against one's own destiny or even towards God. Later he will enter the phase of "bargaining," as if trying to negotiate on the time, praying that he will have more time; however, this cannot be possible. Then, the dying person will close in on himself, in a form of "preparatory depression," manifesting the will to be alone and not to talk to anyone, often even refusing to eat. Once this phase is over — it has variable times depending on the subject —, the final stage will be the acceptance. This could be "passive," meaning resignation, or "active," which occurs when the subject gives a new meaning to death, as an evolutionary phase of the life cycle.

> *"Death that inspires terror and afflicts is for me the announcement of a more joyful life: I fully welcome it."*
> **(Kabir)**

Grieve

The death of a loved one is one of the most tragic events that one can live. We lose the opportunity to share experiences, thoughts and emotions with this person and, above all, to communicate. This is even more painful if there is a bond of affection with the deceased person. Grief, despair and deep loneliness afflict those who remain on Earth. According to psychological theories, mourning includes the conscious or unconscious psychological, cognitive and emotional processes lived by a subject following the loss of a loved one. John Bowlby distinguishes four stages of mourning. The first one is characterized by "stunning:" the subject cannot believe that the loved one has died and seems to be calm. However, sudden outbursts of pain and anger can be experienced. The second phase is characterized by "search and grief:" he begins to be aware of the loss, even if perceived as temporary and is affected by it with insomnia, obsessive thinking, restlessness and anger, which finally culminate in a gloomy sadness. In the next phase, that of "disorganization and despair," the subject realizes that the loss is permanent and the acceptance process begins. In the last phase of "reorganization," which usually takes place one year after the loss, turbulent emotions begin to fade. In numerous cases, despite the final grief elaboration, somehow the subject still perceives the closeness of the loved one. In other cases, this process is blocked, giving rise to a "complicated mourning," which results in difficulties in the psychological sphere. This happens especially when the death was sudden and unexpected, or if there had been relationship problems with the deceased person.

In 1915, Freud stated, "Mourning has a quite specific psychical task to perform: its function is to detach the survivor's memories and hopes from the dead."

According to the psychological theories of the twentieth century concerning mourning, the person who has suffered a loss must be able to free himself mentally from the deceased following an "appropriate elaboration." If this does not happen, it would indicate psychological problems of failure to examine reality. It seems that society has reinforced the idea that ties with the deceased should be cut. Indeed, it is quite difficult to grieve in Western society, which believes that death is the end of everything. It consists of the phase of denial, anger, despair, depression, and then acceptance, following a path that can last from months to years. The idea that death is the end of everything does not allow us to give meaning to both life and death. Death should instead be seen as a passage to other dimensions, being aware that, compared to real life in the spiritual planes, individual earthly lives represent only temporary and contingent roles of our eternal soul essence.

This distorted view in the new century is about to be overcome: we begin to give a new value to maintaining a connection with the deceased, reinforced by multiple subjects who claim to feel the presence of the deceased next to them, as if living in another dimension. This is precisely what emerged from Rees' study, carried out in 1971 on a sample of 300 widows and widowers from Wales: two thirds said they perceived the deceased spouse and received help and comfort from them.

In 1992, Conant conducted another study on women between the ages of 35 and 51, who had been widowed for about a year after a happy marriage that lasted on average almost 20 years. They reported having vividly felt their husband's presence, as if their relationship continued and they took care of them from another dimension. They reported a strong conviction that they were in contact with their spirits, with a visual, auditory or tactile perception. This did not seem to be a hallucination at all, being characterized by reality and vividness. This closeness instilled in them peace, comfort, and the belief that there is an afterlife.

Various studies showed that these phenomena have lasted for many years and were more frequent in the first ten years of mourning. The feeling of the presence of the loved one was more widespread, followed by visual perceptions, while auditory ones were less frequent. The subjects of this research were in normal health, they did not take any drugs that could induce hallucinations. In some cases, these perceptions were experienced independently by more than one subject for the same deceased loved one.

After Death Communication

Mourning can be considered not as a process with a conclusion or a phenomenon from which one will recover, but as something that will continue throughout life, while evolving in modality and intensity.

Bill and Judy Guggenheim have carried out research on ADCs, "After Death Communication" which are experiences of direct and spontaneous contact with a deceased person, without spiritual mediums. It is estimated that about 120 million Americans have had such an experience and thousands of testimonials have been collected. These communications mainly occur between relatives and during sleep or wakefulness. Physical phenomena, such as abnormal operation of physical appliances or flashing lights, have been reported. In these cases, subjects intensely feel the presence of the deceased, in some cases even the touch or their appearance.

The ADC would be caused by the deceased with the aim of comforting and reassuring that they are still alive spiritually. Among the testimonies collected, it happened that the ADCs took place when the living person was not yet aware of the other person's death.

In their book "Hello from Heaven," published in 1997, the two researchers analysed the data collected in 7 years of ADC research on a sample of two thousand subjects and divided them into twelve types, all were positive and instilled comfort and hope.

The first type are symbolic ADCs. Here different natural phenomena unfold as symbols of a message from the deceased, for example a butterfly, a feather, a rainbow or a light beam, an animal or an inanimate object, which do not occur by chance, but at a certain time, in order to convey a message. Another type of symbolic ADC, which I personally experienced, as well as other people I know, is the vision of heart-shaped objects. There are more structured symbolic ADCs too, such as the one told by Dra. Kubler Ross during an interview, in which she talked about an argument with her husband about life after death, while her daughter was there. Her husband turned to their daughter and said, "All right. If what your mother says is true, I will send you a sign from the afterlife. In the first snow you will see after my death, you will see red roses bloom." Five years later, her husband died and it was snowing on the day of his funeral. Red roses had really bloomed in the snow.

Then in the conscious ADCs you can clearly perceive the deceased in the same place where you are, along with emotions and feelings that recall that of an embrace. In auditory ADCs, the voice of the deceased is perceived through an internal hearing, as if it came from outside, in a telepathic communication full of reassuring messages, often encouraging or intended to protect in cases of danger. There are also tactile ADCs, giving the sensation of a caress, a kiss or a hug, and olfactory ADCs, experiencing a smell, aroma of food or drink or perfume reminiscent of that of your loved one. The visual ADCs bring a luminous apparition that recalls the deceased, in an image that radiates happiness and serenity. Other ADCs may occur in a waking state or during sleep, often through an extremely consistent dream. There is also a less common type of ADC, which would even happen on the phone. There are ADCs that produce physical phenomena too, such as moving objects, lights or devices: they turn on, fall, detach from the wall, and so on. Finally, he also identified extracorporeal ADCs, or OBE experiences where, after leaving one's body, one finds oneself in a dimension where it is possible to meet the deceased loved one. According to Bill and Judy Guggenheim, ADCs are not hallucinations, but authentic contact with the deceased loved one. From the testimonies collected during the research, many ADCs provided information regarding the deceased, or concerning particular situations of which one could not in any way become aware. Moreover, in some cases, ADC experiences happened when the death of their loved one was not yet known.

The last type are shared ADCs: in this case, another person lives the same experiences of perception of the deceased at the same time.

These frequently happen a few years after the death of the loved one, when the elaboration process is over.

In order to understand these types of experiences, it is necessary to overcome the prejudicial view that physical-material reality is the only one that exists. We must not forget that our relationship with the world is based on perception, whether it is sensory or extra-sensory, and is always based on our own experience. Experiences and perceptions are also the basis of any scientific theory. Any perception, whether it is physical or mental, expresses something that has the character of existence. We must be open to considering extrasensory perceptions as objective as ordinary sensory ones. It is necessary to overcome the scepticism of the dogmatic materialist paradigm and to question its assumptions, by delving deeper into the meaning of science and analysing the new opportunities of contemporary physics that, investigating further the true nature of matter, puts materialism in serious question, as we will see later.

Psychotherapy For Dealing With Grief

Models of psychotherapy were formulated by Raphael and Bowlby to grieve in complicated situations. These were first of all based on the free expression of emotions related to mourning, such as sadness, pain, anguish, anger, loneliness and guilt. Psychotherapy helps to retrace the events prior to the death of the loved one and, in particular, the emotions triggered. The interactions and experiences shared with the loved one are also retraced, leaving room for the emotions that could arise. The psychotherapist will work in particular on any feelings of guilt, anger and anxiety, and then analyse the existential changes that have occurred following the loss. It is often necessary to help the patient change some irrational and dysfunctional beliefs. Shear developed a structured therapy for complicated grief, based on some strategies, such as writing a grief diary or involving another person as support, and on a work on psychic defences. Another interesting strategy used in psychotherapy consists in leading the patient to an imaginary conversation with the deceased, asking questions and providing answers, giving voice to the deceased in an alternation of roles.

Another model of therapeutic intervention for mourning is EMDR (Eye Movement Desensitization and Reprocessing), a technique formulated by psychologist Francine Shapiro in 1995. EMDR is used for the elaboration of trauma, especially in post-traumatic stress, and was later used in complicated mourning. With the EMDR, the therapist asks the patient to think of an image that best expresses the trauma and to report the type of emotion felt and its level of intensity. The therapist begins to move his hand with his index and middle finger raised, inviting the patient to follow the horizontal movements from right to left and vice versa with his eyes. Following the movements, the patient will say if the level of intensity of the emotion experienced has changed.

Raymond Moody elaborated another method, based on the tradition of the psychomanteum of Ancient Greece, i.e. sacred places where it is possible to communicate with the deceased loved ones. This communication was carried out through bronze basins filled with water, on whose reflective surface the figure of the deceased could appear. They also used a mirror (one meter and twenty meters high), raised one meter from the ground and placed in front of an armchair, so that the patient sitting there can see the mirror without seeing his own image. The mirror reflects the context: the walls are covered with black velvet and a small coloured glass light is placed with a dim light. After a dialogue focused on the memories of the deceased, the patient is guided into a moment of relaxation. Later, he contemplates the mirror, focusing on the deceased and excluding unrelated thoughts. Research conducted on 300 patients showed that 50% reported a contact with the first attempt, while the rest had the opportunity to experience it in subsequent attempts. However, some of them did not meet the deceased they intended to contact, but another deceased — in any case a loved one. This shows that expectations do not affect to the point of suggesting the subject. There are several types and modes of experience, but they all perceive these experiences as more real than the experiences of ordinary reality.

IADC: Induced After Death Communication

The American psychologist Allan Botkin discovered a method that has some analogies with both the EMDR and the mirror room: Induced After Death Communication (IADC). This is based on induction on real communication with the deceased. At the beginning, the therapist leads the patient to talk about his interaction with the deceased and the circumstances of his death. Then, he is asked what part of his story causes him the most sadness and is invited to first come into contact with his pain, experiencing it in the most intense way. At that point, the therapist begins the induction of the EMDR, while the patient is focused on his suffering that will grow further and then eventually decrease after other eye movement sets. Once the intensity of the pain is decreased, the patient will be invited to be open to any experience. A deep relaxation is induced, continuing with the eye movements and "tapping" manoeuvres, so that his receptivity increases. At that point, the patient could have the opportunity to ask questions to his loved one. What happens in that case? Is it suggestion, hallucination, or an authentic communication experience? In this procedure, the answer does not matter, as the therapeutic effect does not change depending on whether the subject believes in the authenticity of the experience of contact and reunification. Those who have experienced the IADC report that it is different from imagination and dreams and it is extremely clear. There can be different perceptions and environmental contexts in which the experience takes place, with large meadows, trees, hills, lakes, seas, with intense colours and a feeling of deep peace. The deceased seems to be calm and smiling, often rejuvenated and communication takes place telepathically, but much more clearly than ordinary voice communications. There are different types of communication between the patient and the deceased, based on different contexts or in case of any situations left unsolved. Generally, they try to reassure those who are still alive, letting them know that they are always close to them and inviting them not to suffer loss, as they are happy in the dimension in which they currently live. Suggestions are often given regarding daily life or appreciation is expressed regarding a specific situation. The experience is always positive and gives deep comfort. These are consistent experiences, often very different from expectations, which carry important messages that could often change one's beliefs, as well as the resolution of internal conflicts still present, due to unresolved issues. In some cases, important information was obtained from IADC's experience, which could not have been known in any way, and whose authenticity was later verified. In some cases the therapist has experienced the same images and words as the patient.

During my psychotherapeutic training, I had the opportunity to carry out the IADC Therapy habilitation training with Claudio Lalla, doctor and psychotherapist, one of the leading experts in Italy of IADC and author of the book "Perdita e ricongiungimento," which means "Loss and reunification." It also included a practical moment playing the role of patient and psychotherapist in turn. When I conducted the IADC as a psychotherapist, my patient told me what she saw in an extremely vivid and detailed way, as if I was also observing from the inside and living all the images she recalled: it seemed a real scene that I could witness and touch. Besides, that IADC culminated in a regression to a past life, which was not planned. When I then played the role of patient, I did not experience a communication with the deceased with whom I intended to have contact. Instead, I had a completely different experience of interaction with a spiritu-al entity, which I then recognized as my own "guide," as described in Weiss, Newton and Cannon's research. My personal experience confirmed that the IADC is not conditioned by expectations or sug-gestions. I found that the state of consciousness achieved allows to "explore" a non-physical dimension, maintaining full consciousness and experiencing it with extreme intensity. This has nothing to do with fantasies or daydreams, but seems to be a way of experiencing reality on other dimensions.

There are many similarities between an IADC and the accounts of life in the spiritual worlds through an NDE or the memories recalled through regressive hypnosis to life between lives: the con-texts, the landscapes, the new wisdom, serenity and peace acquired in those planes, the deep sensation of light and love. On these as-sumptions, the IADC promotes the elaboration of mourning and the overcoming of suffering, as it is an authentic experience, bearer of a mysterious transforming power. The subject seems to have the opportunity to glimpse the beauty of the spiritual dimension that is now the home of his loved one.

As mentioned before, those who follow a spiritual path do not see physical death as the end of everything. Instead, it is a passage, a transformation of human consciousness that continues to evolve in other dimensions invisible to physical eyes. These are not only the-oretical principles of all Western and Eastern spiritual schools: they represent truths that those who have lived spirituality as a practical experience can perceive with their whole being. However, the loss of a loved one leads to a deep mystery that makes us realize that a transformation is still necessary even for those who remain on this physical plane. A step forward is necessary, realizing that the suffer-ing of mourning requires further work on oneself and a change of perspective: one sees one's humanity, accustomed to communicat-ing to loved ones through seeing, speaking and touching. When the loved one is no longer there physically, one feels the nostalgia of the ordinary communication. Precisely at this point, one has the opportunity to develop a new type of spiritual communication with those who have crossed the threshold. This type of communication is essentially based on silence and is therefore an authentic, sincere and immediate communication, which originates directly from the heart.

CHAPTER 11

DREAMS AND OUT-OF-BODY EXPERIENCES

More Than A Physical Body

The Western and Eastern esoteric schools teach us that we not only have a physical body but also subtle 'bodies'. In this case, the word 'body' is just a conventional name; these are subtle and spiritual parts that do not occupy a space as a physical body would. These bodies can be considered different existential planes and states of consciousness.

The physical body, 'soma', is what the Indians call Annamayakosha, made of matter that is energy at a denser and more solid level. Then there is the 'etheric body' or vital body, 'energosoma' or Pranamayakosha for the Indians, which is made of vital energy and keeps the physical body alive. It surrounds and permeates the physical body and its organs and it is animated by a harmonious flow of energy. It is a complex net of subtle energies that interact and infuse vitality into the physical organs. Energy flows through thousands of subtle centres called 'nadis' or 'meridians'. Seven main energy centres called 'chakras' are also recognized, which are like 'wheels' that create swirling movements. This spiritual structure is closely connected to the physical body's organs, through the endocrine system, to the point of directly influencing the state of health.

The most important energy circulation takes place along the central spinal canal, where the main chakras are located. A central thin channel is identified, called Sushumna, and two channels, one on the right, Pingala, and one on the left, Ida. These two channels are like large nadis that enter the central channel at a junction point under the navel.

Traditional Chinese medicine has a deep knowledge of this subtle anatomy and can detect the cause of organic dysfunctions starting from imbalances in the energy circulation along the meridian lines, in order to restore the energy system balance.

The etheric body also connects the physical body to another important subtle vehicle, the astral body, also called the lunar body, place of sensitivity, perceptions and emotions. This connection will be broken at the moment of death, when the etheric dissipates and disintegrates.

After death, the astral body temporarily constitutes the soul shell. The soul is in a state of sleep, as it prepares for the transition and rebirth on the astral plane to which it will have to adapt. At that point, the soul will no longer need the astral body, which was like the counterpart of the physical body. It will therefore remain as an 'astral shell' that will slowly disintegrate. This process is also known as second death.

Then the mental body, Manomayakosha, is the mental tissue formed by the interweaving of thoughts, represented in Western esotericism by the symbol of mercury.

People of the Eastern countries identify other more subtle shells: Buddhi, which is the subtlest intellect, up to the Causal Body, which is our soul and is closer to the Self-Atma, from which creativity, inspirations and intuitions arise.

Rudolf Steiner calls these spiritual vehicles Spiritual Self, Vital Spirit and Spiritual Man.

The energy layer that surrounds the physical body is known as the aura.

It is surrounded by shields that cover every point of entry, protecting it from denser energies. Lighter energies keep the body healthy, while denser energies accelerate its decay. It is like breathing: the aura inhales light and luminous energies, and exhales dark and dense energies.

Seven layers can be identified: the first three layers are the thickest and therefore most easily perceived. The first level is the one most in contact with the body, the physical aura. The second level is the emotional body that preserves all the emotions that affect the physical body and are connected to both this life and the past. The third level is the mental body in which thoughts and abilities, both related to the present and the past life, are stored. The fourth level is the spiritual body, the soul, which contains vital energy and its size depends on the individual's spiritual development. The fifth level is the body of the mental past, which contains traces of previous lives and includes the thoughts and energies stored in past lives. The sixth level is the body of the emotional past, while the seventh contains the energetic traces of past physical bodies, so also health issues.

After death, the layers that previously made up the aura invert and gradually dissolve: the first layer, which was the first physical level, is the first to dissolve. The second emotional layer is the next one that dissolve according to the emotional attachment to things, people or situations. The third layer of thoughts will dissolve at varying times. The fourth layer of the spiritual body remains unchanged, while the remaining three layers are all concentrated in the mental body of the new being, which will be born from the disintegration of that aura. It is as if burdens are removed, through a process of purification. When all the layers are dissolved, the soul will be ready for a new birth. However, the purification is not total, because 'scratches' and deeply rooted energies in the form of unresolved traumas will persist. Only spiritually evolved souls can achieve liberation in life, so as not to bring further burdens into the afterlife, and becoming able to choose independently whether and how to reincarnate in another life.

In order to understand what happens to subtle vehicles after death, we should focus on what Rudolf Steiner says in "Occult Science". After death, both the astral body and the etheric body detach from the physical body. These are temporarily united and the etheric body will let us review the life just ended in a complete picture, until the two bodies detach. The astral body will continue its journey, living experiences perceptible by the ego and taking with it everything it has experienced in the life just spent, together with the ego that is finally free to directly welcome those spiritual revelations that in life were difficult to access due to the influence of the senses. Another world and a new level of existence seem to be revealed. Subsequently, the disintegration of the astral body will take place, as the highpoint of a purification process that will mark the beginning of a new state of consciousness for the Ego, which will now be free from sense perceptions and can therefore fully perceive the spiritual world.

"After death and after having crossed the world just described, however, the man faces a world full of spirituality, which creates only satisfying desires through what is spiritual. And while what surrounds him in life communicates through the sensory organs, the language of the new environment penetrates directly into the intimate sanctuary of the Ego.

Everything that now surrounds him is full of entities, of the same nature as his own ego, because only one ego can enter into a relationship with another ego. As during life the man is surrounded by minerals, plants and animals, which make up the world of the senses, after death he is surrounded by a world made up of entities of a spiritual nature."

Steiner tries to describe the spiritual worlds with images taken from physical reality, suggesting the existence of something similar to colours and sounds, heat and light. However, the perception is different from the physical one, since every spiritual being is intimately connected to everything around him; there is no difference between inside and outside. In the spiritual worlds, thought is a concrete living reality, an active entity endowed with a life of its own.

The soul can perceive the spiritual entities, shaping forces that formed its bodies. At this point, they will work on the essence of previous lives, which is like a germ. Here they will create a new astral, etheric and physical.

"The unborn self and the spiritual hierarchies of the cosmos have been working hundreds of years to prepare the spiritual blueprint of the developing body."

"The astral body is then guided by certain entities towards a pair of parents, who will provide it with the etheric body and the suitable physical body. From this moment, an intermediate state of transition begins, during which the man falls into a state of unconsciousness, which will be interrupted with the reappearance of the physical organs. In this period, when there is no state of consciousness, the new etheric and astral bodies begin to reconnect with each other, to later allow the man to be reborn in a physical body.

[...] before the connection between the astral body and the vital body is made, something extraordinarily important occurs. During the previous life, the man created disturbing forces, which were

revealed to him during the purification process and which acted as
a counterforce to the development of his own Ego. Returning to
physical life, the Ego is faced again with these obstacles, this time
in the form of an image of the future life, with the obstacles that
he will need to overcome, if he wants to progress. This becomes
a new starting point: the image of the pain inflicted on others in
the previous existence becomes a strength; coming back to life,
this pushes the Ego to undo this pain. The previous life thus
influences the new life. The causes of the events of the new life lie
in some way in the previous life. This direct correlation between
the past existence and the new one constitutes the law of destiny,
or Karma."

There is a close relationship between spiritual worlds and the physical world of Earth, because disembodied souls are not only concerned with the preparation for their new life — they work spiritually on the physical world, profoundly influencing it.

According to Steiner's science of the spirit, the Earth, with all that is material, has gradually developed from a spiritual essence, so the origin of matter is spiritual and it remains its essential basis. However, the man cannot see the spiritual essence, since he is more focused on sensory perceptions. According to Steiner, if the human being develops his faculties of spiritual perception, he could not only perceive the spiritual worlds and recover the memories of his incarnations, but also recover the memories of the events of the Akasha — the spiritual heritage in which all the events of the world are imprinted; understanding how the Earth was born, following spiritual events that occurred in the very distant past. The Earth seems to had had different 'planetary incarnations', in more subtle and spiritual forms, which Steiner described in his "Occult Science", recognizing different evolutionary stages of which the Earth would be the fourth, when the spirit has now condensed into matter.

The Mystery of Dreams

During sleep our brain emits delta waves, the same emitted in a coma, when a person is close to death. However, we do not fear sleeping, on the contrary, often we are happy to go to rest. During sleep, a deep part of us persists, a consciousness that continues to exist without interruption.

Rudolf Steiner believes that it is crucial to understand what happens during sleep, in order to understand the true nature of waking consciousness. He describes the sleep process as the separation of the astral body/self from the physical and etheric body. The activity of dreaming is actually the expression of an experience in the spiritual dimensions, disguised under images and contents related to everyday sensory reality. When we dream, we translate spiritual experiences into images taken from ordinary life experience, because we are unable to perceive those contents in their original form. In "Occult Science" Steiner writes,

"This means that the astral body, when we are sleeping, exists but in another state. In order for the human Self and the astral body to also have a conscious perception, it is necessary for the astral body to be united with the physical body and with the etheric body. This is precisely what happens in wakefulness. During sleep, on the other hand, the astral body has a different form from the usual one and super sensible knowledge has to consider this other form of existence. [...]

During the sleep phase, the astral body lives in the universe, outside the physical and the etheric body; this is the same universe from which man himself originates and in which man is harmoniously incorporated. During wakefulness, he moves away from this harmony and returns to physical perception; during sleep, again the astral body returns to its homeland, bringing back renewed forces for man."

During sleep, the physical body and the etheric body are still connected, so that the astral activities continue, while the astral body and the Ego lead a different life.

There are different types of dreams, such us ordinary, lucid, or of the 'clear light' in which one experiences that state of special consciousness of the rigpa, non-dual consciousness.

In the dream, the subject can come into contact with an infinite source of information, becoming receptive to paranormal events such as clairvoyance, that is, knowledge of events that occur at times and places different from the subject's ordinary context. Moreover, precognition phenomena often occur, namely the perception of future events. These are also known as prophetic dreams and we have ample traces in history, for example in Cicero's "Somnium Scipionis".

Ancient history offers us an extensive documentation of prophetic dreams, 'diviners', in which the dreamer could have visions of events that then occur some time later. This does not mean that the future is predetermined; however, in the present, 'seeds' of primary causes of any eventual future situation are formed. The secondary causes of the manifestation of these seeds are instead linked to contingent circumstances; however, we have the possibility to change the secondary causes, and for this reason we can change our destiny at any moment.

In addition, telepathy phenomena are possible in a dream, that is, the transmission of thought between two physically distant individuals. Finally, in the dream it is easier to communicate with the deceased, as our consciousness reaches the spiritual dimensional planes.

Dreams could promote healing from physical or psychic disorders, or they can even teach, because in those dimensions we come into contact with spiritual beings and with all the treasures of knowledge and mind.

The dream is rich in meaning and can become a real path that leads to the deep self. It reflects wakefulness and everything that we will be carried with us after physical death. What is realized in a dream will influence waking life, as we work deeply with the karmic traces, developing a pure, detached consciousness, an empty space that will begin to detach from the appearances of thoughts and the life of the senses. Between dream and dreams there is a mysterious empty gap, the 'clear light' that will be found after death, and which is a union of 'emptiness' and awareness. If you acquire awareness of dreams, preparing yourself with appropriate meditative practices that aim to channel prana into the central channel, you will achieve the goal of becoming aware of the 'clear light of sleep'. When you fall asleep, a process similar to that of death takes place: the white male essence flows from the head to the heart, while the red female essence rises from the lower part of the body towards the heart, until they meet and cause a momentary loss of ordinary consciousness. The training of the dream consists in regaining a state of consciousness and lucidity.

Once lucidity is conquered in a dream, it becomes possible to carry out out-of-the-ordinary experiences, such as travelling to known or unknown places, moving from one place to another, exploring other planets and dimensions, flying, meeting disembodied spirits and guides, transforming objects, having creative inspirations on works of different kinds, or transiting in the state of 'astral projection', seeing the body from the outside. The most important experience will be getting to know the true emptiness and the 'natural state' of the mind.

The spiritual traditions of Tibetan Buddhism and also those of Hinduism, Taoism and shamanism have developed different systems to work on the dream and make it 'lucid'. In this regard, for those who wish to delve into the subject, please refer to my work "Paths for the Spiritual Search".

The dream can become a real path that brings us back to our deepest essence and promotes our spiritual development. We can draw inspiration, insights and wisdom from dreams and navigate the difficult path of life.

For a practitioner of spiritual development techniques, the dream becomes a source of teachings and a door to explore new states of consciousness, dimensions and worlds.

According to Tibetan Buddhism, masters pay great attention to dreams during the spiritual training of their disciples. The Tibetan lama Tenzin Wangyal Rinpoche in his work "The Tibetan Yogas Of Dream And Sleep" has provided detailed instructions on the practice of dream yoga. Tibetans consider dream to be very important, because they are deeply connected to the waking reality and intimately connected with 'karmic traces' that determine the events and destiny of one's life. In the dream, deep aspects of consciousness emerge. According to Tibetan Buddhists, during the dream the prana-energy is brought into the central channel of Sushumna, which they call Avadhuti, as it also happens at the time of death. Dreams are produced by the movement of this karmic prana.

This practice aims to transcend the illusion of ordinary dreams and awaken awareness to rediscover the true nature of the mind. This awareness does not only concern the dream, but the whole life: it will be realized that dreams have the same illusory nature as waking life, and that behind everything there is a true reality, an empty nature. All phenomena are empty and reality is like a dream. Everything is projection of the mind, everything is caused by karma.

"When the dream state dawns, do not lie in ignorance like a corpse. Enter the natural sphere of stable presence. Remember dreams and turn illusion into

brightness. Do not sleep like an animal. Practice in order to combine sleep and reality," the Tibetan lamas say.

According to the Tibetans, the practice of dreaming is not an end in itself, having instead the function of integrating all moments in sleep, dream, wakefulness and bardo with the 'awareness of clear light.'

For this reason, exercising awareness in dreams means preparing to be aware at the moment of death, when one will cross the bardo. Developing awareness during waking through spiritual practices makes it easier to become aware of one's dreams, that is, to wake up within a dream. We can compare ordinary life to a dream state: we are constantly immersed in projections, fantasies and conflicts, we are the victim of fears and habits, we are driven by impulses without knowing who we really are. Ordinary dreaming is nothing more than a reflection of our waking life and it brings us more into contact with unexplored dimensions of our interiority and deep aspects of ourselves, giving us information about any karmic knots that need to be untied.

The process of falling asleep has always been mysterious, despite the physicochemical theories that talk about substances released by the brain in the pre-sleep phase. According to the Tibetan lamas, at the moment of falling asleep, the mind loses awareness of the physical world and begins to create dream content from the karmic traces associated with chakras-energy centres, transforming them into images, colours, lights and emotions.

The ways the experiences arise are the same for both waking and dreaming: the world can be considered a dream, and emptiness is its essence. According to Tibetan Buddhism, waking, like dreaming, has no substance: an illusory projection that can have no real power over the subject. The attachment to these projections, both in dreaming and in waking, would incessantly create karma.

The practice of dreaming is therefore based on the development of awareness, on mind-stabilization and prana in the central channel. With spiritual practice, dreams will acquire greater clarity and meaning, while still retaining remnants of projections and karmic traces. The goal is to achieve the 'dreams of clear light': a state of consciousness free from dreams, images, thoughts, projections, duality, beyond karma and beyond space-time. It will be possible to transform everything we see in a dream and experience the countless possibilities that other dimensions offer, influencing the waking life in mysterious ways. In dreams, we often live complex situations, from both an energetic and psychological point of view, and the work done will then be reflected on the waking life: we will transform it.

We will begin to consider waking experiences as transitory and conditioned by mental projections, as if everything we perceive were part of a dream. Attachment to such projections will thus be reduced and one's reactions to life events will change. We will understand the meaning of our karma as an endless cycle of cause and effect, noting how the past create the present by conditioning it. In their dream yoga, the Tibetans use the figure of the 'tiglè' of different colours to maintain consciousness at the time of falling asleep. As we detach from sensory perceptions, we will connect to these symbols, until we touch pure consciousness.

One of the results of this practice will be to fall asleep maintaining the state of full consciousness, directly entering the dream state, aware of being in the dream.

The dream will become a conscious experience at different levels of lucidity. At the beginning, there will be a vague feeling of being in a dream, but without the possibility of influencing it. There will be occasional flashes of lucidity, which will then leave room for moments of unconsciousness typical of ordinary dreams.

There will then be further levels of lucidity, up to an incredible intensity.

What is most important in the dream experience is the development of awareness. The dream can become an opportunity to access different worlds and dimensions, getting to explore other aspects of what is real.

Awareness of the state of 'natural light' is also a basic condition for becoming aware in the dream state. This would explain the similarities between the practice of dreaming and the states that the practitioner will cross over the edge of death.

Australian Aborigines believe that the dream is real, perhaps more than waking life. It is also a processing in symbolic form of the information and experiences lived in the waking state, so that the soul can obtain information from it. In dreams, communication takes place between the soul and the unconscious. This adds interpretable and applicable meanings to the ordinary reality of space-time.

Dolores Cannon explains that during the state of sleep the soul works, and this seems a kind of training. Our body sleeps, but our soul never sleeps because it never gets tired, so it does not need rest. During sleep, the soul can go to any place on Earth and of the spiritual dimensions and can communicate with guides and teachers. In the spiritual planes so much work is done, but we do not memorize it, except through dreams that do not faithfully show the original contents of the experiences.

We get out of the body every night, when the body is tired and sleepy. But the spirit never sleeps. While the body does, the spirit goes on with its life, going where it wants, flying around the world and other planets, and returning to the spiritual worlds to receive new instructions. It is connected to the body through a silver thread, and it comes back when we wake up, forgetting for the most part the adventures lived in the spiritual dimensions, often disguised as ordinary dreams.

However, there are dreams that are so lucid and vivid, that they seem more real than ordinary reality. Often we need to categorize it as 'dream' and distinguish between dream and reality, imagination and the real world of everyday life. The reason is to guarantee the stability of the world in which we live.

When we are asleep in the dream state, free from the chains of the body-mind, it is easier for a deceased loved one to manifest, because our consciousness is more receptive and momentarily devoid of turbulent thoughts and emotions. In dreams, we can also meet guides, teachers and fellow souls who are often willing to offer solutions to our problems. We live experiences that would be unusual on the earthly plane, precisely because we visit the spiritual worlds or live intense memories. It is often possible to obtain clues about details of existential projects established during the life between lives, often in difficult periods.

The souls of the most experienced deceased would even be able to alter dreams and appear in the dream of the person with whom they want to get in touch. This kind of dream is characterized by such intensity and vividness that it seems more real than the events ordinarily experienced in waking life, precisely because they are. According to Michael Newton, there are two different kinds of contact in a dream: in the first one, for skilled souls, the soul of a disembodied person enters the mind of the one who is sleeping and dreaming, and partially changes the dream. In the second one, the even more experienced soul is able to create a dream, weaving the images according to the message it intends to communicate. In this case, it is necessary that the soul knows how to connect with the person's exact energetic imprinting and that the dream is cohesive and meaningful.

The deceased is always ready to get in touch with their loved ones on Earth, even if they have already reached the highest layers of the spiritual worlds. These contacts can take place in particular environmental contexts associated with their memory.

In dreams, we can find traces of memories of past lives. Comparing dreams with regression to past lives, Bryan Weiss notes that in dreams, about 70% of the content consists of symbols and metaphors, 15% are distortions, while the remaining 15% correspond to actual memories. In hypnotic regression, on the other hand, 80% consists of actual memories, 10% are distortions and the remaining 10% are symbols and metaphors.

OBE: Out-of-Body Experiences

The out of the body experience makes people touch the true nature of awareness independent of physical reality, a unique tool to explore our multidimensional reality.

During an OBE, which is also called 'astral travel', 'lucid projection' and 'mystical journey', the physical body is in a state of deep rest, while the consciousness is perfectly lucid and awake. Consciousness is perceived as if it were outside the body, as if it had a second non-material subtle body and the possibility to explore other worlds, even different from the ordinary one. This subtle vehicle, called by esotericists 'astral body', seems to have very particular abilities.

Several benefits related to this phenomenon have been recognized: promotion of well-being, loss of fear of death, improvement of interpersonal relationships, promotion of health, greater understanding of life and one's own purpose. In these dimensions it is also possible to meet deceased relatives or friends, or spiritual guides, and observe the spiritual dimensions that await us after death. The out-of-body experience fosters spiritual and moral growth. The subject can access information and memories not contained in the brain, living very significant experiences.

Leaving the body is a natural event that happens every time we fall asleep, but we are not aware of it. Dreams would be just memories of out-of-body experiences distorted by projections.

The out-of-body experience can happen spontaneously, often in a sleepy state, or when the subject has just woken up. This unexpected situation manifests itself with shrill whistles and feeling something that forces the person out of the body, as if they were slipping away and floating.

This is precisely what happened to me when I lived an OBE for the first time, after three years of spiritual practices. As I told in "A Mystical Journey: Meeting with Extraordinary Masters, Magicians and Shamans," I did not seek this experience:

> *"On an autumnal night, before falling asleep, I practised the concentration on the fire element, as usual. After the practice, I drifted off to sleep. Suddenly, the sensation of some inner and shrill whistles woke me up. I was awake, totally conscious, but my body was paralysed. These shrill whistles pervaded my consciousness. At that moment, I knew I was before a threshold, as though something 'parted' from me. I had no idea about what was happening to me, but I experienced a deep and undefined terror. I got the distinct impression of fainting, ending up in a vacuum, sliding away, almost like dying. I clearly felt I was partially detached from the physical body. I did everything to stop that unknown and terrifying feeling of 'sliding' and, only after some efforts, I managed to establish again a contact with my body. The whistles stopped and I came back in the ordinary state of consciousness.*
>
> *This had been my first contact, as I knew afterwards, with the consciousness of the 'astral body', that is commonly identified as OBE, or Out-Of-Body experience, 'astral projection'.*

I had already heard about it, and actually I had read a couple of works dealing with it, but I had never considered appropriate the attempt of living this experience.

After few days, I happened again a similar experience. I went to bed earlier than usual and, attained a state of deep relaxation, shortly before falling asleep, at the moment that I heard the whistles, I got again the instinct to halt the experience and cling to the pillow. But, at some point, the 'sliding' overshot and I perceived like being detached from the body. I found myself floating in my room. I passed through the walls and then I ended up outside. I did not know what was happening exactly: it was not a mere lucid dream, but something different, because, shortly before, I was in a state of wakefulness and straight after I found myself 'elsewhere'. And what surrounded me corresponded to the ordinary world, with some alteration and above all, a different brightness. It dawned on me a thought related to Satiel. A movement followed that thought, a jolt: my consciousness went after the thought until the place where indeed Satiel was spending the late evening. I saw Satiel having lovey-dovey attitudes with a girl that recently hanged around with the group of friends we used to meet in a pub. The day after, I told Satiel my experience and he was very astonished. 'I guess you're making progresses. I'm really amazed,' he said, and then he confessed me that what I had actually seen was true! I would resume the 'OBE' speech when my fate would have taken me to the magic meeting with the 'Castaneda's warriors'.

[....]

But that day that I found myself gazing at my physical body from the outside, it was a breaking point, a point of no return. I was lucid and I was in my room. Everything perfectly corresponded to reality, furniture, the chair, the books, and the bed where... I was there. Me? But I was outside, or better my consciousness! In the bed, there was my body and I saw it from outside, one meter far. It was there, inert. For few moments, I had a rush towards my body, as I wanted to touch it, I brushed it with my 'invisible hand', but

I perceived a sudden surge of agony. I turned and, after crossing the walls, I flew off."

Such an experience could instil fear or even terror, evoking the atavistic fear of death and activating the body's natural instinct for preservation.

Then out-of-body experiences can occur, forcibly induced by an external factor, some of which fall into the phenomenon of NDEs, as a result of trauma, accidents, heart attack, anaesthetic and surgical procedures, drowning, illness or drug use. As we have seen, in such cases, the subject is close to their own body. Finally, there is a type of OBE experience that can be developed at will, through techniques that can be found in different books. Once the experience is there, the challenge would be to maintain consciousness and not slip into dreamless sleep or a non-lucid dream. It is also important to remember the experience, because the brain does not always record what happens in an OBE, and in any case such memories are not always accessible. Extra-physical memories are not always transferred into physical memory circuits.

What is the difference between dream and OBE experience? Both experiences belong to the same state of consciousness, but the modality changes. When we dream, we are already naturally 'out of the body,' but we are not aware of it. If we have a lucid dream, we are already out of the body and we begin to be aware of it. On the other hand, the OBE experience that takes place from the waking state or from the sleeping state has a very different dynamic and is characterized by an intense level of lucidity. Lucid dreaming occurs when in the middle of an ordinary dream we realize we are dreaming. These can be considered as the intermediate stage between an ordinary non-lucid dream and the OBE experience, and can become a stepping stone towards lucid projection. A special threshold makes us understand if we are still in a dream that, although lucid, is still affected by subjective projections, or if we are lucid and in full consciousness in the astral plane. In the latter case, we clearly perceive that we are outside the body and have the opportunity to see it from there. During an OBE, we have full mastery of our ordinary identity, all memory is intact and the mental-logical faculties are sometimes even of higher intensity than those experienced during wakefulness.

Among the scholars of the OBE phenomenon is Dr. Waldo Viera who, after years of research, founded the "Projectiology." He collected different information about OBEs from different parts of the world and found out that this is a universal phenomenon, which is an intrinsic part of human nature. Countless cases of OBE are described in different civilizations, including China, Japan, Egypt, India and Mesopotamia.

The astral body is the energy body when it is outside the body; when it is inside, it constitutes the aura. It will leave the body at the time of death, but at that point it will not be able to return to the body. When we live, the astral body is connected to the physical body by a silver thread attached to the crown chakra. It is not a real thread, but seems a magnetic-energetic connection. The astral body carries consciousness. It can pass through physical obstacles such as walls, ceilings, floors and doors.

The astral body has clarity of thought, clear perceptions with high awareness of the environment, is able to make decisions, distinguish and choose between different options, is able to control, remember past events, act according to ethical and moral principles. The astral body can fly, is changeable and can change shape at will. It is invincible, cannot feel pain, hunger or fatigue, and does not need to breathe.

The astral dimensions perceived by those who travel there, have been created by the energy of thousands of consciousnesses, which brought to subtle structures of houses, buildings, mountains, roads and cities. These structures are made of energy, which are no less real than what we experience in the physical world. During the exploration, we can move towards specific places or people, or reach unexpected places.

There are a lot of spiritual entities in these dimensions. The extra-physical population is nine times larger than the intra-physical one. In recent centuries there has been an increase in the physical population on the planet. This does not mean that new consciousnesses have been created, but simply that the proportion has changed.

In those dimensions there are many guides willing to help us. We are connected with them and have a link with them from past lives. We could also meet new guides who can give us insights into the type of activity we are doing in life. The helpers are at a higher evolutionary level and show us deeper aspects of reality than those we can see in physical reality.

Another researcher of the OBE phenomenon, Robert Crookall, a British geologist, scientifically examined the evidence that some people leave their physical body and travel with an invisible 'thin body'. He analysed 700 accounts and testimonies of out-of-body travel from different parts of the world. Despite the different cultures to which they belong, there were clear concordances.

However, the American engineer Robert Monroe is one of the most important researchers in this field, and I have already had the opportunity to mention him as he had carried out research together with Dra. Kubler Ross. He founded the Monroe Institute which deals with research on human consciousness and began his career doing research on the effects of different types of sounds on human consciousness. When he underwent an experiment, he experienced for the first time a spontaneous OBE, that is, he felt that his consciousness had separated from the physical body. That was the first of many experiences, which he detailed in the book "Journeys Out

Of The Body." With his team of researchers, he then began to work on a method to induce and control this kind of experience in a scientific context. They developed the Hemi-Sync technology, a method that alters the state of the brain through sounds. Monroe states that through OBEs it is possible to explore non-physical dimensions, even those where souls live in the afterlife. Through his OBE experiences, he accumulated a vast amount of information, identifying different levels of the subtle extrasensory world. The C1 is the first level which is the ordinary physical world perceptible through the physical senses. This level is surrounded by the 'Focus 22,' where we can find the consciousness of those who are in a coma or those whose consciousness is not fully on the physical plane, such as drug addicts or alcoholics. This level surrounds the Focus 23, inhabited by the deceased who, however, are not yet aware of their state. They are near the Earth and are upset because they are not perceived by the people who still live in the physical plane. Then there are Focus 24, 25 and 26 with groups of souls gathered according to the religious beliefs shared in life. This is like the paradise of all religions, something beyond the illusion of religions, faith, dogmas and beliefs. In Focus 27 there are several activities; often from here the souls choose to guide those who are still alive. From here, we can decide whether to return to physical life, reincarnating to continue from where we left off.

CHAPTER 12:

BETWEEN SCIENCE
AND MYSTERY

"The day science begins to study non-physical phenomena, it will make more progress in one decade than in all the previous centuries of its existence."
(Nikola Tesla)

Beyond the Boundaries of Science

"When paradigms change, the world itself changes with them. Led by a new paradigm, scientists adopt new instruments and look in new places. Even more important, during revolutions scientists see new and different things when looking with familiar instruments in places they have looked before. It is rather as if the professional community had been suddenly transported to another planet where familiar objects are seen in a different light and are joined by unfamiliar ones as well."
(Thomas Kuhn)

In his work "The Structure of Scientific Revolutions," Thomas Kuhn has carried out a historical analysis of the development of scientific thought and the assumptions on which it was based. He focused his attention on scientific revolutions, which consist of paradigm changes, seen as a set of beliefs shared by a scientific community, which include the type of language, the type of problems analysed and the means of validation. The paradigm includes different principles and methodological procedures acknowledged by the scientific community of a given era.

A paradigm is "a philosophical and theoretical framework of a given scientific school within which laws and experiments are formulated." It is a pattern of ideas that researchers refer to when they do their studies.

The scientific community consists of scientists who share the same vision, assessment criteria, methods and interpretive models typical of the paradigm they share. The paradigm is like a disciplinary matrix, which includes symbolic generalizations, metaphysical beliefs, value judgments on theories and solutions used as models.

According to Kuhn, official science is based on the results achieved by the science of the past. These are basic principles that are not questioned; therefore, they are considered the essential basis for subsequent procedures and are expected to be constantly applied and reconfirmed. The shared principles of official science regulate the measuring tools used in the research activity and are closely linked to the system of concepts typical of the accepted paradigm. However, the official paradigm requires the presentation of ever-new results and intends to dissuade any activity that is contrary to the dominant scientific view. Every subsequent result must necessarily be a reconfirmation of the effectiveness of the paradigm itself. Kuhn says,

"Aristotle's Physica, Ptolemy's Almagest, Newton's Principia and Opticks, Franklin's Electricity, Lavoisier's Chemistry, and Lyell's Geology — these and many other works served for a time implicitly to define the legitimate problems and methods of a research field for succeeding generations of

practitioners. [...] Men whose research is based on shared paradigms are committed to the same rules and standards for scientific practice."

Kuhn hypothesizes the possibility of a crisis of a consolidated paradigm and therefore a period of transition to a new one. This could occur if new and unexpected events take place, which represent contradictions and anomalies with respect to the dominant paradigm. Despite attempts to adapt these new phenomena to the rigid structures of the paradigm in crisis, people will realize that it is no longer effective in explaining and interpreting situations that contradict previous certainties. The dominant paradigm will therefore be considerably weakened.

This process cannot save its integrity — it must question it to its foundations; the old paradigm must not project itself onto the new one with all its limitations and expectations, *"the proponents of competing paradigms practice their trades in different worlds. [...] The two groups of scientists see different things when they look from the same point in the same direction."* A total paradigm shift is therefore necessary, and it does not have to be controlled or conditioned by the previous assumptions. The old paradigm will even have to be falsified. The new one must not confirm the results achieved by previous scientific theories but must have the courage to abandon all the pre-established assumptions. It must be able to explain all the phenomena previously explained by the previous paradigms, but it will not be obliged to follow the previous dogmatic theories. There will be a revolutionary break that will entail the abandonment of the old paradigm, with the acceptance of a new way of conceiving the world.

Kuhn argues, however, that mainstream science tends to reject evidence and findings that challenge the dominant paradigm. It seems an instinct of self-preservation of consolidated certainties.

But revolutions in science can happen if a new model or a new perspective is created. A turning point is necessary to progress towards horizons that would have been previously inconceivable.

The current dominant paradigm in science is the materialist paradigm, based on the findings of Newton and Descartes. According to it, the only elements that exist in the universe are matter and energy, which can be transformed into each other, as expressions of the same substance. It follows as an axiom that spirit does not exist, despite the evidence that there is something beyond the physical dimension. Instead, the spirit is mainly seen as mere religious mysticism, from which science must be distinguished or even defended. Academic science, shared by the scientific community, believes that something is real only if it is measurable by instruments or technology. The rest would not be taken into account, as it is neither scientifically detectable nor demonstrable. But if an instrument cannot detect something, this does not necessarily mean that it does not exist. The current scientific paradigm depends on the use of instruments and this leads to deny any kind of non-physical reality. This is clearly a limiting approach.

How can we reconcile with the official scientific paradigm the fact that a subject, which should be considered a mere agglomeration of chemical-biological components that 'produce consciousness', manages to heal from a physical or mental health problem, through the evocation of the causes dating back to past lives? How can all paranormal phenomena, out-of-body experiences, near-death experiences and everything related to the afterlife be explained? Another paradigm could be considered — this would include not only matter and energy, but also extra-physical consciousness. In the absence of instruments that can detect and study our extra-physical nature, anyone who adopts the paradigm of science as the basis for his research should be both the researcher and the subject on which the research is carried out at the same time.

Sceptics dispute the impossibility of using the quantitative method typical of official science to study psychic phenomena. Official psychology does not use this method. All the experiences described above are accounts obtained from testimonials.

Science usually starts from a reality based on an objective physical phenomenon and does not give credit to subjectivity made of thoughts, intuitions, actions, feelings, but emphasizes objectivity, with obvious data and measurable phenomena.

But such a materialistic analysis does not consider the nature of our awareness and therefore the possibility that consciousness is experienced independently of the physical body.

The discovery of steam and electricity was also initially considered a chimera. However, the utopia of the past becomes the reality of the present, just as the utopia of today could become the reality of the future. Nowadays, those who propose new theories different from the official paradigms of science, are subjected to mockery, instead of burning at the stake, going to prison or exile. Official science is accepted because it has been learned since school and, despite the obvious complexity of the mystery of existence, hypotheses about the origin of the cosmos are considered mere philosophical questions. The universe is seen as a machine that operates on its own, which is originated by a sudden explosion called 'Big Bang', supposedly occurred 13.8 billion years ago. This model would be precise and credible. The universe would be composed of elements that are not endowed with an internal intelligence nor are they guided by an external intelligence. So everything would be produced by physical forces such as gravity or electromagnetism. The evidence is that we are aware in a complex world that we call the 'universe'. However, we should also be aware that only 1% of the cosmos is detectable by our telescopes, while the rest is unknown to us. The limit of current scientific cosmology is that, in its attempt to explain the cosmos, it keeps the observer strictly distinct from the observed universe. This is instead questioned by the models of quantum mechanics, as we will see later.

In the past, science underestimated human testimonies; for example until the beginning of the 9th Century, science denied the possibility of meteorites falling from the Earth, despite the popular legend that spoke of rocks falling from the sky. At that time, scientists argued that it was impossible for rocks to fall from the heavens. It was only when two professors from Princeton University witnessed a meteorite falling that studies on the subject began. For this reason, if a phenomenon is not recognized by our current scientific methodology should not rule it out a priori. This could be instead an opportunity to approach new concepts and new discovery methodologies.

The Horizons of Physics

"The invisible universe is a great reality. This is where we all belong and where we will return one day."
(Oliver Lodge)

"Matter is spirit, it is its most sublime expression."
(G. Bruno)

Traditional physics believes that only what can be observed, replicated and demonstrated in relation to visible or measurable particles is real. It is also believed that man can be a mere external observer, detached and distracted from the phenomena he observes.

Aristotle believed that the universe was a single entity in which all parts are interconnected. Everything is animate and has an innate life. Several Greek philosophers believed that the universe was eternal and that it never began. Time does not actually exist, but we perceive it as we become observers of what exists. Parmenides considered time an illusion: reality is timeless and everything is one. All this was discovered several centuries later by quantum physics.

The traditional Newtonian physical paradigm states that time is part of the fundamental structure of the universe, constitutes its own dimension, and is separate from events. On the other hand, according to an alternative paradigm, such as the Kantian philosophy, time is only a category-structure conceived by human beings to organize the information that comes to mind from the external world. The idea is that there is an independent physical universe 'out there', which has nothing to do with our awareness and knowledge of it.

In 1920, a new theory shook the world of physics: Quantum Theory, which redefined the nature of matter, revolutionising our understanding of the world. According to this theory, the world of atoms is far from being understandable; subatomic particles do not follow any path that can be predetermined, they are unstable and unpredictable. What seemed to be a solid and concrete world would be nothing more than a confused agglomeration of incomprehensible and unpredictable particles.

In quantum physics, the rule is the discontinuity of the phenomena of the atom, with the 'discontinuous quantum leap' at the subatomic level, the world of the infinitely small. As a result of this quantum leap, however, matter may no longer be matter turning into a wave. The consequence is that we cannot control nature at an atomic or subatomic level, as Vernon Heisenberg theorizes with his uncertainty principle. According to Heisenberg, it is impossible to distinguish the observer from what is observed. We see the universe as full of objects, which sometimes interact with each other and yet are separate, but on a subatomic level they are actually deeply connected. Consciousness seems to be more real than physical existence, as well as its indispensable basis. The observer and the observed create a single dynamic system.

David Bohm laid the foundations for a physics that approaches spirituality, discovering the 'quantum potential' and theorizing the existence on a subatomic level of something that is under all things and that is actually a single and united fabric, the true essence of everything that in the physical world would seem separated into individual particles or systems.

Max Planck observed that electrons absorb and emit energy, with a specific quantity defined as 'quantum.' He states that atoms can make specific movements between orbits and each time they change position they must transit from one specific orbit to another, without finding a transition space between those orbits. Electromagnetic energy could only be emitted in a 'specific quantity,' which was later confirmed by the Danish physicist Niels Bohr. He believed that all atoms behave this way and that if stimulated, they emit packets of light, called 'photons.'

Massimo Corbucci proved that two electrons that do not come into contact continue to communicate with each other even if they were in very distant places from each other. Corbucci believed in the existence of a 'quantum-mechanical vacuum' and believed that in every atom there is a 'fragment of God', a root cause of life. Atoms are 'shells of a bottomless abyss' that makes them communicate with each other from anywhere in the universe.

A fundamental concept in quantum physics is the 'non-local space' of invisible probability waves, which contains no matter and influences everything, as the basis of force fields that affect the physical world in space-time. Everything that can be perceived by the physical senses would therefore emanate from the invisible. It can be said that non-local space influences the physical world at the quantum level, but it cannot be measured.

Quantum particles can know the states of other particles and instantly assume a behaviour related to them. Quantum entanglement experiments support this theory, as physicists John Clauser and Alain Aspect demonstrated between the 1970s and 1980s, finding that the behaviour of particles is coordinated at speeds even faster than those of light. These principles are based on 'non-locality': no local effect can be the cause of coordination between particles. In this situation, the two particles will share the same wave function equation.

The particles are simultaneously in several states at the same time, until they are observed. Their spin, that is, the quantity that defines their quantum state, is not yet explicit, until it is observed and measured, as if the particle selected one of those superimposed states. Each state is linked to a probability and after different measurements, it will be possible to predict the average result. This probability, however, will still be exactly unpredictable.

Until it is measured, each particle's spin is partly upwards and partly downwards. When the measurement takes place, a 'collapse' upwards or downwards occurs, while the twin particle collapses in the opposite spin. The particles seem to communicate with each other through means that move faster than the speed of light.

The basis of the quantum entanglement theory was the discovery of the formula of photon counting by Leonard Mandel and the demonstration that independent photon beams have an interference: the quantum entanglement of photons. It was thus possible to detect the quantum properties of light, throwing a new perspective on its nature.

Separated particles influence instantaneously each other: if we measure the spin change of two particles generated from the same source, then separated and fired in two different directions, a reaction between particles will occur, without a direct influence.

For example, in a crystal, a purple photon is transformed into two red photons and each contain half the energy of the original purple photon. These two photons share a wave function: if we observe one of them, its wave function 'collapses', that is, it ceases to be an indistinct object and becomes an actual entity that materializes. The same is true for the twin photon, although it is at a considerable distance. The twin photon expresses complementary properties: if one of the two has the spin upwards, the other will have it downwards.

In 1997, Nicolas Gisin, a research physicist from Geneva, created pairs of 'entangled' photons and threw them along optical fibres, in a place about seven miles away from each other. The researcher placed a mirror in front of a particle, which was induced to make a random choice, whether to take one direction or another. The entangled twin at a distance instantly imitated its choice, but in a complementary way. This experiment was then improved by researcher David Wineland, with the use of beryllium ions. But how is it possible for one material object to instantly affect the existence and behaviour of another object at such a great distance?

"There really is a kind of frightening action at a distance," Wineland concluded.

In 2010, Stephen Hawking said, *"There is no way to remove the observer – us – from our perception of the world."*

There seems to be an underlying, invisible reality that connects all parts of the universe, and in which there is no separation. This dimension creates events that materialize in the space-time of ordinary reality. Space and time are created by awareness, which coexists with objects.

"The synthesis of the quantum paradigm is: there is no object in the world that can be isolated."
(Emilio del Giudice)

The wave function is typical of non-local space: a thing that can become a particle by entering a physical world. Here it is clear that matter is made of consciousness.

The phenomenon of 'spectral action at a distance', as defined by Einstein, can be interpreted by assuming that, when a subatomic particle takes a property among the alternatives, it seems to create an alternative universe. With every possible change in the properties of each particle, an infinite number of universes are potentially created. It can be hypothesized that there is an unknown force that determines such phenomena and that completely different principles are involved: a super-determinism that compromises the possibility of discovering any true principle using scientific methods.

According to Bohm, all particles in the universe would then be in entanglement with each other, and the behaviour of one particle would affect all other particles in the universe, even at great distances. All particles share a single wave function that underlies the evolution of the entire universe. John Bell states, *"Bohmian mechanics makes explicit the most dramatic feature of quantum theory: quantum non-locality."* This non-locality would be based on a wave function that connects distant particles into a single reality. Two particles in entanglement act in a correlated and coordinated way, despite the distances, because they are part of the same thing. Everything in the universe seems to be part of the same thing, as mystics mean when they say, "we are all one."

Currently, academic physics accepts the experimental findings of quantum entanglement, although no consensus has yet been reached on the implications of these results in relation to the nature of reality. Until the 1970s, researchers, prompted by Einstein's mistrust, were still divided over whether quantum entanglement was a real phenomenon. However, with the development of new experimental technologies and courageous researchers, quantum mechanics has thus been shown to correctly describe physical reality.

According to quantum physics, everything is interconnected. Emil Schrödinger says that what we perceive as material bodies are variations in the structure of physical space. Matter no longer plays a central role. Based on these perspectives, a particle can have different speeds; according to the principles of quantum mechanics, the speed is opposite to that of space-time in the physical world. When observation takes place, the multidimensional non-local space is reduced to our three-dimensional physical world. This is how observation reduces the infinite possibilities. The wave function has endless possibilities.

Space is for the most part made of a vacuum permeated by magnetic and electric fields, and of photons of all kinds, neutrinos and gravitational waves. In 1998, dark matter was discovered, which pervades everything and prevails in the spaces between galaxies. According to Heisenberg there could be no total vacuum.

The distance between bodies is not as real as it seems: if distant objects can be in contact despite their distance, this means that information can cross the universe without limits of space or time. This vacuum-energy seems to have great power. Provided that there is a correlation between the observer and the universe, 'outer' space would be part of a continuum of awareness. Nothing is detached from the observer.

In ordinary reality there is space and distance, but in a dimension without space-time and matter, everything is in direct contact with everything, as there are no distances. Everything that exists seems to have a soul in direct contact with the soul of everything else, in a field of interdependent forces.

At the subatomic level, the vacuum is full of energy and has numerous movements of quantum microparticles that are continuously created, transformed, destroyed and then recreated.

The 'non-local space' could be interpreted as a hidden and invisible spiritual reality that would influence our physical world. Moreover, the modern theories of psychoneuroendocrinology state that our invisible consciousness constantly influences our physical body.

Quantum theory notes that in the micro dimension, the basis of everything that exists in the macro-reality we perceive with our senses, particles do not behave predictably.

Everett's 1957 theory of the many-worlds interpretation notes that multiple different, arbitrary and unpredictable movements can occur with each movement of an atomic or subatomic particle. Each of these movements is in fact happened. Therefore, beyond the universe that we experience daily, there would be infinite and parallel universes as real as ours.

There Is An Invisible World

The String Theory, a name coined in 1970 by Leonard Susskind, Holger Nielsen and Yoichiro Nambu, based on the mathematical model of Gabriele Veneziano taken from data collected by particle accelerators, suggests that the universe is made up of tiny strings, i.e. vibrating filaments similar to strings. This theory seeks to fuse Quantum Physics with the General Relativity Theory. According to it, all subatomic particles are one-dimensional strings, that can be open, with their ends that do not connect, or closed, i.e. closed loop. This theory detects other dimensions, namely ten dimensions, of which nine are spatial and one is temporal.

The interaction between the strings would explain how the four main forces of nature – gravity, electromagnetism, the strong nuclear force and the weak nuclear force –, create a 'unified theory of everything.' The different strings' vibrations produce different properties of the particles. The universe could be considered as a vibration of energy that creates particles. This theory seems to describe matter and vibrating energy as if it were music. Each string vibrates differently, i.e. protons vibrate in a different tone than electrons, electromagnetism will vibrate at a unique frequency, compared to the strings that make up the nuclear forces.

The physicist Brian Greene says, *"Just as different vibrational patterns or frequencies of a single cello string create what we hear as different musical notes, the different way that strings vibrate give particles their unique properties, such as mass and charge. For example, the only difference between the particles making up you and me – and the particles that transmit gravity and the other forces – is the way these tiny strings vibrate. Composed of an enormous number of these oscillating strings, the universe can be thought of as a grand, cosmic symphony."*

He continues, *"According to string theory, strings vibrate at precise frequencies that create the 4 dimensions you and I call height, width, depth, and time. We live in these 4 dimensions and know them well. But String Theory describes an additional 7 dimensions beyond our ability to perceive."* Physicist David Gross of the University of California at Santa Barbara says, *"It's like we stumbled into darkness in a house that we thought was a 2-bedroom apartment and now we find out there's at least one 19-room villa, and maybe it has a thousand rooms and we're just starting our journey."*

Suddenly, the idea of an invisible world is not so hard to believe.

The subtle body, with the chakras and energy centres, works according to vibrations: the subtle energies are like filaments that vibrate providing nourishment to the spiritual life. Our spiritual part is formed by spiritual atoms and particles that unfold like vibrating filaments. Vibration is the basis of life and produces different results in different contexts. String Theory gives us a new understanding of ourselves as embodied beings: we are made of energy and are in a universe which is actually not as solid as it seems, but is itself energy in motion.

There is a remarkable parallelism with Vedic Indian cosmology – there are countless universes in addition to the one we know and at the basis there is the Universal Supreme Consciousness. The physical dimension that we perceive through the senses is not the only one – there are also multiple subtle dimensions which vibrate at frequencies not perceptible by the physical senses. Indian Vedic cosmology distinguishes three types of worlds in the universe: the physical world, the one perceived by the physical senses, the astral world, the world of subtle forms and thought, and the causal world which is the realm of divinities. In the astral and causal worlds, further subplanes are distinguished according to the level of lower or higher vibrations.

Similarly, String Theory would assume the existence of multiple worlds and dimensions, because three or four dimensions are not enough for strings to realize all their vibrational patterns.

With quantum mechanics and String Theory, a changing and fluid reality is discovered that shows the properties of indeterminacy. The tiny string-filaments can become anything: a particle, an electron, a wave, and so on. When an energy interacts with other energies, it can be transformed. This is true for both the universe and humans, since thoughts, emotions, and intention are energy. We are made of quanta and strings, of invisible energy capable of transformations and changes.

Our physical body and consciousness are deeply interconnected with each other and with the entire universe and they unfold in multiple subtle realities and dimensions that exist beyond the material world. A complex universe can be seen, but it is basically a single field that underlies all forms and phenomena. What seems distinct and separate, actually reveals an intrinsic unity of a unified field. When we are in altered states of consciousness or deep meditative states, we can perceive this deep union with everything that exists. The root of the multiplicity of everything that exists is a unique and infinite reality, which has the nature of pure consciousness.

What makes up matter is far from defined and solid: subatomic elements are not defined particles located in space and time at all – they are fields of probability. Until a particle is observed and measured, it has no real physical state, but is only an abstract probability wave. There is a relationship between the observation of an observer and the existence of physical matter, and consciousness seems to be deeply linked to matter.

According to Eastern philosophies, the waking experience involves three elements: the observing subject, the object being observed, and the act of observation. These three factors are actually the same thing: the consciousness that is linked to the different parts that make up reality. According to quantum physics, when we observe the wave of a particle, we become aware of a reality. However, all other possibilities still exist as alternative worlds, with different quantum outcomes and potentially infinite situation developments.

Our conscious experience of the world, as well as the limited measurements made by scientists, would be nothing more than a very small part of the reality. Everything seems to consist of spiritual energy of quantum fields flowing and interacting with each other. As the Western and Eastern esoteric traditions state, everything that exists consists of energy with different vibrations, lower if it is physical matter, higher if they make up the spiritual worlds. Therefore, all beings, objects, phenomena differ according to their vibration frequency.

The double-slit experiment, which shows that reality is much more than what we can see, aimed at investigating the properties of light. In particular, it was intended to investigate whether light was composed of particles, as Newton stated in the 17th Century, or of waves, as Thomas Young hypothesized. Thomas Young's experiments showed that light behaves more like a wave than a particle. In that experiment, a light source illuminates a plate pierced by two parallel slits. The light passing through the slits is observed on a screen behind the plate and its trajectory is studied. A light separated into multiple brightness lines is displayed on the screen and this indicates that the light is moving in waves that interfere with each other during their journey to the screen. A wave of light passes through each slit, which overlaps the other at several points, with an interference that increases or decreases its strength.

This experiment was crucial to demonstrate the theories of quantum mechanics, according to which subatomic elements behave both as waves and as particles. The experiment was replicated with subatomic particles of electrons and it was found that electrons interfere with each other, behaving like waves. It has been found that electrons behave like physical particles when observed, but otherwise they behave like waves.

Fred Alan Wolf, an American theoretical physicist, has studied the nature of consciousness in relation to quantum physics, seeking a common ground between the contributions of physics, psychology, physiology, spirituality and mysticism. He accepted the theory of quantum physics, according to which phenomena have no continuity, unlike classical Newtonian physics which identifies their continuity with the perspective of gaining control over nature.

Wolf believes in the existence of something higher than the physical plane, which influences the events in it. This would be the spiritual side of reality. Matter can only be understood if one transcends the materialistic point of view, to identify an invisible field of possibility beyond space, which determines consequences that will then become visible in the physical plane. Moreover, as it is not possible to see with the eyes a magnetic field, similarly there are many things that our ordinary physical senses cannot perceive.

Our soul and everything that has to do with the spirituality of a non-physical and non-material universe have a reality. These assumptions would explain the origin of out-of-body experiences, all based on the non-material dimension of realities. According to Wolf, the soul can be perceived if we detach ourselves from the physical reality and sensory perceptions. There is spiritual intelligence that guides everything in the universe. The soul was born together with matter; however, since it is not subject to the laws of physical matter, it can travel at a speed beyond light. This would provide an explanation for the feeling of travelling through a tunnel, experienced by patients who have had an NDE.

According to the physicist Giuliana Conforto, all Western and Eastern religions believe in a single origin of the whole, the only living and intelligent substance, invisible and eternal. Physics would confirm it, particularly with regard to the first moments of the birth of the universe, according to which the universe would originate from nothing as a Big Bang.

Contemporary theories of physics suggest the existence of a single 'Higgs field' from which all types of particles originate, both physically visible and invisible. From the Higgs field, the different non-physical dimensions would originate.

Humans can only see the solid material part of this single substance, which would control only 51% of everything that, while invisible, is nonetheless essential. The modern theory of everything, formulated by Edward Witten, which includes quantum mechanics based on the Superstring theory, confirms that the nuclear particles of quarks are microscopic black and white holes. These would be the particles at the base of 'light bodies.' Conforto distinguishes between the classical electromagnetic field and another field defined by what the human body registers as psychic contents, sensations, emotions, feelings and dreams.

The electromagnetic field, which can be seen through the instruments, includes light and communicates images, colours and frequencies. The human eye perceives only a very small part of this field; instead, x-rays, gamma rays, ultraviolet rays, microwaves and radio waves are invisible to the human eye.

The dark mass, discovered in the 1960s, does not emit or absorb light, does not interact with the electromagnetic field, cannot be observed directly, and contributes to 90% of all existing matter. Dark matter seems to follow supernatural laws.

Several particles from the Higgs field do not make up bodies, in particular twelve particles, of which only four make up the universe that can be perceived through the physical senses and biological bodies. There is life not only in the world that our senses can perceive: a substantial void that is continuously evolving, made of incessant movements and invisible particles, space-time collapse, field fluctuations, infinite dimensions made of waves, impulses, sounds, vortices in continuous evolution.

The body and the psyche can be defined as two layers of the same thing.

According to these perspectives, it is nothing more than a dissolution of the bonds between the physical body and the light body. The biological physical body would only be the mortal reflection of an eternal light body.

The unique substance is first and foremost Consciousness.

Quantum physics believes that consciousness plays a crucial role not only in experimenting, but also in creating the reality we perceive on a daily basis.

The new frontiers of physics are uncertainty and possibilism. There are no isolated systems: the individual field of everything that exists interacts with that of everything existing. The reality of things cannot be seen only with rationality. Everything in space-time has a soul, which comes from a non-space-time and is connected to every-thing that exists.

There is an absolute field of 'pure information' which can be asso-ciated with that of 'God' – pure intelligence with which everything is in constant contact up to its own cells. Every human being is a potential source of new information, both for himself and for the divine absolute field.

The universe seems to be a non-space-time reality that contains 'non-local' information, i.e. not located in space.

Since 1996, Dr. Stuart Hameroff, director of the Center for Con-sciousness Studies at the University of Arizona, and physicist-math-ematician Roger Pen, have been working on the formulation of a theory of quantum physics, based on the hypothesis that there is no real separation between 'inside' and 'outside' of us, and that con-sciousness is everywhere at the same time. Consciousness would not be limited at all by the body and the physical senses.

The Reality Of The Soul

Life and consciousness are central, as Robert Lanza's biocentrism states, one of the most important scientists in the world. They are characteristics of the universe. We cannot understand the cosmos without understanding consciousness. We cannot see the cosmos as a mere collision of atoms. There is no universe without perception, because consciousness and cosmos are the same thing. Conscious-ness cannot be explained exclusively by physical events; by its nature, it is non-physical.

The chemist Lavoisier said, "Nothing is lost, nothing is created, ev-erything is transformed." Life has no beginning or end – it changes shape, first appearing then disappearing, but never losing its essential form.

A 'body' could be seen as a complex of energy created by the soul, composed of several layers that correspond to a particular density of existence, with each ray of one of the seven rainbow colours, as the origin of every manifestation of the universe, both physical and non-physical.

Then there is a 'mind' as an energy complex that connects the 'body' complex with the spirit and allows the soul to work as an individual unit. The spirit is the point of connection between the individual soul and the universal soul, which includes other souls. These three parts are indissolubly interconnected and one cannot exist without the other.

Souls can be compared to photons that make up an invisible field that permeates all space. Each photon is connected with the others and influences their evolution, creating matter and antimatter, thus bringing both the material and the invisible-spiritual aspects into manifestation. The photon seems to be the elementary part that is then at the base of the subatomic particles. It would be possible that the universe was formed when photons, led by spiritual forces, began to attract each other, forming subatomic particles, atoms and molecules, and then manifesting in the natural elements. The basis of the universe is spiritual.

Einstein discovered that matter and energy are the same thing and, with his equation $E=mc^2$, he implies that matter is energy in the solid state. The energy produced is equal to the mass times the speed of light squared. Pure energy is abstract, like a cloud that can be considered to assume a physical body. This energy can be considered as photons with a certain vibration that, in case of slowing down, causes a condensation into subatomic particles, forming atoms, molecules, cells and various forms.

Roger Penrose, an English mathematician and physicist, Nobel Laureate in Physics in 2020, demonstrated the extreme probability of the existence of black holes, developing models that describe how they work and behave. Together with Vahe Gurzhadyan, he elaborated the Conformal cyclic cosmology, which describes the cyclic path of the Universe, whose end corresponds to the beginning, projecting towards eternity. Together with Hameroff, he elaborated the theory of 'Quantum Consciousness', also called 'Orchestrated objective reduction', hypothesizing that unknown quantum phenomena are at the basis of consciousness. These would occur in the microtubules of neurons, which are small intracellular structures in the form of very thin tubes. These structures work in a state of 'entanglement,' which allows the generation of an act of consciousness in consecutive intervals of about 0.3 seconds. Anirban Bandyopadyay, from the National Institute for Materials Science in Japan, later discovered the actual existence of quantum reactions in the microtubules of neurons. Penrose hypothesizes that human consciousness is independent of the body and could therefore survive the death of the brain: the quantum information of consciousness cannot be destroyed, by virtue of the law of conservation of energy and information. While not abandoning scientific rationality, Penrose aims to explain NDEs, without denying such phenomena.

On the other hand, Lanza conceives the afterlife as a dimension parallel to the ordinary one. He believes that the survival of the soul is a scientific fact. Our brain is like a computer where the software of our consciousness is inserted. When the computer stops working, the software continues to live and can be inserted into another computer – a new body with a new brain. According to Lanza's biocentrism, death has no meaning in itself. When we see the body of a deceased, we feel that our loved one is no longer there. When he was alive, asleep and unconscious, we still felt his presence. There is a vibrant and conscious quality. We are not our body: the body dies, consciousness does not. If space and time are categories of our mind and do not exist regardless of who observes them, there is no

space-time in which a body dies. There is no space-time for an energy to be dissipated and for this reason it is always alive.

George Meek searched for evidence of the survival of the soul,
studying Filipino spiritual healers, discovering the importance of
energy in healing processes, an invisible energy that plays a very important role, yet is ignored by official science. He tried to explain the
existence of a spiritual world, using the electromagnetic energies and
radio frequency technologies.

The frequencies of the spiritual world would be subtler than those
of radio, electricity and light and therefore are not only invisible and
not perceptible by the physical senses but also by ordinary appliances. Meek tried to build an instrument capable of tuning in to these
frequencies, the 'Spiricom' in order to initiate a form of 'trans-com-
munication,' with interesting results.

*"It isn't that the world of appearances is wrong; it isn't that there aren't objects
out there, at one level of reality. It's that if you penetrate through and look
at the universe with a holographic system, you arrive at a different view, a
different reality. And that other reality can explain things that have hitherto
remained inexplicable scientifically: paranormal phenomena, synchronicities, the
apparently meaningful coincidence of events."*
(Karl Pribram)

Michael Talbot, author of the book 'The Holographic Universe',
says, *"We should put aside our fears and come to terms with the way the world
really is. For in a holographic universe, a universe in which all things are just
ghostly coruscations of energy, more than just our understanding of time must
change. There are still other shimmering to cross our landscape, still deeper depths
to plumb."*

Talbot's work was ahead of its time, with ideas linking quantum physics to the wisdom of ancient traditions. The holographic theory of the universe sees the whole in every part of this hologram. In a holographic universe the concept of 'space' is illusory, as things and objects are not placed in a precise place, and everything is non-local, including consciousness. Talbot extended his holographic theory to past lives, introducing the concept of 'resonance.' It is possible to find traces of one's past lives not only from psychological or emotional problems, talents, habits and ways of interacting with people, but also in details such as preferences, personality, non-verbal language, facial expressions, food and clothing preferences.

Regarding the disembodied entities that may manifest during the patient's trance state, Talbot believes that further research is needed to establish the authenticity of such information. However, such information and words from these entities provide interesting working hypotheses regarding the existential questions of all time. If all this were really authentic, this would be a really crucial discovery, forcing human beings to restructure their image and the image they have of the universe. From a holographic point of view, overcoming the conceptual barrier of space-time, it would even be possible to hypothesize that, in a non-temporal dimension, several lives are happening at the same time. Therefore, these would be 'adjacent lives' instead of past lives, and it could happen that one of these lives has a greater influence in emotional terms. It would not be a linear time, but a circular one. According to this perspective, past and future lives, although distant according to a chronological point of view, would be close as a psychological presence and coexistence.

The anthropologist Eric Wango believes that future lives influence our behaviour, as a subject could have access to knowledge related to the future. Phenomena such as 'circular situations' could occur, when a precognition of a future situation creates or adds something to a present event, creating a circular pattern between present and future. It is like a 'retro-causation' situation, since time is a continuum in which past, present and future occur simultaneously and the future could therefore influence the present. The reaction would anticipate the action – the opposite of Newton's law, "for every action in nature there is an equal and opposite reaction." The cause of a present event could therefore lie in the future.

The past would still exist and the future would already exist, as the physicist Hermann Minkowsky said in 1908: as if the universe were a fixed block with the illusion that time flows, but actually it is still and the past, present and future coexist in the 'now.' This block, however, is not immutable and everything can be changed. These hypotheses would take us very far!

Claude Swanson, a physicist at the Massachutes Institute of Technology, has come to the conclusion that paranormal phenomena are real. There are levels of reality made up of finer matter than that of the ordinary physical universe. These deep levels of the universe allow us to glimpse forces and principles different from those known to official science. Science should no longer deny consciousness and spirit, but consider the true spiritual nature of reality. Swanson also acknowledges the importance of dark matter that makes up much of our universe.

According to quantum physics, there is no reality until it is observed. Without an observer, energy cannot take shape. The observer is the soul that becomes co-creator of different forms and layers of photons that then make up the three parts of body-mind and spirit in different measures, according to the evolution level. The universe is made of photons that vibrate at different frequencies; the soul is considered as an 'evolved photon' that uses a spiritual and material body to experience life and evolve progressively. The vibrational frequency makes the difference, considering the flexible and dynamic nature of the soul that will adapt to different levels of evolution. The soul-photon contains the most important characteristics of God. It is like an individual spark of God, in different proportions according to the level of consciousness, from minerals to the human being, up to evolved entities of a spiritual-angelic type. The more it evolves, the more the soul can increase its identity with the God-Absolute. The vibrational frequency creates different densities, higher for space-time, lower in the spiritual dimensions of life between lives.

So the soul is our true nature, as a spiritual being that experiences life through a body. The physical dimension that we can perceive with our five senses is one of the dimensions of a multidimensional universe. There are other dimensions that are invisible and important, since these influence our lives.

Quantum physics acknowledges the existence of an invisible side of the world, that cannot be perceived by our physical senses and cannot be measured by our instruments. Countless energetic entities have no physical mass, yet they have a life of their own and are not subject to the laws of ordinary physics and the limits of space-time.

Our senses can perceive only a limited part of the reality that surrounds them and the four dimensions of space, height, width and time, that is, the context in which energy manifests itself through a physical body.

The manifestation of the soul in space creates matter, which in turn generates time. In the space-time reality, one can live experiences that would not be possible in the spiritual dimensions. Here the soul can identify itself in an identity, modifying and evolving according to a temporal perspective. With a temporary physical body, the soul can be enriched with information and by evolving can participate in the evolution of the universe.

Current knowledge of quantum physics suggests that consciousness and memories are stored as 'wave functions' in a 'non-local space.' The mind can be considered as a quantum process; the connection between consciousness and the brain is a quantum physical phenomenon.

The foundations of quantum physics, such as wave/particle complementarity, entanglement, non-locality and probability waves, are important to understand the true mind-brain relationship and therefore NDEs, to be considered as an instantaneous exchange of information in a dimension without space-time.

Can the laws of quantum physics be applied to living beings? Living beings are made of regularly coherent systems, which, however, could sometimes detect irregularities and instabilities. A living system can be defined as an organized chaos, with patterns induced not only by an external world, but by an internal world.

"Science cannot solve the ultimate mystery of nature. And that is because, in the last analysis, we ourselves are a part of the mystery that we are trying to solve."
(Max Planck)

"Hence this life of yours which you are living is not merely a piece of the entire existence, but is in a certain sense the whole; only this whole is not so constituted that it can be surveyed in one single glance.
This, as we know, is what the Brahmins express in that sacred, mystic formula which is yet really so simple and so clear: Tat tvam asi, this is you. Or, again, in such words as 'I am in the east and in the west, I am below and above, I am this whole world'."
(Erwin Schrödinger)

"Once I believed only in what is observable, repeatable and demonstrable, I had a blind faith in science. Then, I realized that it does not take any intelligence

to accept only the phenomena that someone has observed and demonstrated, which are repeatable and are described in many books. True intelligence is demonstrated when you have the courage to accept even what science is unable or unwilling to accept."
(Fabio Marchesi)

Beyond the Boundaries of Psychology

According to Jung, founder of analytical psychology, the psyche is the conscious part or consciousness, plus the unconscious part made up of the personal unconscious and the collective unconscious. The Self is a psychic function that puts the subject in contact with external and internal reality, allowing them to be aware of it and adapt. It is the centre of consciousness, but it constitutes only a part of it, since the psyche is a greater whole that includes factors that escape ordinary consciousness. And here Jung introduces the concept of the Self, which represents the unity of the personality considered as a whole with its conscious and unconscious parts. Self-realization is the ideal goal of Jungian therapy.

The concept of the Self has always been the subject of several disciplines, including philosophy and psychology. The personality includes a conscious and an unconscious part, so the Self includes dimensions that do not always fall within the scope of experience. Here there are lights and shadows, and the Self represents the higher principle of the individual, the nucleus of the psychic personality, the psychic structure that expresses the person's identity and uniqueness. It allows us to think and perceive ourselves.

While the Ego is the centre of consciousness, the Self is the centre of the psyche, which represents the whole personality. It also has the function of guiding the psyche towards its development and the achievement of full awareness of its psychic totality. The Self can be seen an inner guide and we can find it in ancient philosophies:

the Socrates' Daemon in Greek philosophy, the Egyptian Soul Ba, the genius in Latin philosophies and the Self in the Indian spiritual tradition of yoga.

According to Jung, the ego undertakes an individuation process, gradually approaching the Self, seen as the inner core. For this to be possible, an expansion of consciousness is necessary, which is achieved through the integration of unconscious contents at the level of consciousness. The Self is considered both as a guide and as a goal of the identification process. Expanding consciousness means reaching a state of awareness that can lead to understand those parts that are not yet known. This will give meaning to one's own existence, as the process of becoming the Self brings the subject into contact with his personality.

The Self communicates with consciousness through dreams, symbols, fantasy, as it uses a symbolic universal language that goes beyond the ordinary physical world, exploring other abstract dimensions. In this way, the Self creates a bridge between the conscious world and the unconscious world. This is how the psyche reaches a state of completeness and wholeness. In this path from the Ego to the Self, the first one should be sufficiently structured and oriented towards the reality of the world.

The individuation is a dharma, an ethical task for each individual, who withdraws from the world of external projections to enter within himself. Based on these assumptions, the therapist follows the patient's path towards his self-realization, that is, the realization of the Self.

In 1939, Jung held a seminar on Patanjali's Yoga Sutras and later identified some major concepts, including introversion and immobility. Introversion leads from the external world to the internal world, so analytical psychology could be considered equivalent to Yoga, therefore a self-education to introversion. Immobility, the basis of

Eastern meditation, is what Patanjali's Yoga Sutras calls "Yoga Citta Vritti Nirodah", i.e. the suspension of the illusory production of the mind, therefore the point of transition from the Ego to the Self, which let the contents of the unconscious come to surface.

Jung's interest in the Eastern world was fuelled by his awareness of the excessive tendency of Western man to 'extroversion,' or the focus on the external world, to the detriment of the cultivation of inner life. According to Jung, Western man considers intellectual functions superior, as the belief that the Ego is the most important instance prevails. For this reason, he values the elements of Eastern spiritual traditions, namely introversion, the importance of imagination and the centrality of the Self instead of the Ego.

Jung found in the Indian tradition his model of the individuation process, which similarly to yogic psychology involves the shift of personality from the Ego to the self. The Self is a whole without boundaries, just like the Atman in Indian philosophy. This totality includes the harmonious union of conscious and unconscious, rational and irrational elements, which lead to the dimension of universal archetypes. The Self as a whole transcends the boundaries of what can be defined with the instruments of logic.

But several years after Jung, transpersonal psychology moved further away from its boundary. It tried to unite in an epistemological model the scientific rationalist paradigm with contemplative visions, in order to reach the totality of experience in the relationship between the human being and the Universe. 'Transpersonal' was coined by Roberto Assagioli, founder of psychosynthesis, who deepened the concept of the Self as transpersonal, namely beyond the boundaries of the body and mind.

The transpersonal Self seems to exist in a different sphere of reality from that of ordinary life and the biological body and is not affected by psychophysical conditions – it can influence them in turn.

Transpersonal psychology deals with the spiritual experiences and investigates those areas of psychic reality that extend beyond the individual personality, following the method of psychological research.

It is also focused on studying those transcendent inner experiences that over the centuries and in different places have been named in different ways: cosmic consciousness, mystical ecstasy, nirvana or samadhi. These experiences had previously been defined by the main psychological schools as fantasies or pathologies, or as an expression of an Ego unable to distinguish between inner images and external reality. Instead, transpersonal psychology considers these experiences very important for the human being. It has chosen to adopt paradigms that include in human development the states of consciousness induced by the techniques of the meditative traditions, trying to question the individual boundaries of human experience and to identify a structure of consciousness that could accommodate the most varied expressions and potentialities of human consciousness.

According to Charles Tart, transpersonal psychology investigates and explores human faculties and potentialities, to discover the path that leads to the awakening of the spiritual nature of each individual. Tart believes that in order to study states of consciousness, science and spirituality should be integrated, overcoming the assumptions implicit in orthodox psychology and conditioned by Western mechanism. He pointed out the limits of the assumptions on which official science is based, namely the belief that the universe was created by chance, its existence has no meaning or purpose and that only what is perceived by the senses or other instruments is real. According to official science, the researcher does not affect the outcome of the experiments – man is only his body, and consciousness is a product of brain activity, so death is the inevitable end of human life. The supremacy of reason has led us to the logic of control, banishing everything that could hinder it, such as intense emotions, altered states of consciousness, ecstasy, imagination and silence. The transpersonal paradigm with its holistic vision does not aim to deny reason, but to achieve a new integration between science and spirituality, stating the importance of inner experience in every path of knowledge. The need for this integration began from the physical sciences which, investigating matter more and more in depth, found the paradoxical nature of the universe and matter and the need to consider the state of consciousness and the assumptions of the one who investigates. Transpersonal psychology believes in the existence of 'spiritual' events that transcend sensory perception, but are just as real as measurable physical reality. Our understanding of the universe depends on our state of consciousness. Everyone has an essential intimate nature, which however is easily suffocated by social and cultural conditioning. Each individual tends to develop their own true nature or spiritual essence that is hidden under the cumbersome personality produced by education and culture. According to this perspective, consciousness has its own reality independent of matter and uses the brain as its tool. This vision promotes awareness of the interconnection of all things. Life is considered as a school, a laboratory for one's own spiritual growth and development, in which every obstacle and suffering is a stage on the path that leads to personal fulfilment. Transpersonal psychology highlights the potential of the human being and considers his healing not as a disappearance of symptoms, but as a process of rediscovery and reconnection with his totality, through the removal of all obstacles, inner conflicts, unresolved emotions and traumas that prevent him from connecting with his own self.

However, parapsychology went further and studied the so-called 'paranormal' phenomena.

Russell Targ, a physicist well known for his contributions to plasma physics and laser technology, in particular with the development of aerial laser systems for air turbulence, has carried out investigations into psychic abilities, remote viewing and the possibilities of consciousness transformation. He became interested in Eastern philosophies, especially yoga, Buddhism and theosophy, and founded a research group on parapsychology. He was intent on supporting research on ESP phenomena, stating most organizations, such as NASA, were aware of their reality. Targ believed that we are all endowed with ESP abilities, such as remote clairvoyance vision which is the ability to describe events located at a distance of space and time or the out-of-body experiences themselves. He participated in the Stargate project, funded from 1972 to 1995, which developed operational remote viewing investigations for clients of government organizations such as the CIA, FBI, NSA, the Defense Intelligence Agency and the Air Force. The results of research and discoveries on remote viewing have been published in prestigious journals such as Nature. The examples of remote viewing obtained by the participants were impressive, with precise measurements of places and details, starting only from the latitude and longitude coordinates. Moreover, the CIA had promised that it would finance the project, if the remote viewers were able to identify a Soviet place of great interest, providing them its coordinates. Clues were provided about objects that corresponded precisely to the satellite photographs, as well as particular and accurate details that would be confirmed years later. Successful missions were carried out and information was detected that could not have been obtained in any way so distant from space and time. However, Targ left the Stargate project several years before it was closed, because it dwelled more on the usefulness of missions than on ESP research. He took part in different associations and projects. Distance vision had been widely demonstrated with consistent results and the absence of any kind of methodological or statistical problem, so it was no longer necessary to look for evidence.

All these researches that wanted to overcome the limits of official science show that human consciousness is independent of the body and acts in a dimension without space and time, according to laws other than physical ones. It is therefore possible to see consciousness as immersed in a dense network of interconnected meshes. On the one hand, we are bound to the physical body and subjected to space-time laws, while on the other there is something deep within us that is not subject to space-time constraints. This is a great consciousness that can be accessed through altered states of consciousness, or dreams, and leads us back to the dimensions from which we come and to which we will return after the death of our physical body. Our consciousness exists simultaneously in multiple dimensions and is in constant contact with other spiritual beings. However, it happens to lose contact with this essential core, authentic essence, because one tends to identify with one's ordinary personality, one's personal history and the external environment, therefore with something that does not really belong to us. Getting in touch with this essence is crucial to access our resources, authentic needs, talents and transform our life. We have never been separated from the spiritual worlds, which are always here, deep within ourselves. Everything exists within us, but we need to open a window to the other dimensions.

For example, when we find ourselves not thinking about anything, yet we are actually perceiving and becoming aware of many things, in an altered state of consciousness that leads us to expand our awareness into other dimensions.

There are several different layers of reality, such as trance state levels of the physical universe; each of them has a different reality. In order to change a reality, it is necessary to leave one level and enter another. It will be necessary to change the state of consciousness, because each level has a different state of consciousness.

It is therefore clear that the death of the body is not the end of everything, because we are not the body, but the spiritual consciousness that transcends the body. We are the immortal Spirit. The mind is everywhere, because he who knows is always greater than what is known. Therefore, space, as well as time, are nothing but reflections that come from the sense of the ego. The moment the sense of the ego is overcome, we can go beyond space and time. We constantly create the world, as well as our destiny through our own thoughts that float in the 'waves of possibilities.' As explained in contemporary quantum physics, mind and matter are closely connected, creating and modifying multiple possibilities and influencing reality in every moment. There is a state of consciousness where past, present and future exist side by side, defining an atemporal state that is actually our authentic and essential state of being. From that state of consciousness, we can glimpse infinite horizons of possibilities and infinite cause-effect concatenations.

I had come to similar reflections at a certain point in my spiritual journey, as I recall in "A Mystical Journey,"

"I was trying to open my consciousness to energies and information coming from other layers of existence. My inner life became deeper and I felt more and more the connection between my inner consciousness and the cosmos. I saw reality as an energy field in a constant and dynamic change. Everything flows and changes, but deep down, I made out an absolute, unchanging and eternal level. A myriad of dimensions joined on the background of the absolute, and my consciousness seemed to lie right in the heart of this intersection! I considered more and more my consciousness as independent of my body and acting in a dimension where there were laws different from the physical ones: an unlimited consciousness dived into a thick reticulation of interconnected meshes. The key was to gain access to non-ordinary states of consciousness which took me back to perceive the dimension from where I came from. [...]

I thought about how individuals create external reality, deliberately choosing what energies they want to let act in their environment but, because of their unconsciousness, they let themselves be crushed by these forces and follow the current rather than intentionally manoeuvring them. I perceived my consciousness as connected to a larger sphere. However, the heart was still at the centre of my being, regardless of the external environment. In some mysterious way, the inside and the outside came to merge, but on levels of consciousness different from the ordinary one; therefore ordinary science could not carry out observations and experiments using traditional means. My consciousness constantly travelled through many dimensions and, according to the frequencies, thoughts, ideas and vibrations, it attracted shapes, energies and proper beings populating other dimensions. My consciousness was discovering unthinkable dimensions that cannot be described with words: different layers of reality, levels of states of consciousness of the universe itself containing a different reality. For this reason, you need to change state of consciousness. I was trying to investigate more these mechanisms, noticing the reality in my everyday life."

"In relation to what the Quantum Physics states, the observer is fundamental to build the reality, and so the universe acquires a concrete existence in relation to what is perceived. Then, are human beings responsible for the creation of the universe? Physicists have observed that, at the atomic level, the substance stays on a state of 'power' and turned into 'act' only when it is under observation. It is like the atoms were in balanced in more universes, and it is the observer with his observations and his thoughts to define what has to happen in the reality. Following this perspective, then, the concept of casualness is relativized, and it is rather incentivized the concept of 'possibility' or better 'waves of possibilities' with several, multiple, in a certain sense infinite, issues of an event. All of that is determined not only at a physical level, but, at the beginning, at an invisible and subtle level, where proper force fields exist. Therefore, I imagined all the infinite series of casualness, opportunities, choices, real 'decisional windows.' I considered the existence of the infinitude of the chances in 'median space,' and above all, the infinitude of the chances of consciousness, the proper engine, especially if combined with the emotion that allows the passage from the level of possibility to the level of reality. And this is what the quantum physicists define 'collapse of the wave function.'

I considered as thought affects reality by means of vibrations of fear or firmness, and how what you have imagined, especially if vitalized and fed by emotion, can manifest with more chances. And I thought upon the better chance to answer a prayer, in case it is strengthened by feeling and will: prayer is like a catalyst of forces that gets from the 'quantum cloud' what is requested, thought, felt and wanted. This especially occurs if more people pray and work together, and from here the sense of creating 'magic chains' where more people join for the same purpose; in such way the individual's force adds to the resultant force created by the rest of the members. And I had tried it out in person, but at long last, I could grasp the mechanisms, to then overcome them.

Also, the Quantum Physics, as well as the gnostic Occidental esoteric and hermetic doctrines and the Oriental philosophies, has come to state that what we see all around is an illusion. So you need to search for the origin of reality. What we perceive is distorted by our pattern of representation, first sensory then mental. Each single fragment of the universe would contain information about the 'everything,' both past and future, of the universe. So, I was a fragment too! By then, it was so familiar to me the notion of the existence of a multidimensional space made of many dimensions.

I realized more, as I had already started years before, the close connection between mind and substance, that creates multiple chances, influencing reality every moment. In Mexico, for example, I had already lived moments where past, present and future seemed to merge in a state beyond time. I knew, by then, what is the essential and authentic state of being. It is the personality to be restrained in space-time, not our real essence. It is from the true essence that you perform all kind of 'act of magic' that is able to modify the objective reality, because in this way you can draw from the infinite possibilities of the universe, in an unlimited flow. The whole universe was appearing as a mental creation! It was clearer and clearer the dynamic under which your thought and your dispositions call back and attract analogous thoughts due to the vibratory law and fix meetings, situations and events. Actually, in the previous years, I had had evidences about that: the situations I had faced were all products of my own thoughts, emotions, urges that had turned into energy schemes. In some mysterious manner, the world had always reflected as a mirror my inner reality."

CHAPTER 13

THE MYSTERIES OF CONSCIOUSNESS

> *"I regard consciousness as fundamental. I regard matter as derivative from consciousness. We cannot get behind consciousness. Everything that we talk about, everything that we regard as existing, postulates consciousness."*
> **(Max Planck)**

In recent years, consciousness has returned to being a legitimate subject of scientific research, in an interdisciplinary debate that involves different fields: philosophy, cognitive psychology, quantum physics and neurobiology. The investigation of different aspects of consciousness leads to questions concerning the nature of the self and the existence of non-material levels of reality, with an attitude of openness and curiosity.

Eastern spiritual traditions asked existential questions to which any human being, at some point in his existence, is destined: "Who am I really? What will I do now? Where am I from? What is my true origin? Where am I going? What is actually my destiny? What happens when we die?" The assumption is that there is something about oneself and the world that one does not yet fully know. These questions that human beings have always asked themselves have hinted at the possibility that there is something more than mere biological reality. Eastern philosophies want to approach the answer to these questions, which, however, cannot be found on a strictly rational level. Albert Einstein said, *"The intuitive mind is a sacred gift and the rational mind is a faithful servant. We have created a society that honours the servant and has forgotten the gift."*

The great Western thinking minds have been expressing different theorizations about these questions for millennia, without coming to a convincing and satisfactory answer to the mystery of life and death. For this reason, we could seek this answer on other levels of existence of being. Eastern spirituality directs us precisely towards these levels.

On the one hand, Western psychology has provided us with important knowledge about how the mind works, using a rational and scientific research methodology. On the other hand, Eastern philosophy aims to lead us to different levels of knowledge, using different types of tools.

Among the exponents of the Western rational philosophical point of view is Descartes, who with his saying "Cogito ergo sum" or "I think, therefore I am," identifies the essence of the human being with thought. A different point of view, which from rationality would like to reach intuition, is expressed by Patanjali. In his famous "The Yoga Aphorisms", he says "yoga citta vritti nirodhah," which could be translated with "Yoga is the suspension of mental activities," thus meaning, unlike Descartes, "I do not think, therefore I am."

After all, "I think, therefore I am" makes all our considerations on the existential problems of life fall on the mental activity of thought. On the other hand, Eastern philosophies make us believe that there is another dimension beyond ordinary thought.

Both Eastern and Western psychology have studied the mind, but starting from two different assumptions. Western psychology studied the psyche and its conscious and unconscious processes, with the aim of finding a certain balance, a certain form of well-being. Eastern philosophy arises from the study of subjects who have experienced states of 'super-consciousness,' that is, experiences of expanded awareness, of considerable intensity and meaning. That is why Eastern philosophy can guide us through its paths, knowledge and teachings, not only to regain a psycho-physical well-being, but to find an essential nature, which would seem to be even deeper than the unconscious studied by Western academic psychology.

Official psychology focuses more on the study of subjective experience in relation to its neural correlates and on the observation of the mind. It does not dwell on its own interiority, on the ontological principle of psychic activity, which is generally the focus of philosophy. The spirit would therefore be reduced to a mere psychic function, something subjective or arbitrary, since psychic activity is separated from the ontological and metaphysical level. In the West, therefore, a separation of psychology from philosophy occurred, so the question of the nature of experience, subject and reality has been separated from the psychological and neuroscientific approach.

Research on consciousness has raised several problems, which Francisco Varela has tried to solve by creating the "Neurophenomenology," a discipline that studies human experience in the original relationship between mind and consciousness. The experience lived is analysed with a phenomenological approach, which can interface with modern developments in neurology. He fully welcomes the results of neuroscience but believes that they must also be analysed on a philosophical level. In order to solve the problems related to the mind and consciousness, a common ground between scientists of the mind and philosophers is necessary. The experience of consciousness cannot be explained solely in terms of the neuronal system, so the neurobiological explanation cannot be separated from the lived experience, from which self-consciousness develops.

Nowadays, a deep collaboration between spirituality and science is necessary.

The Quest for Consciousness

Contemporary science must modify its paradigms in order to understand the mystery of consciousness. Consciousness is not tangible, it is not visible, but it is a more evident reality, which gives meaning and substance to our existence. Everything exists inside, outside and thanks to our consciousness.

This is the most important experience of human life, and the greatest mystery. There are many psychological, medical and neuroscientific theories about the possible connections between consciousness and the brain, but no one has ever explained how this connection actually occurs. Neuroscience does not yet know what consciousness is. No theories explain its true nature. No instrument penetrates human subjectivity. It seems to be something more than the sense of subjectivity-self-awareness. We must ask ourselves: "Perhaps, I am something more than thoughts, feelings, memories? What really shapes our consciousness? What shapes the surrounding reality?" The universe begins to appear more like a great thought than a great machine. Consciousness is not the mere product of purely neurophysiological and neurobiological processes. What is the true origin of consciousness?

It is not possible to measure or scientifically demonstrate the contents of consciousness: thoughts, feelings, emotions, instincts and the complexity of our inner world in general. Consciousness is a direct, personal, intimate expression and its reality is ineffable, yet extremely real and evident.

The brain is seen as the instrument for experiencing consciousness, which in turn communicates information to the brain and receives information from the physical senses about the external environment. The brain could be compared to a television, a transmitter that works through electromagnetic waves: an instrument of expression and not at all the root and authentic origin of the cognitive process. However, several parapsychological phenomena suggest that human consciousness could have a life of its own, independent of physical-brain support. Moreover, NDE experiences are characterized by a remarkable level of lucid consciousness, yet they occur in a time span during which brain functions have ceased, albeit temporarily.

Many scientists have begun to perceive human consciousness as a form of energy that cannot be destroyed but is susceptible to transformations into further forms of energy that continue their existence on another level.

We know that mind and brain are connected, but we do not know how and what that connection actually is. Over the years, several models have been proposed to explain this correlation, including the one that considers the mind as a product of the brain. But none of them can fully explain the true relationship between mind and consciousness. If the mind is produced by the brain, how does this happen? If the mind were not produced by the brain, where would it originate from? Any activity of awareness, perception, thought, emotion, memory and intention is followed by chemical-electrophysiological manifestations and changes. And certain mental functions are associated with specific areas of the brain. If brain damage is reported or any situation of neurological alteration is suffered, this will affect the cognitive functions. This association between brain activity and mental functions does not mean that thoughts, emotions and our inner world are the mere product of brain activity.

Research in the neurological medical field show that the brain sends electrical impulses through the spinal cord to the muscles to produce movement but we have no idea how the brain produces thoughts, emotions and all conscious awareness. The nature of consciousness is the greatest mystery of science and there are no theories in this regard, nor are there any clues as to the possibility of consciousness and cognitive activity persisting when the brain is completely inactive. The hypothesis that the brain creates the mind has never been scientifically confirmed – it is just a theory that tries to explain the association between the two parts.

Those who have experienced an NDE reveal that they perceived that their consciousness was free from the limits of the mind that manifest when the brain is ordinarily functioning. They claim to have had the feeling that their mind was once again so bound to the brain that they could no longer comprehend what they had been able to see in that other dimension. The possibility that in certain situations, our mind is independent of the brain is worthy of serious consideration and evaluation. Unfortunately, dominant theories seem to be an obstacle to innovation, since they give us the certainty of orienting ourselves in the world.

Among the different experiences of NDE, this evocation of a patient by Dr. Moody highlights the brain limitation in processing the experiences that consciousness has had independently of it:

"There were no walls or boundaries or anything solid, just light and beings. The light was like a magnet. You cannot be detached from it; you want to be with it more than anything you have ever wanted. [...] There was no time at all [...] as if you were completely present, without memories of the past, and there is no future. I had no body, only sight [...] a month later [the NDE] my brain began to work a little. I remember opening my eyes and thinking 'Shit! All I have is a human brain.' I also remember, when I went back, that I knew that as long as I'm on the Earth, I won't be able to understand that, because I only have a human brain. Here, we can think of one thing at a time, while there you really know everything."

If we assume that the mind, with its thoughts and emotions, has an independent existence from the body, we can believe that the brain filters the contents of the mind and selects only the relevant and essential information to manage our daily life situations.

John Eccles, a neuroscientist and Nobel laureate for his contribution to the study of how the connections of brain synapses work, supports the separation between mind, consciousness and brain. In his work "How the Self Controls Its Brain," he refutes the materialist theory that considers consciousness as a product of the brain, a theory that does not explain the mystery of the human Self. The brain is to be considered a tool of the self to communicate with the external world through the senses from which we derive perceptions. According to Eccles, the mind belongs to a non-material world and is composed of a more subtle substance/energy. He believes that, after death, the soul frees itself from the body and from dualistic material existence, entering a new dimension. He thinks that materialism has no foundation and compares it to a superstition held by dogmatic scientists. Scientific reductionism aims to reduce the immensity of the spiritual world to patterns of neuronal activity. *"We must recognize that we are spiritual beings with souls that exist in a spiritual world, in the same way as material beings with bodies and brains that exist in a material world."*

Peter Fenwick, neurophysiologist known for his research in the field of NDEs, studied the relationship between mind and brain and, in particular, the nature and essence of consciousness and its altered states. His research on NDEs led him to the conclusion that human consciousness is independent of the body and survives physical death. In particular, cases of patients who survived cardiac arrest were examined. NDEs occurred when there was no brain activity and no blood circulation. How else would it be possible to explain this, other than that consciousness is independent of brain support? These are not hallucinations, as these would be subjective and arbitrary in nature, while NDEs have objective characteristics. Says Fenwick, *"The evidence shows that we are more than just a function of the brain, bits and pieces of creation, and that something, whether we consider it soul or consciousness, will continue in some way, making its journey to the 'other side'."*

At this point in human evolution, we do not yet have the scientific theories, the language and methodology, to understand and reveal the mysteries of human consciousness. We do not know what really happens when patients in a state of clinical death perceive outside the body and witness events that actually happened.

Roger Sperry, Nobel laureate in medicine and physiology, urges us to give greater importance to subjectivity and mental activity, which cannot be reduced to a neuronal event and a brain process that includes chemistry, the impulse of the nerve, but not cosmic phenomena.

Wilder Penfield, a neuroscientist, spent many years trying to explain the mind based on brain function, and eventually recognized the peculiarity of the mind, which develops independently of the brain over the course of a lifetime, which is like a computer of which the mind is the programmer. The mind-spirit is free and would be active even during states of sleep and coma. The comparison between mind/body and radio and television electromagnetic fields is particularly effective: the voice does not originate from the radio and the image does not originate from the television. When these are turned off, we no longer hear/watch the programs, but the electromagnetic fields persist and the broadcasts continue even if we are not aware of them. Similarly, if the body dies, consciousness and the functioning of the mind with the set of thoughts, emotions, memories still persist.

The true essence of consciousness is 'non-local,' precisely what quantum physics studied. It is a vacuum seen as the source of the physical world, an infinite consciousness. Non-local consciousness is located in a non-local space. It is a transpersonal consciousness connected to everything that exists, in deep unity: a consciousness stored in a non-local space as a 'wave function,' with information accessible non-locally. This non-local space has no structure, no time and space. Here, quarks, electrons, electricity, gravity are all one. It is the basis of an infinite number of possibilities. It could be considered the basis, the foundation of consciousness, a metaphysical substance. Consciousness has a primary presence in the universe, it is the origin of everything.

The scientific investigations carried out in recent decades on NDEs reveal that human consciousness has an existence that can be separated and independent of the brain: the consciousness determines the functioning of the nervous system and not the opposite, as official science believes.

According to quantum physics, there is something beyond the order of the universe made of waves and particles, and our mind has a crucial role in influencing what we perceive.

> *"The ghost universe of dark matter is a template for the visible universe."*
> **(Chung Pei-Ma)**

We therefore have a visible biological physical body, based on organic chemistry, and another invisible body consisting of invisible dark matter. When the physical body dies, the invisible body survives and continues its existence on other planes, evolving and then continuing its existence in a new biological body.

The theory that consciousness is independent of the brain is necessary to explain such deep, precise, sharp experiences at a time when the brain is in a state of suspension. It challenges even the most avid materialism, which usually poses as a cumbersome and fundamentalist paradigm, which claims to be a necessary and infallible truth. A paradigm cannot be changed by a single event or experiment, but by several counter-evidences. For example, numerous cases have been reported of Alzheimer's patients who, shortly before dying, without neurological reasons, regain lucidity, recognize their family members and resume cognitive activities.

There are no scientific explanations to this phenomenon known as 'paradoxical lucidity.'

In the book "Irreducible Mind: Toward a Psychology for the 21st Century" by Adam Crabtree, Bruce Greyson and Emily Williams Kelly, the evidence of the existence of out-of-body consciousness and the authenticity of ESP paranormal phenomena is presented with rigorous scientific analysis.

If we want to know the universe at a deep level, we must realize that consciousness is at the origin of reality. Consciousness is the foundation of all that exists. Reality cannot be explained without considering it. We are all connected to the universe on a subtle level. From the point of view of consciousness, there are no limits of space and time: nothing is really far from us. We cannot see the true spiritual nature of the universe, if we think that matter is the only reality and that consciousness, spirit, thoughts, ideas, emotions are mere products of it.

Methodological Considerations

Researchers could not conduct a traditional study on near-death experiences under controlled experiment conditions, as both procedural and ethical-moral problems would arise. For the purposes of scientific research, it would not be ethically or morally correct to put a number of subjects in an experimental state of clinical death and then subsequently resuscitate them analysing their memories, because there is the inevitable risk that it is no longer possible to bring them back to life.

The collected testimonies are mostly taken from medical emergencies, when the first professional duty for a doctor is to save the patient and bring him back to life with all the means available, without thinking about prospects for scientific research. However, in such situations, thanks to the medical technological progress, it is possible to record multiple data useful for research, such as the reason why the person was in a state of clinical death, how long he remained in such a state, what were the resuscitation procedures, his vital parameters of EEG and EGK, temperature, blood pressure, what type of drugs were administered, and so on.

Greyson continued his research even though the director of the university where he worked did not approve his research on topics he considered only 'anecdotes.' Nevertheless, much scientific research began by collecting, verifying and comparing anecdotes, in order to identify common patterns. From here, the hypotheses to be confirmed will emerge, following a real scientific method. What animates scientific research is not the subject studied, but the way in which we observe and collect data and evidence. If a phenomenon is not believed to be real, this does not make the research on 'pseudoscientific.'

According to medical researchers in this field, the ideal situation would be to form an interdisciplinary study group involving medicine, physiology, philosophy, psychology, anthropology, theology and comparative religions.

Such phenomena reveal the possibility that with decreasing brain activity, the range of thoughts and emotions tends to expand. Doctor Larry Dossey says, *"We are conscious not because of the brain, but in spite of it."*

We are aware and produce thoughts, concepts, intentions, sensations, memories and imaginations. It is something non-physical, yet real: there is nothing in the brain that has the nature of consciousness, which cannot be described in scientific terms. We create and state concepts, we have ideals of freedom and justice, we cultivate an abstract thought not connected to the physical world we perceive. We see things from a personal point of view, from a centre of consciousness that coherently links all life experiences. Despite the continuous change at the cellular level, a sense of self-identity persists that is constant throughout life.

Certain areas of the brain are linked to mental functions; functional MRI results in changes in brain areas, such as increased blood flow to certain areas during specific perception or thinking activities.

Neuroscientist Richard Andersen agrees that, *"we know very little about brain circuits for higher cognitive processes."* The fact that a given conscious experience is accompanied by a specific neuronal action does not prove anything: a correlation does not necessarily imply a process of causation. The question is: how can the thinking subject, not locatable in some brain area, remains the same despite the constant change in cellular structure?

Thought seems to have priority and come before neuronal activity. Neurons do react to certain environmental stimuli, but this does not mean that they have properties of consciousness. He who perceives and experiences life seems to have an out-of-body nature. The Self is not located in a part of the brain.

The human being is body and soul, the latter in the sense of a principle that gives life to the body and gives the sense of consciousness and identity.

According to Schrödinger: *"Consciousness cannot be described in physical terms. Since consciousness is absolutely fundamental, it cannot be described in terms of anything else."*

Sir Charles Scott Sherrington, who was awarded the Nobel Prize in Physiology or Medicine in 1932, says, *"As followers of natural science we know nothing of any relation between thoughts and the brain, except as a gross correlation in time and space. In some ways, this is embarrassing for biology. We have to regard the relation of mind to brain as not merely unresolved but still devoid of a basis for its very beginning."*

The body represents only a mere fraction of what we are. Consciousness is beyond matter; every living thing is a consciousness. Consciousness controls the physical body: it is multisensory, self-aware and has a bioenergetic nature. And we are able to manifest in different multidimensional planes, because there are a large number of extra-physical dimensions waiting to be explored, and this can be done both in OBE but also when we are in the body, if we experience different states of consciousness. Consciousness is the same and it has had other lives, because it has an evolutionary nature: life after life we become more mature, complex and aware, according to the unique and unrepeatable path of each human being.

CHAPTER 14:

ESOTERIC WISDOM

"Having experienced the Infinite, we are free from death and life becomes a game of our earthly existence."
(Swami Vivekananda)

The Western esoteric traditions of hermeticism and alchemy, as well as the Eastern traditions of Hinduism and Buddhism, have given us important clues about the destiny of the soul after death, and above all about the path that the human being can take while still alive to reach a spiritual development that will lead him towards a new perspective of consciousness of the meaning of death.

According to spiritual traditions, the consciousness of ordinary human beings would not continue after the death of the physical body. We have a kind of nucleus that subsists and in which all the memories of lives are deposited, but the consciousness linked to ordinary identity still suffers a temporary interruption with the death of the body. For this reason, in subsequent lives the ordinary mind will not retain at the conscious level the memory of the experiences of previous existences. There is still a partial continuity, but this refers to something that sleeps deep down at the level of the soul. Hence, the need for a spiritual path that, according to the great masters of esotericism, aims to gain a complete continuity of consciousness.

In his "Occult Science", Rudolf Steiner says,

"From this moment, an intermediate state of transition begins, during which the man falls into a state of unconsciousness, which will be interrupted with the reappearance of the physical organs. In this period, when there is no state of consciousness, the new etheric and astral bodies begin to reconnect with each other, to later allow the man to be reborn in a physical body. In this process of connection can take part the Ego which by its own spiritual activity had developed the hidden creative forces of these bodies, in other words, Life-Spirit and Spirit-Man. So long as man has come to this point, more advanced entities must carry out this task in his place."

Steiner's words suggest important clues to what is the Great Work of the alchemists. According to alchemists, birth means coming to life in the world, while death is abandoning forms to immerse in the great sea of being. From the point of view of the Absolute, there is no birth or death, as it is only the relative personal individual in space-time who dies. What can exist instead is that part enucleated in a way of being absolute, which derives its reason from itself, after developing the consciousness of itself as Absolute.

An initiate who walks a spiritual path intends to "To die before you are dead, in order not to die when you have to die," as Sileno said, as long as it has been recognized that life is a mundane unreal representation.

The Mysteries of Alchemy

"That which is above is like to that which is below, and that which is below is like to that which is above, to accomplish the miracles of one thing."
(Emerald Tablet)

The tools provided by esoteric schools over the centuries are intended to transform human consciousness, accelerating its evolutionary process. According to Hermetic philosophy, man is a microcosm that has all the forces of the universe-macrocosm, so he contains all the properties of the kingdoms of nature.

Alchemy uses symbols to describe the evolutionary process of man. Alchemical Gold, also known as Sulfur, is the divine Self, the eternal part, the true intelligent essence that survives from life to life and is independent of the physical body.

The physical body is represented by Saturn and Salt; the lunar astral body is represented by the Moon, the lower mind under the influence of the body and the lunar astral body is the lunar Mercury, also called 'vulgar.' The higher mind under the influence of the Sun-spirit-Sulfur-universal consciousness is the Mercury of the 'philosophers.'

Metals, in particular Lead, represent the human parts to be corrected, such as desires, instincts and passions, everything that forms the ego and the false personality.

There are correspondences between these parts and the elements: Sulfur corresponds to Fire, active Mercury to Air, passive Mercury to Water and Salt to Earth.

Alchemy therefore works on all levels of the physical, etheric and astral. The alchemist must 'extract the lunar Mercury and Sulphur from the body' and then 'dissolve' the body in them, that is, transform the body into spirit. This is what Rudolf Steiner calls 'vital spirit.' Later, the lunar Mercury and Sulfur, which constitute the 'Quintessence,' the basis of the sense of existence and individuality, will 'coagulate,' so the spirit will be 'embodied.' This is the meaning of what Steiner calls 'Spirit Man.'

The alchemical work intends to transform metals into Gold, then purify the lower parts and sublimate them into a consciousness that will become a 'solar body,' a conscious and eternal spiritual body made of pure energy.

It intends to produce and maintain full continuity of consciousness after the death of the physical body. A physical body represents an opportunity, as it is the sense of self, the sense of identity, which otherwise would not be compact. The true alchemical laboratory is found in one's body and, above all, in one's spiritual essence. The alchemical vase is nothing more than the human being himself.

Alchemical work is carried out through alchemical fire, which is a state of consciousness, a will external to the psycho-physical complex, independent of body and mind, a state of purifying observation.

According to the Hermetic philosophy, the human being has in his depths a 'historical man' who has lived different lives and retains all memories, ideas, impressions and emotional states. It is the essential nucleus that contains the product of all lived existences. It is completely different from the ordinary personality and can hardly be heard by our mind, unless we learn to recognize its voice. For this reason, the system of spiritual development suggested by all esoteric schools is meditation, which aims to silence the mind. This essence voice will become our guide: as an inner master, the Socratic Daimon, who will communicate through indefinite moods, which we will have to learn to interpret. It is not easy, since our ordinary personality is distracted by the pressures of the social environment, the demands of the chaotic world, the collective psyche of humanity and worries of everyday life. The ordinary personality is shaped by the process of education, by the opinions of others, by the education received and by the social demands.

The ordinary man is not aware of this deep core that would put him in contact with the Absolute, as he is identified with his own personal individuality and passively follows its programs. He can sporadically come into contact with this core in states of deep meditation, in the state of lucid dreaming or OBE, or through altered states of consciousness.

Spiritual work aims to reintegrate this deep essence with the conscious personality, producing a detachment of one's consciousness from the chaotic turmoil of the world and a radical change in oneself. Work will be done to purify the lunar-astral body, which would usually be a reservoir of images, external impressions and memories, making it a reflection that can cleanly reflect the essence of the inner Sun. The initiatory traditions symbolize this process as a gradual 'dying to self,' because it seems to be a sacrifice to polarize one's attention on one's inner spiritual essence rather than on the external stimuli and on everything that ordinary people consider essential needs. There will be a process of 'disidentification' from one's personal individuality to understand one's true essential core, in close contact with the existential and archetypal structures of the universe. Esotericists speak of 'initiatory death' because the 'metals,' that is, the 'psychic crystallizations,' will disintegrate under the fire of consciousness, in a purification process that at times will prove painful. The outcome will be the extraction of a 'quintessence' that will be the basis of consciousness of the spiritual body.

'Fixing the volatile' for alchemists means stabilizing the consciousness of the true absolute deep essence within the ordinary individuality. The cross horizontal line would represent the material life bound to space-time, while its vertical line the infinite divine universal life.

"Do not identify yourself, by not identifying you find yourself in the universal nature," said the Buddha; this shows the close connection between Western esoteric schools and Eastern spiritual traditions.

The focus of one's being will be shifted from the individual sphere to an absolute, impersonal cosmic context that reflects one's real origin and truth. The sacrifice will bring the liberation from the cycle of rebirths, as the Eastern traditions of yoga and Buddhism state. Western esoteric traditions express the same foundations and procedures as those of the East, albeit with different words and concepts. Subtle spiritual faculties will be developed to move into other dimensions and planes of existence. One's individual consciousness will unite, in a yoga, with the Principle, the Absolute, which we can call God, Great Spirit, That, ineffable and unspeakable: it will be the awareness of the One in All. One's authentic spiritual core-essence is the bridge and point of communication between the personal individual and the transpersonal consciousness. Lead, that is, the individual personality, will be transformed into Gold, or the consciousness of the Principle. The person will come into contact with an impersonal energy field and therefore full of all the potential of the Absolute, 'empty of everything but full of all possibilities,' as the Italian alchemist Giammaria said.

The initiatory work is like a 'descent into hell,' which is nothing more than a descent into the unexplored depths of oneself, illuminating the way through the light and fire of Consciousness.

In alchemy, three stages are practised: Nigredo (the blackening), Albedo (the whitening) and Rubedo (the reddening). During the Nigredo, the conversion of land into water will take place; in the Albedo, the conversion of water into air; and in Rubedo, the conversion of land into water.

The reader does not need to interpret symbolisms that seem objectively complex, but, 'reading between the lines,' he will understand the meaning and purpose of alchemical work: to bring to light the deep part of the human being that is independent of the physical body and to form a spiritual body, metaphorically speaking. The Work consists in identifying one's consciousness with the divine

Principle when one is still alive, so that it will persist out of time and space.

In the depths of our being we have a piece of consciousness, not yet explored, which is Eternal and is in close contact with God because it is the same thing.

By creating the 'whiteness,' the alchemist will be able to have a 'body of light' that can exist without the support of the physical-Saturn. Later, there will be a further integration of the purified mercury that will join in Sulfur, when 'the Christ will become one with the Father': Redness.

Following the alchemical-hermetic symbolism, the Moon (the astral-lunar body) and the Earth (the physical body) will be separated from the Sun (the spirit-soul) and from Mercury (the mind-intellect). What is physical will be spiritualized and vice versa: the physical-psychic complex will move from the lower mind to the mercurial and solar spiritual intellect, forming an individualized spiritual body, which will persist out of time and space. This spiritual body is called 'body of glory,' or by Tibetan Buddhists 'rainbow body,' independent of physical support. From the ashes of initiatory death, the Phoenix will be born. That is why in the Emerald Tablet, Hermes Trismegistus teaches to 'fix the volatile,' that is, to fix the divine, stable and permanent spiritual consciousness in the 'volatile, falling' individual human consciousness.

"You will separate the earth from the fire, the thin from the thick, slowly with great care."

Among the alchemists of the 1500s was Robert Fludd, first a theologian then a doctor and chemist, who approached the occult sciences and esotericism, in particular the Rosicrucian movement. He specialized in the production of chemical remedies, with a mystical approach, and delved into alchemy, incorporating its ideas into his

medical profession. Fludd intended to see the spiritual world directly, both personally through ascension and intellectually, through science.

He joined a school of mystical physicians who claimed to hold the
key to the universal sciences. In the early seventeenth century, the
Rosicrucian Manifestos of the Fama Fraternitatis and the Confessio
Fraternitatis spread in Germany. According to Rosicrucian philosophy, humanity had the opportunity to join a scientific and spiritual
reform, in the name of understanding spirituality as the essence of
matter and the relationship with the Divine. It was initiatory knowledge transmitted from generation to generation and in secret to protect its integrity. Rosicrucian society held the secrets of alchemy. In
the Tractatus Theologo-Philosophicus, Fludd addresses the themes
of creation and alchemy: "the earth is dense water and the water is
dense air... the air is nothing but dense and coarse fire." He dwells
on the divine principle of man, which is considered a perfect work
of God that can return to a state of being before the biblical Fall.
Everything is together a macrocosm and microcosm and the divine
light spreads into all the realms of creation, while descending into
darkness as the lower world of the elements separates from the celestial realms. In all the realms there are beings, of a spiritual type
in the subtle planes and of a material type in the material plane. All
beings have a divine spark and a hierarchy is established depending
on how much the degree of light brings the being closer to God.
For Fludd, the universe is a series of circles that surround a centre,
God, in a concentric flow in which, however, 'the circumference is
nowhere.' God is also represented as a triangle within a circle. Within
the triangle, there are three circles representing the elemental, ethe-
real, and angelic worlds. The human being is the image of God and
is a mirror of the divine harmony that is expressed in the three kingdoms; there is deep harmony between body and soul, both animated
by divine essence. For man to rise to the contemplation of the di-

vine, he must undergo a process of purification, which will lead him to be aware of the presence of God within him.

"The divine architect who created the universe, made man equally perfect and complete, the image of his own greatness. The circle of existence has been made complete. The circle of existence that formed the worlds, formed man... what perfection the world received, which man also received. Heaven and earth have their counterparts in the body and soul of man. As the universe is one, so the body and the soul are one. Thus, man is properly called the image of God, the other world, microcosm; thus man, regularly proportioned, can be delimited by a circle, at the center of which are the organs of reproduction. Thus, man is the 'mundus minor'."

There is an analogy between the cosmic Consciousness of the universe and human consciousness, recognized as 'Christic' in the sense of perfect knowledge of the Divine Mind. The goal of alchemy is the conjunction between these consciousnesses. Man needs to have a pure heart to get in touch with high entities.

"Our gold is not the gold of the vulgar, but the living gold, the very gold of God... There is a spiritual chemistry, which purges with tears, sublimates with customs and virtues, decorates with sacramental graces, makes the rotten body and the vile ashes to become alive, and makes the soul capable of contemplating heaven and the angelic world. This is the application of spiritual chemistry [...]."

Fludd argues that throughout history, several men have devoted themselves to spiritual research. He says that the alchemical work is the separation of light from darkness, the pure from the impure; it is the key to understanding life.

"Yet some seek the tree of life, which is in the paradise of God, the hidden manna, the white stone, the white robe. Their names are written in the book of life and become pillars in the spiritual temple."

The Journey of Dante Alighieri

In several literary works, there is an esoteric message that reveals deep meanings regarding life and death. However, this message is not understandable at a rational level, but conveyed through symbols and allegories. Dante Alighieri, who was part of the secret initiatory order of The Fedeli d'Amore (The Faithful of Love), in the Divine Comedy shows us the path that the human being still alive can take to achieve a form of spiritual knowledge that aims at reuniting with the Divine, therefore at enlightenment. He reveals an initiatory path that starts from the darkness of the unawareness of the ordinary human state towards the spiritual Light. It is the same spiritual path presented by other Western or Eastern esoteric traditions.

> *"I found myself within a forest dark,*
> *For the straightforward pathway had been lost.*
> *Ah me! how hard a thing it is to say*
> *What was this forest savage, rough, and stern,*
> *Which in the very thought renews the fear.*
> *So bitter is it, death is little more; [...]*
> *I cannot well repeat how there I entered,*
> *So full was I of slumber at the moment*
> *In which I had abandoned the true way."*

The human being starts from a state of 'fall,' namely from a deviation from the only supreme divine Principle, which made him a prisoner of a world made of illusions.

In the Divine Comedy, Dante goes on a spiritual path, led by Virgil, to a symbolic 'death' of his individual self, descending to Hell, where he will meet all kinds of human miseries and face different trials. He needs to purify his soul and therefore must first become aware of his dark parts, gradually dissolving the darkness that exists within him. The 'dark forest' stands for human passions and instincts, the chains of karma and destiny. Hell includes circles that go downwards and, as you descend, you find the darkest tendencies of the human soul that hold it back in the chaos of the ordinary world, preventing it from perceiving the truth and light of the divine Principle. The adventures of the human being characterized by passions and instincts are told using metaphorical and symbolic images, which must be known and faced and then overcome and transcended. This is precisely Blackness, the alchemical Nigredo: the spiritual Fire of awareness that is able to purify all the psychic-egoic complexes that prevent us from perceiving the reality of the soul and becoming aware of our own true forgotten divine nature. It is a symbolic initiatory death, to be reborn to a different life, no longer conditioned by the instincts and passions of the ego, but guided by one's eternal inner spiritual part:

"How frozen I became and powerless then,
Ask it not, Reader, for I write it not,
Because all language would be insufficient.
did not die, and I alive remained not;"

As alchemy suggests, it can therefore be interpreted that matter is then spiritualized and Lead becomes Silver, in a process of transmutation in which light purifies the darkness.

Later, Dante will face his purification through the long path of Purgatory, with other trials that will lead him towards light. The soul begins its climb of a symbolic mountain, made of ten circular shelves, which will lead him towards the liberation and awakening of his immortal spiritual part. It is a spiritual work of introspection and purification and it will bring the spiritual qualities opposed to previous 'sins' to life. The previous burdens are gradually lightened, to make way for that light that will awaken one's true divine nature. The bonds that bind the ordinary world will be gradually dissolved, detaching from passions, mental crystallizations, ordinary thoughts and thus transforming the most instinctive energies into spiritual awareness. At this stage, the Ego chains are still lurking and there are still obstacles and opposing forces trying to imprison the soul again. The soul will have to face several trials before glimpsing the first lights of the alchemical Albedo. Dante will then ascend from heaven to heaven until he reaches the Empyrean, eternal light of God, where he will meet Beatrice, with whom he will enter into spiritual communion. Beatrice represents Light and Truth. This is Paradise, which represents the enlightenment and the perception of the Divine, difficult to express in words:

> *"Eternal Light, You only dwell within*
> *Yourself, and only You know You; Self-knowing,*
> *Self-known, You love and smile upon Yourself!"*
> *"Here powers failed my high imagination:*
> *But by now my desire and will were turned,*
> *Like a balanced wheel rotated evenly,*
> *By the Love that moves the sun and the other stars."*

Paradise represents the Redness, the alchemical Rubedo, the conjunction of the mercury-soul with the Sulfur-spirit, which represents purification of the soul now separated from the body and therefore no longer enslaved by passions and instincts. Now Dante will be able to continue his journey through the nine planetary skies that will gradually lead him to see 'the light of God.' Here, Dante will meet the angelic hierarchies and souls who can contemplate God. The divine Empyrean is described as perfect, eternal, and motionless, imparting a rotary motion to the heavens below. He moves progressively to higher states of consciousness, in a process of total transmutation of being from matter to spirit, from sleep to awakening. In the vicinity of the Empyrean heaven, Dante's final purification takes place, to make him finally ready to welcome the vision of God, described as 'very intense light.' Everything that was apparently separated is actually united in Unity. Dante penetrates into the mystery of the divine incarnation and the divine that is present in all human beings: God who made man to His image and likeness, as described in the Book of Genesis. The previous lead from Silver has finally become Gold: the awakening to one's real divine essence, the identification with one's true Self, original nature, in total harmony with God.

The symbolism and allegories described here not only suggest analogies with the spiritual path, but also with the path that the human soul will face beyond the threshold of physical body's death.

Swedenborg's Clairvoyance

Emanuel Swedenborg, a Swedish clairvoyant of the seventeenth-century, believed in the existence of other dimensions and wanted to explain how matter is closely related to spirit. During his mystical-spiritual experiences, induced by his clairvoyance skills, he had direct experience of the spiritual world, so he claimed to be able to speak with the dead. According to historical testimonies, Swedenborg gave the Queen of Sweden a demonstration of his abilities, telling her a message from her deceased brother, which revealed something whose content no one else, other than the Queen and the deceased, could ever have known. Swedenborg reveals how the soul survives death: *"After the spirit has separated from the body, that person is still alive, just as before."*

He wrote works about out-of-body experiences, providing very detailed descriptions of the spiritual worlds of the afterlife, describing the universe similarly to the description of the quantum physics two centuries later.

Swedenborg talks about life after death, describing the separation of the soul from the body: *"Man only passes from one world to another when he dies."* He tells of his experience of NDE, when he maintained the ability to think clearly, perceiving that his spirit was being 'pulled away' from the body. During this experience, he met angelic creatures, with whom he communicated telepathically, in a sort of universal language.

Swedenborg also refers to the initial confusion of the subject who does not immediately realize that he is dead, since he is still alive spiritually, with a body that resembles the physical one, but has considerable advantages, not being bound by space and time. He talks about meeting deceased spirits known in life and who will assist him in the passage to the afterlife. He also refers to the review of life, stating that every detail is remembered and there is no possibility of lying or alteration regarding the memories of the events. This review takes place with spiritual entities. Swedenborg describes the bright light, which he calls 'light of the Lord' and cannot be described in words, made of truth, love and compassion.

Assuming that spiritual entities can see, and taking into account that 'seeing' is a function that is exercised in space, one could imagine that in the spiritual worlds there is something like space, as a 'state,' not fixed and immutable like the material one, but dynamic and susceptible to changes and alterations. According to Swedenborg, space in the spiritual world is not like ours: spiritual entities can travel enormous distances in no time to reach a human being. This is precisely the idea of quantum physics: two objects are aligned and can influence each other, regardless of the distance between them.

Moreover, spiritual concepts are not so much inherent in space, but rather in the state, since they are related to wisdom, love, goodness and truth. The spiritual environment resonates and changes according to thoughts and emotions, states of love and wisdom. The similarities between Swedenborg's thought dating back to the 18th Century and the current perspectives of quantum physics are interesting. He describes the interaction between souls in the afterlife, *"The movement in the spiritual world is the effect of changes of inner states, so movement is nothing but a change of state. Since this is the nature of movement, we can see that approaching is similarity of the inner state and distancing is dissimilarity. That is why those who are close have a similar state and those who are far away have different states. The space in the sky is nothing but the outer states that correspond to the inner ones. This is also why in the spiritual world an individual is present only when it is intensely desired. This is because one person sees another in thought in this way and identifies with that individual's state. On the contrary, in case of resistance, one person turns away from another; and as it comes from an opposition of affections and disagreement of thoughts, many people can appear together in one place as long as they agree, but as soon as they disagree, they vanish."*

Swedenborg emphasizes that the interaction between two souls is based on similarities in what they love, that is, it is an emotional, spiritual state that can bring spiritual beings closer or farther away. Just like quantum particles, so spiritual beings can resonate according to their inner qualities.

The Indian Tradition of Advaita Vedanta

Advaita Vedanta is based on Gaudapada and Shankara's teachings, which refer to those found in the Indian sacred texts of the Vedas and the Upanishads. It has then evolved throughout history, up to the last century with Ramakrishna and Vivekananda's teachings.

The Advaita doctrine is based on the principle that the Absolute reality is Brahman, Existence, Consciousness, Infinite: non-dual, immutable, without attributes, without mind, without cause or effect. Human beings perceive a universe made up of many objects, bodies and minds, with different names and attributes — these are nothing more than unreal forms, overlapping the one authentic reality of Brahma. This overlap occurs because of the illusion, Maya, which is what we perceive through our physical senses. The true nature of the human being is Atma, which is identical to Brahman as an expression of the same indivisible awareness. The human being, influenced by his ignorance, believes in an external world made up of multiple objects with which he interacts. This gives rise to the cycle of Samsara and the cause-effect law of Karma. However, there is a way out of Samsara: with a long spiritual journey it is possible to achieve liberation, Moksha, discovering one's true nature which is the identity between one's Individual Self and the universal Self. Along this path, the researcher will realize that the mind is a prison and that it is nothing more than an ephemeral and changing flow of thoughts that are held together by memory and a false sense of identity, therefore it is a cause of limitation. Beyond thoughts, however, there is something else — "I am," that is the gateway to a state of pure and deep awareness that will reunite the consciousness of the subject with that of the Absolute, making one experience identity with Brahman on the realization of "I am That," reported in several works of the Upanishads.

The Atma-Brahma is like the Sun that remains untouched and unchanged if it is reflected by water; even if the water is moved or if it is reflected in millions of different bodies of water. Similarly, Brahma remains unchanged, pure, undifferentiated, eternal awareness, albeit reflected in the millions of different individuals. When the individual transcends his identification with the body-mind complex, realizing his real identity with the infinite absolute Brahma, his karma is destroyed. He will then be freed from the cycle of Samsara, thus finding the Absolute in his deepest interiority.

The human soul must go through several cycles of birth and death in order to evolve. It gradually overcomes attachment to the desires and pleasures, heading towards Nirvana, considered as the dissolution of the Self in the Absolute.

The Eastern masters believe that it is necessary to continually contemplate our divine Self-Nature and our death. When the Purusha, the being, "I am," is recognized in Prakriti, the primary manifestation, through the Buddhi intellect, becomes "I am That," expression of the divine intellect.

In the Upanishads, the identity between the individual conscious principle-Self (Atman) and the divine cosmic Brahman (Absolute) is established. This unity produces Ananda, the divine Bliss, with the attainment of Samadhi, contemplative ecstasy. Gaudapada talks about the 4 stages of consciousness — the first three are wakefulness, dream, dreamless sleep. These are affected by the limits of the mind. The fourth transcendental state of being, the Turiya, is real and marks the realization of absolute truth: it is not a fading of consciousness, nor a state of sleep, but a lucid contemplation of absolute truth.

The Turiya, which is located between a state of wakefulness, dream and sleep, between two thoughts, two breaths, is a state of being, and here there is silent awareness, extreme peace.

Meditation practices will let us know that transcendental state of Being, but above all our essential core of the Self.

The tools of this path are reported in my work "Paths for the Spiritual Search," for those interested in learning more.

At the moment of death, the Indian sages suggest that we keep in mind the words of the Bhagavad Gita, *"However, if we remember God at the time of death, we can definitely attain Him."*

> *"He who has perceived that which is without sound, without touch, without form, without decay, without taste, eternal, without smell, without beginning, without end, beyond the Great, and unchangeable, is freed from the jaws of death."*
> **(Katha Upanishad)**

Robert Lanza refers to Advaita Vedanta, quoting his individual path, when he had realized that there is really nothing in the mind, but only a flow of thoughts, memories and experiences. So we have to find the person who wants to know these things. Who experiences this? There is nothing or there is the whole universe, because we are not distinct from the rest. The universe is the Self, the true Self, not the individual reflected Self, the Self is the Universe. We do not come from the Universe — we are the Universe.

According to this perspective, there is no death, no space and time, but only life and consciousness as a single living entity that includes everything. Consciousness has neither a beginning nor an end. It is everywhere and it does not take place.

Mystery of Tibetan Buddhism: Death as a Liberation

Buddhism, especially Tibetan Buddhism, one of the most complete esoteric traditions, offers us a collection of wisdom and in-depth knowledge related to the mystery of death.

Buddhist philosophy believes that the body's nature is based on change and degeneration, and that death is inevitable. One realizes the impermanence of the body and the sufferings one experiences in life, both physical and mental and emotional: illness, pain, anger, depression, confusion, anxiety, loneliness, and so on. One is aware of the difficulties met during existence in the ordinary world, such as poverty, unemployment, political oppression, violence and wars. All human beings want to escape from suffering and evil and desire happiness. Buddhism believes that experiences are not lasting and that all things in the world are transitory. When human beings get what they wanted, they experience dissatisfaction. Suffering is incessantly generated by this vicious circle that feeds between cause and effect, between attempts to repeat certain experiences by incessantly seeking pleasure and fleeing from pain. However, one realizes that this kind of happiness is ephemeral and creates further suffering.

The Buddhist tradition has proved to be the most suitable for starting a confrontation with Western science.

Buddhism does not dwell on the relationship between soul and supernatural entities, but studies the mind and states of consciousness. The Buddha's teachings on the mind were deepened by scholars of Buddhism and meditation, for example in the Abhidhamma Pitaka, "Basket of Further Doctrine," a collection of canonical texts, which describes mental processes, including perception, feelings, attention, emphasizing the interdependence between body and mind. What appears to our senses, including the image we have of ourselves, as something fixed and unchanging, is actually a dynamic process and subject to change. According to Buddhist contemplative traditions, experience is not a predetermined event, but a flexible and changeable process. The mind itself proves to be a dynamic and changing process, of which one can become aware through practice and exercise.

All Buddhist schools are based on the four noble truths, expressed in the sermon "Setting in Motion the Wheel of Truth": suffering originates from human beings seeking fulfilment in transitory things. Ordinary life, even a pleasant and satisfying one, is pervaded by a vague feeling of dissatisfaction, due to the fragility and transience of all things. The cause of suffering is adhering to an idea of perfection or permanence, or to an alleged absolute and immutable reality. The four noble truths reveal that there is a happiness that does not depend on controlling the outcome of things and offers us a way out of human suffering, teaching us that it is possible to change the way we relate to what happens to us and within us, making possible a different relationship with transience and fragility. There is a solution to suffering: a path to follow to free oneself, namely the Noble Eightfold Path, formed by eight stages that lead to three perfections: morality (sīla), wisdom (prajñā) and concentration (samādhi). This last point is reached through right effort, concentration and precisely the 'sati,' mental presence.

In Tibetan Buddhism, the mind is described as clear, luminous and pure, and it has the potential to free itself from the obscuration that covers it and from cognitive distortions. The meditation masters of this tradition have been carrying out mental training practices for centuries, a real investigation into the nature of the mind. The practice of meditation is intended to reveal the true nature of the mind. The master (lama) is necessary, as he helps to recognize this nature, and the disciple must become more and more familiar with this true essence through the practice of techniques that will weaken the mental contents that obfuscate and obtain this purity. The natural state of mind anticipates any intervention of intentional modification of experience, as Namkhai Norbu says.

In the Sutta Pitaka, the concept of Dharma is constantly recalled, considered as something similar to an ever-growing scientific knowledge, constantly changing but endowed with methods, observations and discoveries of natural laws that were elaborated during millennia of inner exploration conducted through self-observation and self-enquiry, empirical findings of what was found during the introspective investigation of the mind.

The Dzogchen teachings harmonize with the assumptions of Buddhist philosophy, according to which the human condition is based on suffering, which is due to attachment to phenomena and desires that strengthen the existence of an ego as an entity separate from the external world. But the phenomena of the world do not have an intrinsic nature: there is a substantial emptiness behind them, a void that lies at the origin of everything that exists. The primordial state, pure consciousness, is at the origin of the entire universe, and the manifestation of phenomena is nothing more than a projection. The problem is to lose contact with one's origin and identify with external phenomena, falling into the confusion of dualism, conditioned by karmic mechanisms. According to the Dzogchen masters, all phenomena have an empty essence. Spiritual fulfilment consists in the direct experience of one's true nature. There is nothing outside, there is no external world, it is just an illusion. Once the illusion is overcome, the individual will experience their true nature: infinite mind and energy beyond the limits of any form. In Dzogchen meditation, a state of contemplation is reached in which one rests in the natural state of perfection of full and pure presence, Rigpa, which does not follow and does not reject thoughts. We must distinguish between the ordinary and rational mind from the nature of the mind, which is beyond the intellect. This practice has Vipassana as its starting point, but aims to reach even deeper levels of consciousness.

Buddhist cosmology acknowledges that there is a deep essence that is the basis of everything that exists, both Samsara and Nirvana, which has no kind of obscuration, is intrinsically lucid, pure and perfect: the Kunzhi, the Clear Light, Rigpa. It is at the origin of human consciousness and, in particular, of that pure essence of empty awareness within us, which is in the cavity of the nerve of the heart. Rigpa is what persists after physical death.

Death is inevitable, and nothing lasts forever in the cycle of births and deaths. The life of the physical body is very fragile, as it can be easily damaged by diseases, accidents and disasters. Death could occur at any time, although every human being has a predetermined life span, but an early death is not excluded. Our life-span shrinks at every moment with every breath and brings us closer to death.

Buddhists believe that human life is precious and therefore should be lived fully. It is like a gift to be valued and dedicated for the benefit of all sentient beings.

Much of the Tibetan Buddhist funeral ritual derives from the Bon religion and follows the tradition of the Bardo Thodol, which means "liberation by understanding the plan that follows death." The Bardo Thodol is a text on death written in the 7th Century, based on sources of Nepalese Tantrism but dating back to the ancient Bon religion, with subsequent additions of typically Buddhist elements. The word 'Bardo' also means what happens in life, sleep and dreams.

After death, ceremonies are performed and in some cases an effigy of the deceased is built and placed in the same place as the body. Food offerings are then made until the end of the forty-nine days of the Bardo. During those days, lamas sing day and night and read the text of the Bardo to accompany the deceased on his journey and in his visions.

The Bardo Thodol has the function both of helping the dying person to remember the nature of what will live in the bardo, and of helping those who remain alive to develop positive thoughts, avoiding retaining the deceased with their own emotional attachment. It is important that the dying person leaves behind any worries or distressing emotions.

The book describes the states through which the soul will pass immediately after death. First of all, the soul detaches from the body and momentarily finds itself in a kind of emptiness, perceiving relatives and friends close to its body. The soul does not realize that it is dead, which is why it tends to stay close to the physical, familiar places. It soon discovers the potential of being in an invisible and immaterial body, it lives a new lucidity of mind, with perceptual faculties superior to those of his physical senses. It meets other beings and goes towards the clear light, increasingly feeling light and warmth. Reference is made to a 'mirror' in which its life is reflected. There are further stages, but it is interesting to dwell on those just mentioned as they have considerable points of connection with some testimonies. Sogyal Rinpoche in his "The Tibetan Book of Living and Dying" compares the NDEs to ancient Tibetan knowledge.

According to the Bardo Thodol, 'liberation' consists in clearly recognizing that the heavens, the hells, the gods and the demons are nothing but creations of our imagination. At the time of death, one must have no desire and be aware that the visions one will see in the bardo are illusory.

According to Tibetan Buddhists, at the time of death, the body is returned to the elements that had sustained us in life. A process of dissolution of the elements connected to the physical organs takes place: the earth is reabsorbed into the water, the water is reabsorbed into the fire element, which in turn will be reabsorbed into the air, which will finally be dissolved into space-ether. At the same time, the body loses its strength, the sharpness of the physical senses is gradually reduced, heat decreases, one has visions. One is no longer able to hold breath in one's body. All thoughts are dissolved in the void space of the nature of the mind, clear light, of which we must strive to maintain awareness, bringing consciousness out of the head. Meanwhile, the karmic traces, with all the thoughts and memories, will remain near the dead body for three days.

Going into more detail in the dynamics of the bardo, it should be noted that the deceased is an actor and spectator of what he sees.

The event has form, colour and sound. The mind, which is now pure consciousness, can finally grasp the subtlest vibration of energy.

"Now that the Bardo of the Dharmata emerges in me, I will abandon all thoughts of fear and terror, I will recognize everything that appears as my projection, knowing that it is only a vision of the Bardo. Now that I have reached this crucial point, I am not afraid of peaceful or angry forms, my projections."

The first phase is a vision of nature in lights, colours and sounds. The five elements are manifested in the vibration of five colours: ether in blue, air in green, fire in red, water in white, earth in yellow. It is an immense and dynamic space, in which one has the opportunity to grasp the unity of the divine manifestation and merge into it. This is how, according to Buddhists, liberation takes place: the discovery of the Rigpa, what we really are. What we witness, we are at the same time. The doors of the Absolute open. If this opportunity is not seized, the lights will be transfigured into tiglè-spheres and we will have visions of a being who welcomes us, like God in human form, similar to our closest religious ideal, as in the experiences of NDE. The Tibetan Book of the Dead talks about forms of peaceful or angry deities, but these are only manifestations of our mind. In the third phase, these spheres of light will come together in carpets of light that will vibrate according to the various colours, giving the experience of the basis of creation, in its immense wisdom. One will still have the opportunity to free oneself by directly experiencing the meanings expressed by these lights. The lights are connected to the five dhyana buddhas of Tibetan Buddhism. The blue tiglè light is Dharmadhatu, substance, essence of the nature of being as an expression of balance and justice, expressed by the syllable Hung. Later the blue light will be transformed into white light, Vajrasattva, Om syllable, which expresses the wisdom of the immense all-encompassing divine nature. The light will then turn yellow, Ratnasambhava, So syllable, to express equanimity, purity and divine stillness. Later, there will be the red light of Amitabha, Ah syllable, shining with the wisdom of discrimination, the essence of the divine mind. Finally, the green light of Amoghasiddhi, Ha syllable, will be given way as "wisdom that does everything" and that works miracles, an expression of divine harmony.

In the next phase of the bardo, there will be the presence beyond time and space, inconceivable. Lights give way to a union and the vision of the being of light. Also in this case we can recognize the origin of the phenomena, then obtain liberation, otherwise we will be attracted to other worlds. We will regain contact with everything that we were at the time of death, except the body: personality, memories, inner senses and, as Buddhists say, samskara and klesha in the sense of mental agglomerations and karmic energy, everything that has been recorded in Sushumna. Here the life review takes place, as explained in the NDE. The importance of intention and love emerges, in a global vision and in an awareness that leads to a judgment that is not condemnation, but knowledge, which arises from within.

Then the souls go to different worlds, depending on their karma, which can be a bright and heavenly plane, called 'Svarloka', or Bhuvarloka by the Indians, or the bardic world of becoming; otherwise to the Patala Loka, which is the hell. The soul meets the 'absolute possibilities,' with the recognition of its reality, the possibility of realizing the relative in the absolute.

Those who are familiar with the spiritual practices and teachings of the masters, will be led to easily recognize and manage the bardo experiences. Untrained people, on the other hand, will perceive those experiences as manifestations of sounds, lights, and rays in the form of illusions that will arouse attachment, desire or fear. There is a difference between those who stay in the bardo and those who gain liberation. The former will go to the bardo of rebirth, seeing previous lives, familiar places and then planning a future rebirth. Those who maintain the awareness of the Clear Light, perceiving the bardo as an illusion, will get out of the cycle of deaths and rebirths. For those who practice the Dharma teachings during their lives, the experience of death is not terrible — it is an event whose steps and processes are known: they will know what to do and how to avoid pitfalls at the time of death.

Those with a firm spiritual practice have the possibility to reach the state of spiritual liberation within a few seconds of death, without going through the bardo. Various illusions are experienced in the bardic state. However, when the subject realizes that these are only a game of the mind, he can quickly free himself from them, reaching the pure state of mind. If one understands that thoughts and emotions are only illusory expressions of the mind, one will no longer follow those movements. The secret is to keep awareness alive 'in the central channel' and not be overwhelmed by the waves of thoughts.

For this reason, Buddhist practitioners practice the achievement of the natural empty state of the mind, also through the channelling of prana, of the 'winds,' along the paths of the energy centres and, in particular, of the energy centres of the spine. It is the same meaning and objective of the Indian practice of Kriya Yoga.

The Buddhist practice teaches how to control the mind, so that it is free from the influences of the thoughts that arise in it. Awareness is exercised, so that one remains present and alert, no matter what happens.

Death is therefore fundamental, as consciousness finds itself momentarily free from any attachment to the body and the world, it is empty and therefore very powerful. The smallest thought or emotion in that situation would be capable of transferring consciousness to a corresponding realm in the bardo.

Consciousness leaves its body but is not yet in the other spiritual body, it is in limbo without supports. The moment of death is a threshold and it can be a moment of liberation or suffering, depending on the karma and personal history of the subject.

The Tibetan book of the dead says that at death the state of the Absolute, the Dharmakaya of the Clear Light, will be experienced, but in the most comfortable form for the subject. A Christian will see this absolute light as Jesus, a Muslim will see it as Muhammad, a Buddhist as Buddha Shakyamuni and a Shaivite will see it as Shiva.

According to Tibetan Buddhists, if one recognizes the visions after death as illusions, one will no longer have rebirth in the material dimension.

However, this does not mean that the spiritual levels described in the previous chapters are an illusion. The spiritual planes after death are as real as our physical world in which we ordinarily live. Tibetan Buddhism, however, considers even physical life itself in the ordinary world to be illusory. In order to understand the horizons of spiritual traditions, we should make a leap from relative planes of existence — the physical world, the astral world and all the spiritual planes to which the researchers have referred through their investigations — to an Absolute plane where a complete union takes place with the source of everything that exists, a state of consciousness in comparison to which everything else is just a mere illusion. It is that mystery connected to what cannot even be defined 'God,' as reductive; that mystery that is glimpsed behind the light of the Council of Elders in "Life Among Lives."

There is an absolute universal, which is origin and goal of any soul. Michael Newton stated that not even the most advanced souls have direct experience of it. But there is a desire to merge again with it. The Absolute seems to be a great sun, and every ray is an individual soul. Even if the ray identifies with an existence, it has never really detached itself from the Sun. We are all One, in a collective consciousness in which each individual does not cease to exist and to feel unique in his or her identity. Every human being could perceive the universe as part of his body and feel himself as part of the universe.

According to Tibetan Buddhists, advanced souls maintain consciousness through the passage from death to new birth, having control over the circumstances in which they will be reborn. Their function is to help human beings to alleviate their suffering.

Nirvana does not involve the loss of individuality, but liberation from the wheel of rebirth. Everything we live is based on the law of cause and effect that dates back to previous lives.

There is a Tibetan practice, called Phowa, which allows the transfer of consciousness at the time of death and which must be transmitted by a qualified lama. Its purpose is to achieve liberation from karma, otherwise after the detachment from the body at the time of death, consciousness would wander into the bardo. So it is about achieving liberation at the moment of death. A transformation takes place from a place where one is crushed by karma, that is Samsara, to the pure Sanghye dimension, what is called 'freedom from suffering.' This practice must be learned well to be carried out at the last moment with lucidity. Consciousness matters; even when the body loses its energy, the spiritual mind retains lucidity; unification with the true natural state takes place and thus the bonds with Samsara will be severed forever.

At the moment of death, the inclinations and habits stored in the depths of the mind come to the surface, and precisely these projections will determine the images that will be in the bardo. The last thoughts and emotions before death greatly affect our immediate future, so a positive attitude is essential, making sure that every attachment or desire is let go.

The awareness of the Rigpa arises from the centre of the heart, like a tiny sphere of light that comes out through the top of the head, in an experience made of sounds and lights. The senses gradually withdraw from the outside world. When the soul detaches from the body, there is a momentary black-out in the void in which the clear light, the true nature of the mind, will be revealed, a moment in which enlightenment could be achieved. This essence never dies, because by its nature it is eternal and untouched by birth or decay.

The awareness help us to connect to the 'clear light,' to 'dwell in the rigpa' before the sensory experience dissolves.

Sensory perceptions will gradually fade, until a different state of consciousness arrives. This state will no longer be comparable to the ordinary state of mental consciousness, linked to sensory perceptions. It will be a state of awareness of 'natural light.' Later the dying person will enter a bardo whose substance is very similar to the dream state. The more the practitioner has developed the 'practice of natural light' during his life, the more he will be prepared to maintain the presence and awareness of 'natural light' at the time of death.

When great practitioners die, atmospheric phenomena may occur related to the elevation of the person who has left the body. The 'rainbow body' occurs when the elements dissolve in their luminosity connected to the very source of all things, so the body will be transformed into light. The rainbow body is one of the highest achievements in Dzogchen, which consists of integrating the parts that make up the physical body into the essence of the five elements, five rainbow lights. The supreme realization consists in reaching the 'rainbow body' at the time of death and as a result no material body remains. Several documented cases of people being transformed into light bodies were reported. For example, Francis Tiso documented the Tibetan monk Khenpo A-Chos, who died reciting the mantra "Om mani padme hum", on his right side, and began to shine. He was wrapped in a yellow dress for seven days, and when it was removed, the body was gone. Padmasambhava also reached the light body, having acquired the ability to fly, turn objects into gold, and leave footprints on Himalayan rocks. The physical body dissolves in the natural state of clear light, while the elements of the body are purified and transformed into their pure essence like the colours of the rainbow. Immediately after death, only nails and hair will remain.

Truth is the Void, on which one can meditate, in which one can rest and from which the thoughts that give life to forms and sensations arise. All reality is in the mind. The mind is in space. Space is nowhere to be found.

The highest level of the rainbow body, reached by the masters of Zhang Zhung and Bonpo Dzogchen is the Tib, in which the practitioner becomes like Buddha: his physical body is transformed into the essence of the five light elements, it can disappear and reappear in any place or time. The second type of realization is when, at the moment of death, the body splits into the rainbow lights of the essence of the five elements, leaving no physical remains. In the third level, there is a shrinking of the physical body and finally only hair and nails are left. Although it seems incredible, there are many testimonies about these phenomena, which reveal the mystery of the energetic nature of the matter of the physical body.

At the Moment of Death

When we divide into mind and matter, there is an interval in which consciousness, without material support, finds itself in its true transcendental nature. This is a great chance to gain enlightenment. We must ensure that we are no longer bound to attachments, both emotional and material. Not having affective attachments does not mean giving up love, on the contrary, it means transcending the idea of love as a possession. Conquering a detachment means achieving the awareness that we are neither our body nor our mind with its thoughts and desires, but rather we are the Self, from whose perspective we can observe our body and mind without being involved. Around the dying person there should be a peaceful environment, without strong emotions, and all unresolved problems should be estimated. We should understand the meaning of death, in relation to the awareness of the meaning of life. Those who follow a spiritual path can turn their thoughts to remember their master, who guided us along the path of knowledge to make us achieve its results: the realization of the Divine within us.

For this reason, the last thought and emotion before death is focused on the Absolute. This also applies to an atheist, who could focus on something not divine, such as the origin of life, or on any idea or image that has particular meaning for him.

"At the moment of death, there is no 'real' death, because our innate nature is beyond time. In the bardo, flames cannot burn us, weapons cannot hurt us,

everything is illusory and devoid of substance: everything is emptiness. [...] The experiences that will appear at the time of death are inconceivable. The most important thing is not to be sad or depressed, there would be no reason. Rather, we must have the attitude of a traveller returning home. We are all, more or less, prisoners of our habits, fears, illusions. Sufferings should induce us to abandon the ego, which closes the way to return to our divine nature."

(Franco Battiato)

'Franco, what does it mean to cross the Bardo?'

'By alluding to the Tibetan Book of the Dead, I reflect on the fact that nothing ends forever with death because our energy has the spiritual characteristics of eternity. So dying is just turning into a passage from one dimension to another.'

'The lesson is: nothing is as it seems.'

'Exactly, we are as infinite and eternal as the cosmos. Actually we are prisoners of our habits, fears and powerful illusions, so we cannot consciously consider ourselves to be a completely universal part.'

'What limits us in this research?'

'Suffering due to arrogance, greed suggested by the ego, responsible for closing the road to return to our divine nature. Human beings are too proud of an alleged free will and woe to those who question this freedom.' [...]

'There are people, special beings, who have already understood in this life and at great sacrifices the meaning of the fatal passage. They consider the abandonment of the body as the expected Prize, so the crossing will be much more important for them than the stay.' [...]

'The Knowledge of God helps us to know ourselves better and if we feel akin to that source, death accepted with awareness will perhaps be able to definitively heal us from the disease of rebirth.' (from: Philosophical interview with Battiato, We are made for eternity, 2015)

Beyond Reincarnation

There are life paths in other spheres or planets, and all souls currently involved in the cycle of human incarnations tend to the goal of climbing further up the evolutionary ladder, until the attraction to Earth will no longer be felt. The latter, in fact, is just one of many schools, as there are millions of different worlds. There are many souls who are facing the last states that anticipate liberation from the cycle of earthly incarnations. What is life like in the higher spheres? It goes beyond the mind and anything conceivable by human concepts. The soul ready for this leap is the one that has realized its true divine nature and its relationship with the whole, as well as the illusory nature of earthly life: it will no longer have any kind of earthly bond, it is awake and freed, and it has transcended its human ego. This is achieved through different paths, including a path of spiritual development, or even a form of wisdom that leads to receiving profound insights.

The human soul is immortal. The life principle is in us and outside of us, and it is eternal. Every human being has his own law, and any reward or punishment can only come from himself.

CHAPTER 15

MUCH MORE
THAN A BODY

Our human consciousness seems to be part of a larger, infinite, immortal consciousness.

Eastern philosophies have always believed that the physical world is an illusion, that the world is not as concrete as it seems, as indeed our body is not as solid as it seems. Human beings constantly receive frequencies and transform them into physical perceptions, but what we actually do is create one of the possible worlds of the infinite universe. All individual minds are nothing but parts of something great, in which everything is interconnected with others, in an infinite network. According to this perspective, we can believe that consciousness can be independent of the brain and its physical-biological mechanisms, and thus survive the death of the body. What we call 'paranormal powers' should be considered natural facts, explained by physics and the consequence of a deep interconnection between physical reality and a more subtle and invisible level. According to these perspectives, contacts with deceased people would not be hallucinations or imaginative delusions caused by the pain of loss, but manifestations of natural laws of a physics that also studies the invisible plane of reality.

The spiritual world is ineffable, infinite, immeasurable, it cannot be conceptualized, so it is difficult to communicate it with the rigidity and materiality of the scientific method. There are facts and truths that transcend materiality; these are part of the realm of thought-spirit, what we cannot measure with scientific instruments, yet they are more real than what we see and touch every day.

But we are ordinarily so involved in existential affairs, worries, anxieties, so related to our status, external appearances, our reputation, the opinions of others, to the point that we forget our spiritual origin and our inner power.

Accepting the assumptions of the Western and Eastern esoteric schools, we realize that we have a Master Self within us, a divine spark that we can awaken and follow, an inner God. We have to find our guide within ourselves. Each subject is the result of a long journey, an individual who wants to answer questions, who is driven by impulses and emerges conditioned by his past.

We are much more than a physical body and the material world. Death is not the end of our being: it is nothing more than a passage to a greater existence. Dag Hammarskjold says, "Our idea of death defines how we live our lives."

Those who believe that death is the end of everything are led to focus on the material and temporary aspects of existence, regardless of the destruction of the planet on which we live and the depletion of natural resources. Also, they do not think that we are all interconnected, and the damage we do to another person is as if it were done to ourselves.

Our life here seems to be a very limited period and during this time there is so much that can be done and so much to learn, before returning to that other dimension from which we come and which has the characteristic of eternity.

Scientists have not been able to provide an explanation for the NDE phenomenon, since they use research tools and methodologies that refer to the material world; however, that phenomenon pertains to another dimension.

Robert Klauber states that two subatomic particles can coexist as two waves crossing the ocean heading in opposite directions and passing through each other, occupying the same space on the water surface. This view goes against the assumption of classical physics, according to which two objects could not occupy the same space at the same time. Quantum physicists therefore argue that at an elementary level, all matter is made of energy that can be diffused like a field. Billions of neutrinos, tiny subatomic particles that are not affected by electromagnetic forces, pass through bodies at all times, yet no one is able to detect them and be aware of their presence. It can be that these particles are the basis of the existence of other invisible worlds coexisting with our physical world. According to physical theories, the negatively charged neutrino that rotates clockwise can be detected if it interacts with another particle; positively charged neutrinos, as well as quark particles, and maybe other particles not yet identified by science, escape detection, but still exist, despite being imperceptible. We could think that everything that pertains to the mind, to everything that concerns thought and spirit and that we do not see, is most likely composed of those same particles. How many dimensions and worlds are made up of such tiny, elementary particles, so invisible to the physical eyes that they are not even detectable by the scientific instruments. Yet they exist even if we do not realize their existence! String theory recognizes other dimensions beyond the three dimensions in which the official scientific model is trapped, and in such multidimensionality, countless particles can live, wander, and take their course without being seen. Carl B. Becker, a researcher at Kyoto University, in the article "Extrasensory perception, near-death experiences, and the limits of scientific knowledge," states the existence of other dimensions of the universe, objectively real but accessible only to individuals who are in particular states of consciousness. Here he refers precisely to the NDEs: "*If mental states can influence the external world, or if alternative dimensions of reality are accessible only in certain states of consciousness, then important aspects of the universe cannot be detected by current scientific instruments. The exploration of NDE phenomena requires a new scientific paradigm.*"

The phenomenon of NDEs can therefore be associated with the nature of subatomic particles and the possibility of expansion of consciousness, also taking into account the peculiar nature of mental events that occur in a context-space different from that occupied by physical bodies, which is generally isolated and protected from the intrusion of other people's thoughts, except in cases of telepathic communication.

It would be possible to apply the theory of dark matter to human beings, assuming that they have two connected brains: one made of matter, the one studied by official medicine, and another made of dark matter. It is as if humans have a 'twin body' made of lighter dark matter. This would explain the phenomenon of OBEs and NDEs, produced by the separation between the physical body and the dark matter body. The latter, obviously not endowed with physical senses, would perceive the surrounding physical reality through photons.

Dra. Laurin Bellg in her collection of "Near Death in the ICU: Stories from Patients Near Death and Why We Should Listen to Them," admits that doctors tend not to expose themselves too much when they address such topics, as they have a reputation to defend and fear losing respect and credibility. In this way, they maintain a facade of truth, hiding very different beliefs about the possibility of survival of something beyond death. On the other hand, there is a tendency to maintain the supposed certainties of science and not to want to question a shared and predictable world-view. This at least until some event occurs that collapses the castle of apparent dogmatic truths and forces us to look beyond.

It may be tempting to consider these phenomena as dreams and fantasies, yet it is undeniable that for people who have lived that kind of experience they have a character of reality greater than both a dream and even ordinary reality. However, the most important aspect is that they occur when brain and heart functions are suspended. This is precisely what makes these phenomena not only mysterious and fascinating, but also worthy of serious consideration, so that they continue to be the subject of research.

> *"Reality is what you see. When what you see changes, moving away from the reality of any other person, it is still reality for you."*
> **(Maria Hornlachle)**

Perceiving from outside one's body and then being able to accurately report details cannot be explained with the current means of scientific knowledge, since these perceptions are not processed through the physical senses.

According to Bellg, considering an NDE as a mere neurophysiological phenomenon is totally disrespectful, since it is so significant for the patient and a harbinger of important changes, and it even occurred when their body had been declared clinically dead.

There are multiple ways of interpreting such experiences, however all this gives us a glimpse of a greater truth than the one we are ordinarily accustomed to conceiving.

Carl Sagan says, *"Absence of proof is not proof of absence,"* criticizing those scientists who do not accept what is outside their ordinary field of knowledge.

We have all consolidated beliefs about reality, which are necessary to orient ourselves, so everything we encounter on our path is interpreted according to this frame of reference, so that it makes sense to us. But everything that does not fit into these constructs is often considered ridiculous, 'impossible,' probably because it threatens our security and confronts us with the uncontrollable unknown. The beliefs acquired by science are so cumbersome that they prevent us from understanding other laws than those of ordinary physics and official medicine, and therefore from conceiving that there is more to human beings than mere physiological and electrochemical reactions.

We must be open to the possibility of the existence of what we cannot currently explain scientifically, and above all respect such mysteries, as well as have an open mind, awe and wonder.

Scientific knowledge is uncertain as it is subject to change, so science should be considered as a 'work in progress.' We must be willing to abandon our certainties, or at least rephrase them, we must be ready to doubt our preconceived ideas and keep an open mind. Throughout history, new ideas have opened new horizons not only in literature, philosophy and art, politics and economics, but also in science.

We should bear in mind that the best developments have occurred precisely in relation to those phenomena and events that did not correspond to our preconceived ideas.

In 1633 Galileo was prosecuted by the Inquisition for his theory that the Earth revolved around the sun and not the other way around, thus refuting the dominant geocentric theory. The Church considered it a heresy!

In the past, people scientifically affirmed that the Earth was flat, or believed int the Ptolemy Theory. With the study of scientists who changed their point of view and engaged in constant and objective observations, it was discovered that our planet is instead round – despite the recent claims of flat-earthers. If we look back, it is inconceivable, almost ridiculous, that the dominant thought identified the Earth as flat.

When Isaac Newton resumed the Galilean theory to develop his mechanical theory of the universe, moved by physical forces, finally the Galilean theories were accepted. This shows that truth can be found by following one's own thoughts and intuitions without being conditioned by the opinions of others regarding what is true according to them. We must be open to the idea that what we have been taught since childhood may not have such firm roots. It is advisable to keep an open and curious mind, and accept to give a chance to what does not fall within our certainties and the frames of reference acquired.

We must respect and consider what cannot be measured with ordinary scientific canons, rather than considering them unreal. This is the true scientific spirit: keeping in mind that scientists do not hold the final answer.

Every generation of scientists surpasses the previous one, smiling at their ingenuity.

Neuroscientists must not get rid of their models of the 'brain-produced mind,' but must recognize that it only works under certain conditions.

Perhaps the doctors, psychiatrists, psychologists who have approached these seemingly bizarre perspectives, challenging their professional reputation and the dogmatism of the community, could be regarded as the new mystics of the 21st Century.

After his many years of research, Bruce Greyson is convinced that there is no incompatibility between science and spirituality. He also believes that scientific investigation, with its methods based on evidence, does not preclude us from valuing the spiritual aspects of our lives, in order to seek meaning. The fact that we cannot explain this kind of experience with scientific methodologies does not mean that we must pretend that it does not exist or, worse, ridicule it.

Science must not be on the side of the researcher – it must remain impartial. Rather, researchers should be on the side of science.

Experiences such as NDEs can be considered as the function of a non-physical mind. Those who have lived such experiences are convinced that the mind is not at all a product of the brain and that therefore it can act independently of the brain and persist after the death of the body.

Doctors and scientists who have conducted research in this field have humbly admitted that they do not have all the answers.

There are also changes in values and behaviours in those who have learned of the existence of NDEs, or who have come into contact with them indirectly through people, books, conferences. Ken Ring defines it as a 'benign virus' contracted by those who have experienced it; it causes less fear of death, growing interest in spirituality, a re-evaluation of the meaning of life, the development of compassion and acceptance of oneself and others. It also leads to a reduction in anxiety and negative emotions, and greater involvement in life, with the ability to live more in the present moment, without dwelling on the past or the future.

We must focus not only on the body, but more on the evolution of the soul.

If now we can recover information such as the memories of our past lives, it is thanks to hypnosis, a method that allows thousands of people to recover those deep unconscious fragments that were not affected by amnesia and that instead stored everything: their Higher Self. We would not have the same opportunities for growth and learning if we arrived at each new existence with the weight, conditioning and limitations produced by the full memory of our history.

According to Dr. Newton, it is no coincidence that these regressive hypnotic techniques have been developed in the last century: an era characterized by the limits induced by the excessive use of medicines, drugs, alcohol and other impediments that increase the 'mental fog,' further imprisoning the soul inside the body and reducing its possibilities of expression and communication with the mind. Today contemporary man needs to contact the spiritual worlds to make sense of an existence that, given the difficulties, contradictions and negativity, seems to have been emptied of all meaning. There is a need for a new and authentic spirituality more than ever; not that of religious associations, but something that arises from the deepest roots of our true essence. Deep inside ourselves we can find the way to know the answer to the question: Why am I in this world?. We must therefore rediscover the divinity within us and begin to listen to our guides.

"Coming to Earth means travelling away from our home to an unknown land. Some things seem familiar but most are foreign, until we get used to them, especially situations that are unforgivable. Our true home is a place of absolute peace, total acceptance and complete love. As souls separated from our home, we can no longer assume that these beautiful features will be present around us. On Earth we must learn to face intolerance, anger, sadness as we seek joy and love. We must not lose our integrity along the way, sacrificing the good for survival and acquiring attitudes superior or inferior to those around us. We know that living in an imperfect world will help us appreciate the true meaning of perfection. We ask for courage and humility before our journey into another life. As we grow in awareness, so will the quality of our existence. In this way, we are put to the test. Passing it is our destiny."

The purpose of life seems to be to achieve the soul's objectives that wants to evolve through a body and later with other bodies that are always different and evolved, capable of living in new contexts and situations. Hence, the need for a cycle of deaths and rebirths, which starts from the actual evolutionary level reached by one's soul, instead bringing the mind to a state of reset. Resetting, a new beginning, allows us to fully live new experiences and learn lessons, without influences or conditioning. It is therefore necessary that there are increasingly evolved physical bodies with more complex brains. In the future, the brain could reach higher levels of complexity, with greater possibilities of becoming a further effective tool for the manifestation and expression of a somewhat evolved soul. Without the evolution of the body, the evolution of the soul would not be possible. It is difficult to imagine a world without death, in which every tiny being is immortal and with infinite possibilities of reproduction. Death seems to be necessary to life, so that it is constantly renewed and improved. Humanity evolves thanks to individual differences; regardless of one's body and contingent situation, everyone can realize the meaning of his life if in alignment with his soul in a constructive way.

From the point of view of the soul, the death of the body is an opportunity for change and evolution, not therefore a painful event. A highly evolved soul can still achieve its goals, whether with a physical body or without. The human being can produce new information through his thoughts and this is a great opportunity for evolution.

CONCLUSION

How would the contemporary world, philosophy, religion, psychology change if official science admitted that consciousness does not die with the death of the brain? The survival of the spirit is not linked to a religious faith, but is a fact that can be studied scientifically. There is a lot of evidence collected over decades, as we have seen.

Talking about all the phenomena we have seen throughout this book means coming across topics that have often caused confusion and non-acceptance. However, we must not forget that in the Middle Ages, it was science itself that was rejected. We must not even forget that those who were accused of witchcraft for having paranormal abilities were persecuted or, worse, killed.

Many people are convinced that there is no life after death. But why not believe that there is existence after the death of a physical body? How is it possible that once something exists, the energy that represents that existence can be destroyed? Is it possible to destroy electricity? The energy is always there, albeit in a different form. The same is true for the human soul, which is anything but energy. "What exists cannot cease to exist," says the Bhagavad Gita.

The English psychologist David Fontana, director of the Commission for Survival Research at the Society for Psychical Research, said, *"I am happy to be a psychologist, this is important to maintain a scientific approach to things, but we must never allow science to blind us to other possibilities that we cannot always explore with the scientific method."*

There is non-refutable evidence, such as children meeting deceased relatives they did not meet, encounters with people who thought they were alive but were actually dead, blind people who see, brain-dead patients describing in detail the surgical procedures they witnessed from outside the body, and many other such situations.

NDE experiences reveal to us the mystery and depth of our consciousness, because it still remains alive and active despite the death of the brain and biological physical body.

The basis of all that exists is not mere matter, but consciousness.

There are many aspects of our lives that we do not understand, indeed we have not even begun to understand. We should not deny the existence of something just because we are not yet able to understand it. We considered 'paranormal' what is not understood by 'normal' laws. But there is no progress with a close mind.

We have had many lives, but we only have one soul and our care and attention must focus on this. What matters is what we add to our soul in each life.

At a deep level, all things are part of a great unity: what had been affirmed for millennia by Eastern spiritual traditions was then confirmed by quantum physics.

Giordano Bruno wrote, "a single true Light illuminates the worlds and a single Sun makes them alive."

It is desirable that it may one day be possible to accept intellectually, albeit without obvious scientific evidence, the existence of another dimension, where the soul goes after death. Those who have lived that experience are not interested in demonstrating it.

A psychiatrist interviewed by Raymond Moody says, "People who have had these experiences know. Those who did not, should wait."

Nowadays, contrary to what happened in the past, people have less resistance to talking about their inner experiences and visions. There seems to be a new openness about non-ordinary experiences and altered states of consciousness, which was very familiar to our ancestors of bygone eras.

We are now looking for a new type of more personal, inner spirituality, which does not involve external mediators as happens in religion. Something that originates from a universal awareness and that help us to understand the reasons for our existence on Earth. The mystery of life seems to go far beyond what the official religions have indicated to us and far beyond the limits of the rational mind.

We are divine sparks: there are young souls beginning to grow, and old souls near the end of a long cycle of human births. Human life is closely interconnected with divine life.

We are like beings of light who temporarily disguise themselves as actors on Earth's stage, as if it were a film, glimpsing a truth beyond the opposites of good and evil. We carry in our depths, although clouded by oblivion, the memory of the beauty of the spiritual worlds and the sense of union with the whole, while we face the limits, challenges and trials posed by the earthly world, which is also full of opportunities.

The first cause must not be sought in the past as scientists do, but beyond space-time.

As Arthur Findlay, one of the most important researchers of psychic phenomena, suggests to us, the human being should just understand the meaning of the mystery of life, in order to lay the foundations for a new humanism, a new philosophy that is based on a worldview totally different from the one currently dominant. Current official science must meet with what is considered 'paranormal,' in order to solve the enigmas of existence and begin a new science dedicated to the knowledge of the entire universe and not only its material part. With the progress of scientific knowledge, what cannot be explained today will be interpreted tomorrow; just as what can be explained today was still unknown in the past.

The meeting between science and spirituality makes us reflect on the deep mystery of the human soul. Heraclitus said, *"Travelling on every path, you will not find the boundaries of soul by going; so deep is its measure [logos]."*

Human life cannot be reduced to scientific principles and methods. Different opinions must be put together, in a discussion between knowledge: philosophy, psychoanalysis, psychiatry, anthropology, sociology, which do not claim to reach final answers. Questions make sense when they amplify, not when they close. This allows a dialogue between the different branches of knowledge, with the awareness that none of them holds absolute truth but only relative.

And here it is possible to add 'spirituality,' which today is attracting considerable interest, although considered as an 'alternative' field, but which in reality contains interesting perspectives and potential.

Important discoveries in basic research were made, as well as methodological challenges, when new attention was paid to the inner experience that, at the beginning of psychological research, was mainly considered as 'subjective.' The value of first-person experience has therefore been redefined. A systematic investigation of inner experience could assume the characteristics and requirements of an epistemology, being an essential and basic phenomenological dimension of human knowledge.

Taking into account Kuhn's suggestions, which indicate that changes in science occur when new ideas and paradigms force us to change our way of seeing things, we can state that science has accepted possibilities that previously would not have been admissible. Looking at reality through alternative lenses, we can therefore glimpse new possibilities.

It is appropriate to reflect on the development in science over the centuries and also on the science of psychology. Science must be valid for everyone, but it can be historicized, so its validity is relative to a given historical moment and linked to the knowledge of that time. Psychology has acquired greater possibilities nowadays, thanks to techniques and tools that allow us to get closer to the unknowable. However, we should bear in mind that the human being is far from knowing reality directly, but with the mediation of tools; however, these are still related to the historical period.

All scientific disciplines move within a paradigm related to the historical period and with the tools at their disposal. A more complete awareness of our world and interiority is possible only with a collaboration between different fields of knowledge. Science and spirituality together provide us with new ideas that will give rise to new questions and new paths.

Themes, such as values, ethics, the meaning of life and everything that pertains to spirituality are part of an area beyond scientific observation. And spirituality embraces even deeper themes because they involve that part, defined as 'spirit,' which is intimate.

Quoting Nicola De Carlo, a professor at my school of psychotherapy, who passed away at the end of my four-year specialization, *"The limit of rationality seems to be mystery."* Indeed, precisely that mystery is an integral part of our human life! The psyche is the place of uniqueness, but also of mystery, and the mystery of life and death leads us through the mysterious paths of the human psyche. As Jung says, *"If the psyche of man is something, it is enormously complicated and of unlimited multiplicity, impossible to understand with a simple psychology of instincts. I can only contemplate with silent admiration, with the deepest wonder and fear, the abysses and peaks of psychic nature, whose a-spatial world conceals an immea-*

surable amount of images, which millions of years of evolution have accumulated and condensed organically. My consciousness is like an eye that welcomes the most distant spaces, but the psychic non-Ego is what a-spatially fills this space. I could not compare this except to the vision of the starry sky, because the equivalent of the inner world is the outer world; and as I reach this world through my body, I reach that through my soul."

Writing this book was for me a journey of discoveries, revelations and synchronicity, which led me towards important awareness. My intent was to bring together the different contributions of the experts, with the aim of offering the reader a more complete and rich frame.

During the study and research between the different sources, as I proceeded in the writing of the book, the memory and evocation of certain truths that had always been known by my deep being took place. The reader could perceive the same feeling, as long as there is an open and curious mind on his part. Even just hearing about these topics could have a transformative effect.

It is interesting to highlight how each person mentioned in this book has come to the same truths, while following different paths. What really matters is the personal path that each of us travels in our own existence and that will make us rediscover the traces of those knowledge that we have never really lost. In fact, we may find the truth of our immortality in the depths of our being.

"Death is not the end of life. It is an aspect of life. It is a natural incident in the course of life. It is necessary for your evolution. Death is not the opposite of life. It is only a phase of life."
(Swami Shivananda)

"My soul is from elsewhere, I'm sure of that, and I intend to end up there."
(Rumi)

"May your own spiritual eyes become opened, that you may perceive these truths for yourself, and through your own experience."
(Yogi Ramacharaka)

"The soul changes from form to form and the dwellings of its pilgrim are many. You lay down your bodies as clothes, and as clothes you go back to wearing them. You have existed for a long time, O soul of man, indeed you have always existed."

ACKNOWLEDGEMENTS

Marco, my true and only love from life to life.

Paul Aurand and Sophia Kramer for your inspiring and precious teachings

My mother, who always wonders about the mystery of life.

My dad, who did not believe in an afterlife.

All my loved ones who are always there, even without a physical body.

The spiritual masters and scientists who had the courage to abandon their certainties: the credit for this book goes to them.

He who, invisible, guides me and watches lovingly over me.

REFERENCES

Albert Einstein, *Opere scelte*, Bollati Boringhieri, 1988

Alex Raco, *Non è mai la fine*, Mondadori, 2017

Alex Raco, *Non c'è vita senza amore*, Mondadori, 2019

Allan Botkin, *Induced After-death Communication: A New Therapy for Healing Grief And Trauma*, Hampton Roads Publishing Company, Inc., 2005

Allan Kardec, *Che cos'è lo spiritismo*, Gattopardo Editions, 1971.

Amit Goswami, *Physics of the Soul: The Quantum Book of Living, Dying, Reincarnation and Immortality,* Hampton Roads Publishing, 2001

Angelo Bona, *Il profumo dei fiori d'acacia*, Pendragon, 2012

Angelo Bona, *L'amore dopo il tramonto*, Mondadori, 2005

Angelo Bona, *L'amore oltre la vita*, Mondadori, 2004

Angelo Bona, *L'arte della levatrice*, Mondadori, 2017

Anita Moorjani, *Morendo ho ritrovato me stessa. Viaggio dal cancro, alla premorte, alla guarigione*, Mylife, 2013

Aristotele, *Opere. Collezione di 20 libri*, Laterza, 2019

Arthur Findlay, *On the Edge of the Etheric: Survival After Death Scientifically Explained*, Psychic, 1970

Becker, C. B. *Extrasensory Perception, Near-Death Experiences, and the Limits of Scientific Knowledge*. J Near-Death Stud 9, 11–20 (1990)

Bhagavad Gita, *Il canto del beato*, Asram Vidya Editions, 1974

Bill & Judy Guggenheim, *Hello from Heaven: A New Field of Research-After-Death Communication Confirms That Life and Love Are Eternal*, Random House Publishing Group, 1996

Blackmore S. J., *Beyond the Body: An Investigation of Out-of-the-body Experiences*, Heinemann, London, 1982

Brian Greene, *The Fabric of the Cosmos: Space, Time, and the Texture of Reality*, Knopf Doubleday Publishing Group, 2007

Brian Weiss, *I miracoli accadono*, Mondadori, 2012

Brian Weiss, *Lo specchio del tempo*, Mylife, 2012

Brian Weiss, *Molte vite, molti maestri*, Mondadori, 1997.

Brian Weiss, *Molte vite, un'anima sola: Il potere di guarigione delle vite future e la terapia della progressione*, Mondadori, 2007

Brian Weiss, *Oltre le porte del tempo*, Mondadori, 1998.

Bruce Greyson, *After*, Penguin Random House Uk, 2021

Budd Hopkins, Carol Rainey, Sight Unseen. *Science, UFO Invisibility and Transgenic Beings*, Pocket Star Books, 2004

Budd Hopkins, *Intruders: The Incredible Visitations at Copley Woods*, August Night Press, 2021

Budd Hopkins, *Missing Time*, CreateSpace Independent Publishing Platform, 1981

Carista Luminare-Rosen, *Parenting Begins Before Conception: A Guide to Preparing Body, Mind, and Spirit For You and Your Future Child*, Inner Traditions, 2000

Carl Gustav Jung, *Memories, Dreams, Reflections*, Collins Fount Paperbacks, 1978

Carl Sagan, *In the Valley of the Shadow*, Parade, March 1996.

Carol Bowman, *Children's Past Lives How Past Life Memories Affect Your Child*, Random House Publishing Group, 2012

Cesare Boni, *Dove va l'anima dopo la morte*, Amrita, 2008.

Charles Tart, *Psicologie transpersonali*, Amrita, 1994

Claude Swanson, *Life Force, the Scientific Basis: Breakthrough Physics of Energy Medicine, Healing, Chi and Quantum Consciousness*, Poseidia Press, 2010

Claudio Lalla, *Perdita e ricongiungimento. Comunicare con i propri cari oltre il tempo della loro vita*, Mediterranee, 2015

Crabtree, Greyson, Williams Kelly, *Irreducible Mind: Toward a Psychology for the 21st Century* , 2007

David Chamberlain, *The Mind of Your Newborn Baby*, North Atlantic Books, 1998

David Fontana, *Life Beyond Death: What Should We Expect?*, Watkins Media, 2016

David Jacobs, *Secret Life: Firsthand, Documented Accounts of Ufo Abductions*, Simon & Shuster, 1993

Dj Kadagian, Pim Van Lommel, Gregory Shushan, *The Crossover Experience: Life After Death / A New Perspective*, Four Seasons Productions LLC, 2022

Dolores Cannon, *Between Death and Life*, Gill & Macmillan, 2003

Dolores Cannon, *Keepers of the Garden*, Ozark Mountain Publishing, 1993

Dolores Cannon, *Legacy from the Stars*, Ozark Mountain Publishing, 1996

Dolores Cannon, *The Convoluted Universe: Book One*, Ozark Mountain Publishing, 2014

Dolores Cannon, The Convoluted Universe*: Book Two*, Ozark Mountain Publishing, 2015

Dolores Cannon, *The Custodians: Beyond Abduction*, Ozark Mountain Publishing, 1999

Dolores Cannon, *The Legend of Starcrash*, Ozark Mountain Publishing, 1994

Dolores Cannon, *The Search for Hidden, Sacred Knowledge*, Ozark Mountain Publishing, 2014

Dolores Cannon, *Three Waves of Volunteers and the New Earth*, Ozark Mountain Publishing, 2011

Eben Alexander, Proof of Heaven: *A Neurosurgeon's Journey into the Afterlife*, Simon & Schuster Books, 2012

Edward Burnett Tyler, *Primitive culture*, Dover Publications, 2016

Elisabeth Kübler-Ross, *Sulla via dopo la morte*, l'Età dell'acquario Editions, 2018

Elisabeth Kübler-Ross, *The Wheel of Life*, Transworld Publishers, 1997

Elizabeth Carman, Neil Carman, *Babies Are Cosmic: Signs of Their Secret Intelligence*, North Atlantic Books, 2019

Elizabeth Carman, Neil Carman, *Cosmic Cradle: Spiritual Dimensions of Life before Birth*, North Atlantic Books, 2013

Elizabeth Kübler-Ross, *La morte è di vitale importanza*, Armenia, 2004.

Elizabeth Kübler-Ross, *La morte e la vita dopo la morte*, Mediterranee Editions, 1991

Emanuel Swedenborg, *Cielo e inferno. L'aldilà descritto da un grande veggente*, Mediterranee Editions, 2005

Erich von Däniken, *La storia si sbaglia. Dal manoscritto Voynich al libro di Enoch, le prove che il mondo non è quello che crediamo*, Armenia, 2017

Etienne Gilson, *La filosofia nel Medio Evo dalle origini patristiche alla fine del XIV secolo*, La Nuova Italia, 1997

Fabio Marchesi, *La fisica dell'anima*, Tecniche Nuove, 2004

Francesca Scarrica, *L'aldilà esiste: lo dice la scienza, 89 Scienziati e Ricercatori lo Confermano, 5 Campi Di Ricerca Differenti Indagati, 1 Sola Grande Verità Che Cambierà per Sempre la Tua Vita*, Independently Published, 2019

Fred Alan Wolf, *Mind and the New Physics*, Simon and Schuster, 1985

George Meek, *After We Die, What Then?*,Ariel Press, 1987

George Ritchie, *Return from Tomorrow*, Baker Publishing Group, 2007

Giammaria, *L'alchimia questa sconosciuta*, Amenothes Editions, 1997

Giuliana Conforto, *Il gioco cosmico dell'uomo*, Noesis, 2001

Gregory Shushan, *Conceptions of the Afterlife in Early Civilizations*, 2009

Greyson, Bruce and Stevenson, Ian (1980) 'The Phenomenology of Near –Death Experiences' American Journal of Psychiatry 137, 10, 1193-1196.

Hermelinda, *Il segreto del Buddha*, Streetlib, 2022

Hermelinda, *Paths for the Spiritual Search: Methods for the Awakening of the Inner Guide*, Cerchio della Luna, 2012

Hermelinda, *A Mystical Journey: Meeting with extraordinary masters, magicians and shamans*, Harmakis Editions, 2015

Hermelinda, *Oltre l'orizzonte dello spirito*, Harmakis Editions, 2021

Ian Stevenson, *Twenty Cases Suggestive of Reincarnation*, The University Press of Virginia, 1974

James B. Craven, *Doctor Robert Fludd*, William Peace & Sons, 1902

Janet Lee Mitchell, *Out-Of-Body-Experiences: A Handbook*, Ballantine Books, 1981

Jean-Luc Achard, *Enlightened Rainbows*, Brill, Leiden-Boston, 2008.

Jeremy Wooster, *Quantum Physics For Beginners*, Independently published, 2021

Jim Alexander, *New Lives, Old Souls: Fascinating reincarnation evidence from case studies using Hypnotic Regression*, Independently published, 2019

Jim Sparks, *The Keepers: An Alien Message for the Human Race*, Wild Flower Press, 2008

Jim Tucker, *Life Before Life: A scientific investigation of children's memories of previous lives*, St Martin Griffin, 2008

Jinpa Thupten and Coleman Graham. Il libro tibetano dei morti. Integrale Editions, Italia, Mondadori, 2007.

Joe Keeton, *The Power of the Mind*, Simon Petrick Edition, 2012

Joel Whitton, *Life Between Life. Scientific exploration into the void separating one incarnation from the next*, Grand Central Publishing, 1988

John Eccles, *How the Self Controls Its Brain*, Springer-Verlag, 1994

John Mack, Abduction: Human Encounters with Aliens, Scribner, 2009

John Myrdhin Reynolds, *Selections from the Bonpo Book of the Dead*, Bonpo Translation Project (privately printed), San Diego and Copenhagen 1997.

John Searle, *Il mistero della coscienza*, Raffaello Cortina, 1998.

Julius Evola, *Maschera e volto dello spiritualismo contemporaneo*, Mediterranee Editions, 1978

Kenneth Ring, *The Omega Project: Near-Death Experiences, Ufo Encounters, and Mind at Large*, Morrow, 1992

Kerr CW .Donnelly JP , Wright ST , Kuszczak SM , Banas A , Grant PC , Luczkiewicz DL (2014) *End-of-Life Dreams and Visions: A Longitudinal Study of Hospice Patients' Experiences.* Journal of Palliative Medicine, 17(3):296-303

La Bibbia, San Paolo Editions, 2014

Laurin Bellg, *Near Death in the ICU. Stories from Patients Near Death and why We Should Listen to Them*, Sloan Press, 2015

Lawrence, M and Repede, E (2012*) The incidence of deathbed communications and their impact on the dying process.* The American Journal of Hospice & Palliative Medicine 30(7), 632–639

Leon Denis, *Che cosa ci attende dopo la morte? Il capolavoro del successore di Allan Kardek,* Mediterranee Editions, 2018

Lorna & John Jackson, *Soul Regression Therapy*, The Jackson Institute, 2016

Luis Maio Ruiz, *L'esoterismo della Divina Commedia*, Irfan, 2020

Luis Minero, *Demystifying the Out of Body Experience: A practical manual for exploration and personal evolution*, Llewellyn Publications, 2012

Mary C. Neal, *To Heaven and Back: A Doctor's Extraordinary Account of Her Death, Heaven, Angels, and Life Again: A True Story*, Waterbrook Press, 2011

Melvin Morse, Paul Perry, *Parting Visions: An Exploration of pre-Death Psychic and Spiritual Experiences*, Piatkus, 1994.

Melvin Morse, Paul Perry, *Where God Lives: The Science of the Paranormal and How Our Brains are Linked to the Universe*, HarperCollins, 2000

Michael Newton, *Destiny of Souls*, Llewellyn Publications, 2001

Michael Newton, *Journey of Souls: Case studies of life between lives*, Llewellyn Publications, 1994

Michael Newton, *Life Between Lives*, Llewellyn Publications, 2004

Michael Newton, *Memories of the Afterlife*, Llewellyn Publications, 2009

Michael Sabom, *Light and Death. One Doctor's Fascinating Account of Near-Death Experiences*, Grand Rapids Zondervan, 1998

Michael Talbot, *The Holographic Universe*, HarperCollins, 1991

Michael Wolf, *Catchers of Heaven. I guardiani del Cielo. Una trilogia*, Verdechiaro Editions, 2015

Milton Erickson, *The Collected Papers of Milton H. Erickson on Hypnosis, Vol. IV, Innovative hypnotherapy*, Irvington Publishers, 1980

Morris Netherton, *Past Lives Therapy: Past Life Regression Special Edition with Past Life Regression Center*, Past life therapy center, 2014

Namkai Norbu, *Lo yoga del sogno*, Astrolabio Ubaldini Editions, 1993

Nick Pope, *Open Skies, Closed Minds*, Simon & Shuster, 2014

Nick Pope, *The Uninvited*, Simon & Shuster, 1997

Oliver Lodge, *Linking Life After Death To Subatomic Physics*, in The Queen's Hospital Annual, 1933

Oliver Lodge, *Why I believe in Personal Immortality*, Cassell & Co London, 1928

Osis K, Haraldsson E. , *Deathbed Observations by Physicians and Nurses: A Cross Cultural Survey*. J Am Soc Psychical Res. 1977;71(3):237–259.

Osis K., Haraldson E., *Quello che videro nell'ora della morte*, Armenia, Milano, 1979.

Paola Giovetti, *NDE: Testimonianze di esperienze in punto di morte*, Mediterranee Editions, 2007

Paola Harris, *Esopolitica. E' già nel vento*, Verdechiaro Editions, 2009

Paramahansa Yogananda, *L'eterna ricerca dell'uomo*, Astrolabio-Ubaldini, 1980

Patanjali, *Aforismi sullo yoga*, Melita Editions, 1992

Paul A. LaViolette, *Secrets of Antigravity Propulsion: Tesla, UFOs, and Classified Aerospace Technology*, Inner Traditions, 2008

Paul Aurand, *Essential Healing: Hypnotherapy and Regression-Based Practices to Release the Emotional Pain and Trauma Keeping You Stuck*, Reveal Press, 2021

Paul Hellyer, *La luce alla fine del tunnel*, Verdechiaro Editions, 2013

Peter Fenwick, *The Art of Dying*, Continuum, 2008

Peter Fenwick, *The Truth in the Light*, Headline Book Publishing, 1995

Philaletes, *L'esoterismo Rosacroce nella Divina Commedia*, Bastogi Libri, 2014

Philip Corso, William Birnes, *The Day After Roswell*, Gallery Books, 2017

Pim Van Lommel, *Coscienza oltre la vita. La scienza delle esperienze di premorte*, Amrita Editions, 2017

Pim Van Lommel, *Near-death experience in survivors of cardiac arrest: a prospective study in the Netherlands*, Lancet 2001

Platone, *Tutte le opere*, Newton Classici, 2013

R.A. Bertlmann, *From Bell to Quantum Information*, Springer Berlin Heidelberg, 2013

Raimon Panikkar, ed., *I Veda. Mantramanjari. Testi fondamentali della rivelazione vedica*, Rizzoli, 2001

Raphael, ed., *Le Upanishad*, Bompiani, 2010

Raphael, *La triplice via del fuoco*, Asram Vidya Editions, 1986

Raymond A. Moody, *Glimpses of eternity: An investigation into shared death experiences*, Rider Ebury Publishing, 2010

Raymond A. Moody, *Life After Life*, Mockingbird Books, 1975

Raymond A. Moody, *Reflections on Life After Life*, Mockingbird Books, 2011

Raymond A. Moody, *The light Beyond*, Mockingbird Books, 2011

Rekhaa Kale, Past Life: *A Mystique Reality Uncovered*, 2012

Richard Andersen, *Frontiers in Cognitive Neuroscience*, Mit Press, 1995

Richard Dolan, *The Secret Space Program and Breakaway Civilization*, Richard Dolan Press, 2016

Richard Dolan, *UFOs for the 21st Century Mind: A Fresh Guide to an Ancient Mystery*, Richard Dolan Press, 2014

Robert C. Baranowski, *Past Life Journeying. Exploring past, between and future lives*, BookBaby, 2023

Robert Bruce, *Astral Dynamics: A New Approach to Out-Of-Body Experiences*, Hampton Roads Pub Co, 1999

Robert Klauber, *Student Friendly Quantum Field Theory. Basic Principles and Quantum Electrodynamics*, Sandtrove Press, 2013

Robert Monroe, *Journeys Out of the Body*, Doubleday, 1971

Robert Schwartz, *Your Soul's Gift: The Healing Power of the Life You Planned Before You Were Born*, Whispering Wind Press, 2012

Roberto Lanza, *Oltre il biocentrismo. Ripensare il tempo, lo spazio, la coscienza e l'illusione della morte*, Il Saggiatore, 2016

Roger Lipsey. *Hammarskjöld: A Life*, University of Michigan Press, 2013

Roger Penrose, *L'universo è ancora un segreto*, Rizzoli, 2017

Roger Penrose, *La mente nuova dell'imperatore*, Rizzoli, Milano, 2000.

Ron Pearson, *Intelligence Behind the Universe*, Headquarters Publishing Company, 1990

Roy Abraham Varghese, Raymond A. Moody, *There Is Life After Death: Compelling Reports from Those Who Have Glimpsed the Afterlife*, New Page Books, 2010

Rudolf Steiner, *La scienza occulta*, Edizione antroposofica, 2002

Russel Targ R, *Miracles of Mind*, New World Library, 1998

Russell Targ, Harold. E. Puthoff, *Mind Reach*, Delacorte Press, 1977

Russell Targ, *Remote Viewing at Stanford Research Institute in the 1970s: A Memoir.* Journal of Scientific Exploration, 1996

Sam Parnia, *Erasing Death: The Science That Is Rewriting the Boundaries Between Life & Death*, HarperCollins, 2013

Sam Parnia, *What Happens When We Die?: A Groundbreaking Study into the Nature of Life and Death*, Hay House, 2008

Sam Parnia, *What Happens When We Die?*, Hay House, 2006.

Shapiro F., *Desensibilizzazione e rielaborazione attraverso movimenti oculari*, McGraw-Hill, 2000.

Shar-rdza bKra-shis rGyal-mthan, *The Natural Arising of the Three Enlighted Bodies* - collected works

Sir Arthur Conan Doyle, *The History of Spiritualism in two volumes*, Psychic Press, 1989

Sogyal Rinpoche, *Il libro tibetano del vivere e del morire*, Astrolabio-Ubaldini, 1994

Steven M. Greer, *Hidden Truth, Forbidden Knowledge*, Ztt Consulting

Swann Ingo, *Penetration: The question of extraterrestrial and human telepathy*, Swann Ryder Production, Llc, 2019

Tenzin Wangyal Rinpoche, *The Tibetan Yogas of Dream and Sleep*, Snow Lion, Ithaca NY 1998

Thomas S. Kuhn, Joseph D. Sneed, Wolfgang Stegmüller, *Paradigmi e rivoluzioni nella scienza*, Armando Editions, 2015

Thomas Vazhakunnathu, *Spiritual Theory of Everything. A unique blueprint to discover the origin and purpose of life, awaken your counsciousness and lead a blissful life*, 2020

Verner Heisemberg, *I principi fisici della teoria dei quanti*, Bollati Boringhieri, 2016

William James, *The Varieties of Religious Experience*, Penguin Classic, 1982

Yogi Ramacharaka, *The Life Beyond Death*, Yogi Publication Society, 1937

ABOUT THE AUTHOR

Hermelinda graduated in Philosophy in 2004 and in Psychology in 2016. She is a psychologist-psychotherapist with a cognitive-constructivist orientation. She graduated from the four-year ISFY Yoga Instructor Training School and works as a high school teacher.

She began her spiritual journey when she was fourteen years old, led by several Masters and Guru of both Western and Eastern spiritual traditions. Constant spiritual practice and yoga, performed in the higher forms of Raja and Kriya, have always been at the centre of her life. Fundamental landmarks of her path were Anthroposophy, Alchemical Hermeticism, the Fourth Way of Gurdjieff and the Shamanism of Carlos Castaneda. Her studies and practices, over the years, have led her to a great synthesis of the teachings of different schools and traditions, in a constant search for a common background: a Unique Spiritual Tradition, which has taken different forms in time and space. In recent years, as she met new Masters and Tibetan Lama, she had the opportunity to complete this synthesis by exploring the paths of Advaita Vedanta Yoga and Bon Dzogchen Buddhism.

Made in United States
Troutdale, OR
05/09/2024

19741496R10206